A PHILOSOPHY OF EVIL

lars svendsen
A PHILOSOPHY OF EVIL

TRANSLATED BY KERRI A. PIERCE

dalkey archive press
champaign and london

Originally published in Norwegian as *Ondskapens filosofi* by Universitetsforlaget, 2001
Copyright © 2001 by Universitetsforlaget
Translation copyright © 2010 by Kerri A. Pierce
First English translation, 2010

Library of Congress Cataloging-in-Publication Data

Svendsen, Lars Fr. H., 1970-
[Ondskapens filosofi. English]
A philosophy of evil / Lars Svendsen ; translated by Kerri A. Pierce.
    p. cm.
Includes bibliographical references.
ISBN 978-1-56478-571-8 (pbk. : alk. paper)
1. Good and evil. I. Title.
BJ1405.N67S8413 2010
170--dc22
                        2009050785

Partially funded by the University of Illinois at Urbana-Champaign and by a grant from the Illinois Arts Council, a state agency

This translation has been published with the financial support of NORLA

www.dalkeyarchive.com

Cover: design and composition by Danielle Dutton, illustration by Nicholas Motte
Printed on permanent/durable acid-free paper and bound in the United States of America

TABLE OF CONTENTS

FOREWORD

When I first seriously took up the subject of evil many years ago, I faced a particular challenge. I had to prove that the idea in general was still relevant to philosophical discussion. Back then, of course, the idea was undergoing a nascent "renaissance."[1] However, among most of my colleagues in philosophy, and even more so among my colleagues in other disciplines, the idea of evil was seen as a holdover from a mythical, Christian worldview whose time was already past.

Initially, as I began to attempt this "rehabilitation" of the concept of evil, the idea itself was still an object of fascination for me.[2] This fascination was a result, most especially, of our tendency to regard evil as an *aesthetic* object, where evil appears as something *other* and therefore functions as an alternative to the banality of everyday life. We're steadily exposed to more and more extreme representations of evil in films and such,[3] but this form of evil doesn't belong to a *moral* category. Like most other things in our culture, evil has been aestheticized. Simone Weil writes: "Imaginary evil is romantic and varied; real evil is gloomy, monotonous, barren, boring. Imaginary good is boring; real good is always new, marvellous, intoxicating."[4] In fiction, evil feeds off its fictional nature. It poses a contrast to the banality of everyday life and represents a transcendence of the same. "Evil" is translated as "transgression," "the sublime," etc. When such aestheticization becomes dominant, we lose sight of the *horror* associated with evil. For the purely aesthetic gaze, there is no actual *victim*. As a purely aesthetic phenomenon, evil becomes a game without consequences, something we can gorge ourselves on, play around with, or shed a tear about without worrying that the knife will cut too deep.[5]

Eventually, however, my rehabilitation of evil took a more serious turn. In Europe, we paid close attention to the events in the former Yugoslavia: the reports of mass murder, rape, and extreme forms of torture. So much meaningless brutality, we thought, as we read about the Serbian troops who forced Muslim fathers and sons to have sex, or the male prisoners who were forced to stand naked and watch women undress—anyone who got an erection had their penis cut off. Yes, Yugoslavia was a shock to us. We thought such things didn't happen in the light of day, at least not in our part of the world. It's difficult to find an explanation for *why* such things happen ... "Evil" was the only word that could begin to express the horror of these events.

Then came September 11, 2001, and suddenly the idea of evil assumed a prominent place in political discourse. That day, George W. Bush declared: "Today, our nation saw evil." Tony Blair remarked that "mass terrorism is the new evil in our world today" and that "we, like them, will not rest until this evil is driven from our world." Ariel Sharon was quick to hop on the bandwagon. He announced: "There is no 'good' and 'bad' terrorism—it is all horrific, all evil, all lacking in human values."

The events of September 11, as well as the years that have followed, have shown us how potent the idea of evil still is, and how dangerous the use of the word can be. As I sit and write these words, Palestinian civilians in the Gaza Strip are suffering under an Israeli attack. It is difficult to regard this attack—with its systematic destruction of civilian targets such as schools, greenhouses, and mosques—as anything other than a collective punishment directed against the Palestinian people. The magic word used to justify this invasion is "terrorism." And since terrorism is defined as evil incarnate, and Hamas is a terrorist organization, any and all means may be employed to eliminate this threat—no matter the suffering it may cause to Palestinian civilians.

A lot has changed since I first began working on this book. In the beginning, I wanted to leave out almost all material regarding sadists[6] and genocide, because I wanted to focus on ordinary, as opposed to extraordinary, evil. It soon became clear, however, that our concept of evil is so closely tied to these extreme phenomena that they had to be included. Extreme actions undertaken by "monsters" are among the clearest ideas we have of evil. Perhaps there really are human "monsters" in the world—and by that I mean people whose actions are so extreme that we simply can't identify ourselves with them—but there are far too few of these to explain the abundance of human evil in general. In the end, it is we—we normal, more or less decent, respectable people—who are responsible for most of the damage. We are the only explanation for all the evil in the world. From this point of view, it is "normal" to be evil. Of course, we aren't eager to describe ourselves as such. If anyone is evil, it's always "them."

I emphasize the Holocaust in this book because such a wealth of research is available concerning the perpetrators that it allows us a unique insight into how completely ordinary people can become involved in the greatest evil imaginable. When I discuss the Holocaust, my focus will not be on Hitler, but instead on the "normal" people who participated in the mass exterminations. This is because I'm most interested in the relevance the idea of evil has for an understanding of ourselves as moral agents in the world. When it comes Hitler, most of us have little reason to identify ourselves with him; on the other hand, it is easy enough to identify ourselves with those who participated in his program. For this same reason, I don't focus on serial killers and the like—though I will not claim that there is any categorical difference between "us" and such "monsters." For example, Jeffrey Dahmer's father, Lionel Dahmer, has described his inability, at first, to understand how his son could become one of the worst serial killers in the history of the United States: he seemed, at first, like a complete stranger. Slowly but surely, however, the father began to recognize how something could have turned Dahmer "into the person my son became."[7] I believe it's possible, then, for all of us to discover these sides of ourselves—sides that find an extreme expression in cases such as Jeffrey Dahmer's. But I also believe that the grounds for identification with people such as Dahmer—who was obviously a seriously disturbed young man—are tenuous enough that there is more to be gained by focusing on the evil done by normal people. I am interested, that is, in what the idea of evil can contribute to an understanding of *us*.

It would be intellectual hubris to think that I could make evil completely intelligible. My own understanding of evil has changed during the time I've spent working on this book. In the beginning, as I've said, evil was first and foremost an object of fascination. Then it became something more terrifying, and finally something simply, enormously, sad. And perhaps that's the essential characteristic of evil: it is terribly sad. As far as basic intelligibility, I assume that my reader will be able to picture in detail the events I discuss. Those who are looking for graphic descriptions of crimes, however—instruments of torture past and present, what serial killers did to their victims, brutal methods of execution, etc.—will be disappointed: For the most part, I've left such things out. Perhaps the book would have been more "entertaining" if it contained such descriptions, but my primary goal wasn't to write an entertaining book. Besides, I believe that the essential details, presented soberly, are hair-raising enough.

I recognize as well that the subject of this book is too extensive, too complex, and too ill defined for any representation to do it justice in a truly satisfying way. It was never my intention to give a *Gesamtdarstellung*, a complete picture, capturing evil in its full complexity and providing a solution to all the problems evil presents us with. But even singling out the aspects I felt were especially pertinent to the discussion proved to be more problematic than I ever imagined. I thought that, academically speaking, I was well prepared to write this book, but when I began to survey the source material I felt like I was drowning. I've never worked on any project that called for such extensive research; I was only able to cover a fraction of the literature on the subject, leaving out, in the process, many things that I found particularly interesting. Nevertheless: I hope I've included the most important works.[8] This isn't a *History of Evil*, even though I do track changing notions of evil through my historical sources. A complete history of evil from the Old Testament (or even earlier: from the Epic of Gilgamesh) to the present day would prove a far too comprehensive task. Instead, I've chosen to limit my discussion to certain topics and theories that I find especially relevant.

There are four traditional explanations concerning the origin of evil: (1) People are possessed or seduced by a malevolent, supernatural power; (2) people are predisposed, by nature, to act in a certain way that might be described as evil; (3) people are influenced by their environment to commit evil acts; and (4) people have free will and choose to act in accordance with evil. Of these four explanations, I will focus most on (3) and (4), while (2) will be handled more succinctly. On the other hand, I will not discuss (1) at all. In my opinion, this is not a subject for rational debate, but is purely a matter of religious belief. That is to say, I will not debate the existence of Devils and Antichrists, because I consider these subjects to belong to theology or to the history and sociology of religion much more than to philosophy.[9] In the course of the eighteenth century, the Devil lost his place as a convincing explanation for evil.[10] Religious, magical, and mythical themes do not occupy a central place in this book, even though I do engage in a relatively in-depth discussion of the problem of theodicy—that is, how God's existence is compatible with all the evil that is found in the world. In this book, I'm more concerned with humanity than God—something that's clearly related to the fact that I'm not a believer. The choice to take humanity as my point of departure, however, does not mean that I think I've found the *root* of all evil. It's simply that evil makes itself known, first and foremost, in human interaction.[11] While it's clear that, where evil is concerned, the boundaries between philosophy and theology are blurred, I've steered clear of the theological issue—aside from in Part I, which is devoted to traditional, theological solutions to the problem of evil—more so than is common in other literature on this subject.[12] For myself, evil is about interhuman relationships, not about a transcendent, supernatural force. When we call evil acts "inhuman," we completely miss the mark. Evil is human, all too human. As William Blake writes: "Cruelty has a Human Heart."[13]

Again, the goal of this book is not to unearth "the root of all evil" or trace evil to its source, but first and foremost to describe certain characteristics of human action, and the positive and negative possibilities it contains. One problem we face, in life, is that the negative possibilities so much outnumber the positive. In terms of causality, it's always easier to do evil than to do good; easier to hurt another human being in ways that will haunt them for the rest of their lives than to provide a comparable amount of help; easier to inflict an enormous amount of suffering on an entire nation than to bring about a comparable state of prosperity. In short, there's an asymmetry between our ability to do good and our ability to do evil. This may be a defining condition for human action, but it's still our responsibility to do more good than evil.

Finally, because it was my desire, in writing this book, to understand the perpetrator more than his victim, I have, necessarily, put greater emphasis on evils committed than on evils suffered. Some people will perhaps say that the victim deserves a greater share of our attention, but it should be obvious where my sympathies lie.

I have had extremely generous support from friends and colleagues. Anne Granberg, Thomas Nilsen, Hilde Norrgrén, Helge Svare, and Knut Olav Åmås offered constructive commentary, pointed out weaknesses and suggested some important revisions. Helge Jordheim suggested a number of improvements, among others the reorganization of sections in Part II, which has made the book clearer. Einar Øverenget commented on the chapter on

Arendt. My editor, Ingrid Ugelvik, has gone above and beyond the call of duty. A hearty thanks to them and to all who have made the book better than it would have been otherwise. Any mistakes or omissions are naturally my own.

INTRODUCTION

WHAT IS EVIL AND HOW CAN WE UNDERSTAND IT?

Even if the idea of evil seems outdated, a holdover from a pre-modern era when the world was interpreted by way of Christian doctrine, evil is still a reality for us. We see, do, and suffer from evil. This is true even when we manage to forget—sometimes for quite a long time—that evil does exist; sooner or later, something always comes along to serve as a brutal reminder. In 1939, Thomas Mann remarked that we'd again discovered the difference between good and evil, and that this was a good thing.[14] It seems the recognition of evil surfaces again and again, only to be forgotten. E. M. Cioran writes: "I have less and less discernment as to what is good and what evil. When I make no distinction whatever between the two, supposing I reach this point some day—what a step forward! Toward what?"[15] Toward catastrophe, I should imagine. We recognize evil when it has a face, an identity. That's what happened in the former Yugoslavia during the early 1990s and in the United States on September 11, 2001.

In his introduction to the book *The Death of Satan*, Andrew Delbanco observes that today there's an enormous gap between our experience of evil and our intellectual capacity for understanding it.[16] We see social need and vicious acts, but aside from certain extreme cases—that have a clear perpetrator—we have no real idea of where evil actually *resides*. In the Christian culture, Satan was the scapegoat—but when God died, Satan followed suit, and we, Satan's murderers, lost the ability to talk about evil. Because how can you talk about evil without the aid of evil incarnate?

Jean Baudrillard asks what's become of evil in our day and age, and answers that it resides *everywhere*.[17] This idea is reminiscent of H. C. Andersen's fairy tale "The Snow Queen," where the devil's mirror—which warps everything it reflects, showing its worst possible manifestation—splinters, and the splinters land in every human eye and heart, dooming mankind to see something evil or corrupt everywhere we turn.[18] For most of us, the idea of evil isn't something we associate with our everyday reality, with our day-to-day experiences and routines, but we do nonetheless come into contact with it almost constantly by means of the mass media: We are always watching and reading reports of genocide, famine, unmotivated violence, and traffic accidents, living in a paradoxical situation where evil is both absent and omnipresent—absent in our concrete experience, but everywhere in the reality we perceive in the media. Thus, for Baudrillard, evil is everywhere—and since it's everywhere, we've lost the capacity to talk about it.[19] Evil has become decentralized; it's no longer located in a single image. We live in a world where foolishness triumphs on all fronts, and such foolishness is the root of all evil.[20] Baudrillard goes further, however, saying that this omnipresence of evil is made possible precisely *because* we don't know how to talk about it. He argues, therefore, that it's imperative to restore dualism and resurrect the principle of evil, as it is found in Manicheism and other mythologies, and oppose it to the principle of good.[21] On the other hand, Andrew Delbanco maintains that our understanding of evil should be renewed instead of restored—though he makes no practical suggestions as to how such a renewal might take place.[22]

We might object to all this and say that evil has always existed everywhere, but "evil" can refer to such a diverse number of phenomena that the concept seems beyond our comprehension. Perhaps, then, the idea of evil can indeed only be grasped through mythological representation? This is the departure point for Paul Ricoeur's theory on the symbolism of evil. Ricoeur maintains that evil is more or less inaccessible to philosophical reflection because reason presupposes a meaningful context that has no room for the idea of evil, whereas myths and symbols act as recourses to aid our understanding.[23] The danger is that myths are easily transformed into ontology. That is, what starts out as a means of representation is confused with an actual, active force. In this way, myth comes to function as *explanation* rather than as *symbol*. Ricoeur insists that the dissolution of myth as explanation is necessary for the return of myth as symbol.[24] But what symbolism of evil would still be relevant to us today?

We certainly don't need the idea of an otherworldly hell. Nazi and Communist concentration camps, for example, have already done a fairly good job of embodying on earth the same notion of hell we inherited from our religious traditions. Likewise, we don't need the idea of a supernatural devil to understand what an evil agent is: they are everywhere, living among us. Still, though we can't continue to locate evil in a single place or actor, surely we can recognize that it manifests itself more fully in certain places and actors than in others?

There are few who will deny that evil exists in the world, but there are many, in fact, who will deny that there is such thing as an evil *person*. Ron Rosenbaum points out that there are amazingly few Hitler specialists today who are willing to call Hitler evil.[25] It's striking that there's such a widespread reluctance to use the word "evil" to describe the person who in modern times has come to incarnate evil more than any other. This says a little bit about how low the idea of evil has sunk, and how little it's used. I myself agree with Alan Bullock, who remarks that if we can't say that Hitler was evil, then the word "evil" lacks all meaning.[26] Do evil people exist? If doing evil to others suffices for one to be called evil, then the answer is a resounding "yes." The same holds true if we further insist that evil, to be evil, must be committed with *intent*, not accidentally. On the other hand, if we go on to insist that evil is only properly evil when it is committed *because it is evil*—that is, that the motivation for an evil act must reside in the very fact of its being evil—then I would have to be a little more cautious, and will simply assert that things which can in some way be defined as good can also become grounds for doing evil.

The idea of evil seems to be making a comeback, lately, in the field of ethics—in both the continental and analytical traditions. People were reluctant, on the whole, to discuss evil during the twentieth century, because the term was largely associated with theological problems beyond the scope of a more scientifically oriented philosophy. This trend has a long history: in keeping with what Max Weber called the *Entzauberung der Welt*, the "disenchantment" of the world, and the waning influence of religion, we have seen the idea of evil gradually shuffled to the periphery since the sixteenth century. In his excellent discussion of religion's political history, Marcel Gauchet writes:

> God's withdrawal, which initially caused the evil objectively present in the world to be pushed back into the unoccupied inwardness of the sinner, logically led, at a later stage, if not to evil's total expulsion from the world, at least to a radical relativization of its influence. Evil still existed, but it said nothing about the ultimate nature of things or about the being of humans. It no longer originated in ontology but in pathology. [27]

The idea of evil could find no place in a rational and scientific view of the world. It was no longer religion but science that determined the truth about the human condition. Today this task falls particularly to biology. However, biology has no room for the concept of moral evil. In *The Moral Animal*, Robert Wright asserts:

> The concept of "evil" [...] doesn't fit easily into a modern, scientific worldview. Still, people seem to find it useful, and the reason is that it is metaphorically apt. There is indeed a force devoted to enticing us into various pleasures that are (or once were) in our genetic interest but do not bring long-term happiness to us and may bring great suffering to others. You could call that force the ghost of natural selection. More concretely, you could call it our genes (*some* of our genes, at least). If it will help to actually use the world *evil*, there's no reason not to.[28]

Wright's position is in every way incompatible with the idea of evil as a moral concept. Moral evil vanishes into natural evil; Wright has replaced original sin with genetic material. The difference between moral and natural evil isn't easy to map out, but we can tentatively say that moral evil begins with free will, while the causes of natural evil are purely natural. Biology doesn't have the capacity to define the *moral* concept of evil and at most can only *explain away* the phenomenon. What tools does biology employ to distinguish good from evil? Nothing aside from the fact that "good" can be understood as "useful for an individual's reproduction," while evil can be understood as anything that is correspondingly useless. Lyall Watson writes that we don't necessarily have to be selfish, even if our genes are. However, he also veers off and latches onto

Augustine's doctrine of original sin, ultimately arguing that, like the rest of nature, we are born evil.[29] But neither good nor evil are located in our genes. Instead, both represent concrete possibilities for each of us.

Traditional, theological vocabulary has long been considered a historical relic. In its place, we attempt to use a more "scientific" vocabulary. Instead of evil, we talk about asocial tendencies, dysfunctions that can be corrected—dysfunctions usually considered to have social or chemical causes. The problem, however, is that our vocabulary doesn't match our own experiences. We can blame a perpetrator, but we can't blame a dysfunction—a dysfunction can merely be corrected. In fact, this idea robs the perpetrator of something essential, namely of his freedom and dignity. As Dostoevsky writes:

> In making the individual responsible, Christianity thereby acknowledges his freedom. In making the individual dependent on every flaw in the social structure, however, the doctrine of the environment reduces him to an absolute nonentity, exempts him totally from every personal moral duty and from all independence, reduces him to the lowest form of slavery imaginable.[30]

One of the best-known fictional serial killers, Hannibal Lecter, refuses, in just these terms, to let himself be imprisoned in a flaw located outside himself. He insists upon his own evil, because it forms an essential part of his dignity: "Nothing happened to me [. . .]. *I* happened. You can't reduce me to a set of influences."[31] We have a tendency to redefine evil in such a way that social evil is seen as a "social problem" and individual evil becomes a "personality disturbance."[32] We look for the *causes* of evil and these causes are often located outside the discussion of morality. They can be either natural or social, and can range from natural inclination and illness to poverty and traumatic childhood experiences. However, if you attribute all human evil to such causes—causes located outside the individual understood as a moral subject—simply to provide a "scientific" explanation for evil, you've suddenly reduced moral evil to natural evil, and thereby done away with all moral standards. Such reductionism is, however, completely contrary to our experience of ourselves and other human beings as moral agents subject to ideas such as guilt and responsibility.

My insistence that ideas such as guilt and responsibility are unavoidable may seem old-fashioned. David B. Morris suggests that evil has changed its character in the postmodern era, and that evil can no longer be understood as the cause of suffering: Instead, suffering itself should be regarded as evil.[33] A number of theoreticians likewise have the tendency to separate evil from individual responsibility. As a result, evil is exclusively attributed to outside causes, for example to "society."[34] Odo Marquard describes how an "Entbösung des Bösen" takes place in modernity—how, that is, evil is de-eviled.[35] We traditionally distinguish between evil that is committed and evil that is suffered, between active and passive evil; however, according to Morris, only the passive aspect, suffering, now remains. Not only evil incarnate, but also *evil itself* has vanished from the world. The only things to remain are the *evils* that we suffer. Of course, these evils do have causes, but the causes themselves are not considered evil.

The concept of evil evaporates in scientific debate. Human misdeeds are not considered *sins*, but are instead the *effects* of various *causes*. In Hitler studies, a whole host of causes are typically put forth as explanations for Hitler's actions—for example, Hitler's relationship to his father, his later affair with his niece Geli Raubal, or else his insecurity complex resulting from a physical defect (first and foremost the much-discussed thesis of whether or not he lacked a testicle).[36] The choice of cause depends on a given researcher's discipline and runs the gambit from genes and chemistry to social relationships and political ideologies. However, Hitler was not simply the sum of a certain set of causes, but also a person who acted freely. There is always something else, something irreducible, something that doesn't simply vanish without a trace into the chain of cause and effect—something that allows us to makes choices, a thing we can call *free will*. Without free will, moral evil simply doesn't exist. (I don't mean to assert here that every scientific explanation is illegitimate, but simply to underscore that they have limited validity.) Thus, our attempts to explain away evil, to rationalize it, have never been completely successful. The fact that an individual is free means that in a given situation they *could have acted differently*; it follows then, when we commit evil, that we can be *accused* for not having acted differently.

It is clear, despite everything, that we continue to have a general, if vague, understanding of "evil," and can use the word to refer to events, actions, and people. These events, actions, and people might also be described using other terms, of course; the question is whether or not the word "evil" aids our understanding. In my opinion, it certainly does. The idea is a valuable tool when we attempt to orient ourselves in the enigmatic landscape we call "the world." I further believe that "good" and "evil" not only refer to the way a person evaluates different phenomena, but also to a given phenomenon itself, to the object of our evaluation. In other words, I don't agree with Hamlet that "Nothing is either good or bad, but thinking makes it so."[37] The decree that "X is evil" is true if and only if X *has the characteristic* of being evil. So what does it mean, then, to say that "X is evil"? All people hope to live a good life, but living a good life is not always possible—and in the broadest sense of the word, evil can be understood as everything that hinders the realization of a good life. This understanding of evil encompasses natural catastrophes and sickness as well—and there were many who considered the earthquake in Lisbon in 1755 as an expression of the earth's inherent maliciousness.[38] In a narrower sense, evil signifies those premeditated human actions that are intended to cause harm to others. Earlier, the expression was often used in the broader sense, but today we mainly use it in the narrower.

Evil is not simply a single overarching problem. Instead, it represents a number of concrete phenomena that all contribute to making life less than good. Yet we humans have always wanted to discover an *unconditional* concept of evil that allows us to relate all our misfortunes back to it. As Novalis concludes: "We seek everywhere the unconditioned, and always find only the conditioned."[39] That is, we are always seeking *the ultimate evil* and finding only *evils. Ultimate evil* simply does not exist. What does not exist, in my estimation, is evil as something autonomous—whether understood as something present or something lacking. "Good" and "evil" are relative concepts; that is, something is only good or evil in relation to something else, not in and of itself. Evil is not a substance, a thing, but rather a *characteristic* of things, events, or actions. Evil is *not* something definite and well defined, nor does it have an essence. "Evil" is a broad concept we use to describe actions and suffering. In fact, the idea refers to such manifold phenomena—for example, illness, natural catastrophes, death, war, genocide, terrorism, the drug trade, slavery, rape, child abuse, etc.—that it can appear to be so broad as to lose all specific content. All these various evils, however, are recognized as evils *suffered by humanity*, and the idea of evil is therefore applicable, even though it is difficult to pin down the necessary and sufficient conditions of its use. Of course, in order to reconcile ourselves to the existence of these evils, we tend to seek a *meaning* behind evil. Such meaning would ensure that *the world's* existence was justified and allow us to hope that things could change for the better. We find such meaning in different places: in religion, in our belief in progress, in political ideology. My general attitude, however, is that evil neither can nor should be justified, and that every attempt to reconcile ourselves to the suffering in the world is wrong. There is simply no meaning to be found in the countless tragedies of human history. They cannot be justified by any divine plan or active historical force.

Indeed, one of the things that fascinates us most about evil is its apparent incomprehensibility—which is both seductive and repulsive. By incomprehensibility, what I mean is that the idea of evil has a certain opaqueness about it; even though, as a philosopher, it's my business to understand things, so I must act on the assumption that my chosen subject is understandable. Still, just because I think it's *possible* to understand the phenomena doesn't mean that I'll be able to do it. Raimond Gaita claims: "Good and evil are essentially mysterious, which is why no metaphysical or religious explanations will penetrate their mystery."[40] I doubt that "mystical" is the right word, because it implies a special depth that can only be plumbed by a certain type of insight, by a special intuition. But isn't it true that anyone can recognize evil? We *see* evil in the form of persecution, starvation, torture, murder, etc. If we read a kind of depth into these events, it's precisely because we long for a dimension of meaning that evil's manifestations actually lack. Again, the purpose of this book is not to "plumb the depths" in order to find the root of all evil. Instead, I've tried to stay as close to the surface as possible; close to the place, that is, where the phenomena of evil tend to show themselves. If I'm going to understand evil, I have to begin on the surface, at the place evil appears in our lives. Ricoeur argues that the price we pay for clarity, dealing with a demythologized concept, is the loss of depth.[41] However, when dealing with the idea of evil, the surface is so demanding that it seems premature to "go in depth." Of course, evil also invites "in-depth" consideration because it appears to defy given forms and frameworks and eludes our control. Emmanuel Levinas, for instance, describes evil as something that can't be integrated into the world, something that doesn't fit when we try to grasp the world as a whole, something that's always on the outside: the radical Other.[42] Evil appears to us as something chaotic, defying comprehension—and perhaps it's this experience of evil that forms the basis for the many privation theories, according to which evil is simply understood as the absence or lack of the good. These theories seem to explain our difficulty in grasping evil, because there's *nothing* there to grasp. An attempt to grasp evil would literally be to reach out into an empty nothingness. The problem, however, is that these privation theories cannot fully account for the "positive" moments in our chaotic experience of evil, where something is actually *given*, not simply lacking.

We can recognize evil without having a *theory* of evil. Evil is an unavoidable aspect of the world. It precedes philosophical reflection, because it's found in experiences that form the basis for such reflection. In this respect, philosophy itself is understood as the act of reflecting on a meaning or experience that already exists.[43] Philosophy takes its content and legitimacy from what is already understood. This viewpoint is methodologically significant because it requires philosophy to maintain contact with the pre-philosophical if it's to retain its legitimacy. On the one hand, therefore, evil is something abstract and elusive; on the other hand, something concrete and tangible. An abused child, a bomb that kills innocents, a people slaughtered—all these things are concrete events. But when we attempt to understand the evil inherent in these events, we often lose ourselves in greater and greater abstractions that become steadily less tangible. Ultimately, we remain lost in abstraction and therefore lose sight of the concrete evil that was the basis for our initial reflection. Most explanations of evil simply *explain it away*. This is especially evident in the countless theodicies that compose the greatest percentage of the literature on evil. To avoid losing sight of concrete evil has been a goal of this book, and I have therefore attempted to write a comparatively *concrete* study of it.

In part, this book can be described as a *phenomenology* of evil, as a consideration of how evil manifests itself. The phenomenologist Heidegger's reflections concerning evil, however, take an almost entirely different direction than the one I have chosen. Heidegger primarily wants to see evil as an ontological, rather than a moral or political problem.[44] He tries to plumb "the depths" of evil, whereas I've chosen to remain on the surface. For Heidegger, morality is something derivative,[45] but for me it's fundamental for an understanding of evil. My own approach to the subject—plainly stated, that evil is first and foremost a practical problem and that we have a duty to do our utmost to prevent the suffering of others—would for Heidegger be an expression of the decay of reason in modern times.[46] In fact, as Heidegger understands evil, such a view of evil would itself be evil.[47] Heidegger wants to uncover an ontological evil that penetrates deeper than the moral, but in my opinion he fails in his attempt. However, a detailed discussion of this topic would take up a disproportionate amount of space.[48]

The main point of this book is quite simple: evil is not first and foremost a *theoretical* concept, but rather a *practical* problem. The question of how evil entered into the world, whether it has actual being, or can only be understood as an absence, etc., is less important than the question of how evil can be prevented. In my opinion, philosophy—and to an even greater extent theology—has erroneously prioritized the theoretical over the practical. Today's analytical philosophy of religion is especially extreme in this regard.[49] When we're suffering, theodicy isn't the most pressing issue. And it certainly shouldn't be the most pressing issue when others are suffering. Nevertheless, I'm a philosopher, and therefore this book also makes a contribution to theory. At the same time, large parts of it are also devoted to removing what I consider to be *theoretical blind spots*. The movement of this book is from the theoretical to the practical, from the problem of theodicy to politics. Along the way, political questions replace classical ontological questions concerning evil.

In the twentieth century, hundreds of millions of human lives were lost because of war, genocide, and torture.[50] This means that multiple human lives were lost per minute on *political*, that is, ideological grounds. Between 1900 and 1989, around eighty-six million people were killed in war. When compared to the number of people who starved to death during the same period, that number may not seem large; however, it should be stressed that many hunger-related catastrophes have ideological causes as well, such as in the Soviet Union under Stalin and China under Mao. And, certainly, in itself, the number is enormous. Around two thirds of these people lost their lives in the two world wars; if we distribute these deaths equally over the entire eighty-nine-year period, however, we still find that for every hour that passed during the twentieth century, an average of one hundred people were killed in war.[51] Of course, it's nothing new for people to lose their lives in war—if we look at the last 3,400 years, we find that there were only 243, all together, in which mankind was not at war.[52] A study of eleven European countries showed that, on average, these countries were either involved in a war or some other kind of military confrontation for forty-seven percent of the last millennium. In the last century, there was an average of three conflicts resulting in significant loss of human life taking place on the globe at any given time.[53]

According to Hobbes, violent death is the greatest of all evils.[54] There are a number of other great evils, and living with chronic pain due to some illness is not necessarily the least of them. But violent death is clearly *among* the greatest, however we look at it, and Hobbes's assertion has far more resonance today than Augustine's claim that eternal death is the greatest of all evils.[55] Eternal death seems a rather tempting alternative to the kind of things that living people inflict on one another. But, on the subject of violence, my focus will remain on the *individuals* who perpetrate and are the victims of these crimes, rather than on general political relationships. I don't believe that Auschwitz or Bosnia can reveal any deep metaphysical truths about modern, Western culture, about civilization's *telos* or the like. What happened was that a group of individuals acting under certain political, social, and material conditions persecuted, tortured, and murdered other individuals. There's no good reason why an understanding of such events should require us to refer to historical-metaphysical principles, the "deepest" levels of a person's spiritual being (what that person "really" is) or the like. We're dealing with concrete *agents* in a concrete socio-material space—and it's important to maintain the agent perspective. A socio-material space never unfolds by itself. It's made up of *individuals* who act in accordance with the possibilities and limitations imposed by that space. Genocide is only possible if a relatively large number of individuals are willing to murder a large number of other individuals over a long period of time. We can put forth a host of explanations on different levels, and these can all shed some light on the phenomenon, but ultimately we cannot escape the fact that the *individuals* in a group must be willing to murder the individuals in another group *because* they belong to the other group. As Hugh Trevor-Roper points out, in the context of witch-hunts: They were only possible because a large portion of the population supported them and took part. No tyrant or dictator *acting alone* can bring about the persecution of large groups of people.[56] For the most part, too, those individuals who take part in persecutions know the difference between right and wrong. They know that people shouldn't torture and murder their fellow men, but they don't let this insight influence their actions. How is that possible? If we're going to understand the majority of the participants in genocide and other such crimes, we have to direct our focus to a side of evil not often discussed, away from the usual argument that agents of evil do evil *because* it's evil. Instead, we need to turn our sights toward idealistic and "stupid" evil, respectively—where, on the one hand, agents consider their actions to be good because those persecuted are themselves considered "evil," or else, on the other, agents simply neglect to reflect upon whether their actions are good or evil.

The Holocaust forms a decisive orientation point in relation to all later thought concerning evil—even though, at the same time, it's often upheld as a singular event that won't tolerate comparison. A paradoxical aspect of discussions concerning the Holocaust, therefore, is that it is considered a unique event, without parallels, while being used simultaneously as the standard by which all other evil must be measured. In my opinion, the thesis of uniqueness, which considers the Holocaust to be an absolute singularity, should be discarded entirely, once and for all.[57] More than implying that nothing like the Holocaust has ever before occurred in our history, this thesis also implies that nothing like it will ever happen again. Adorno, for one, maintains that Hitler has forced a new categorical imperative upon humanity, "to arrange [our] thoughts and actions so Auschwitz will not repeat itself, so that nothing similar will happen . . ."[58] It's interesting that Adorno allows himself this "nothing similar," because it weakens the thesis of uniqueness that he otherwise embraces. This addition, however, is vitally important: it obliges us not only to prevent another Auschwitz, but also another Srebrenica, Rwanda, Congo, and countless other situations. Adorno also suggests that the thought that life could proceed "like normal" after the Second World War and the eradication of the Jews is "idiotic."[59] For the most part, however, life *has* proceeded like normal. Instead of standing for the end of history, the Holocaust has *become* history . . . albeit a part of history that obliges us to prevent it from ever repeating itself. In the meantime, however, despite our obligation, it has indeed gone on repeating itself—and will probably do so again.

The Holocaust represents an extraordinary evil, certainly, but it was completely ordinary people who carried out the mass exterminations, who gassed and cremated others, who slaughtered whole towns, who conducted medical experiments on other human beings, who murdered Jews so that their skeletons could be donated to an anatomical institute at a German university, etc.—and the morality of these perpetrators can't be used to differentiate the Holocaust from other genocides. The Holocaust stands as one of the worst cases of genocide the world has ever seen—perhaps the worst, by certain standards—but it can indeed be compared to other genocides: Everything can be compared to something else. On empirical grounds—that is, the number murdered, the technology used to commit the murders, its effectiveness, etc.—the Holocaust is simply not a unique event. As compared with earlier genocides, the Holocaust *does* demonstrate some characteristics theretofore unrecorded, but none of these signify that we're dealing with an absolute singularity or historical discontinuity—quite the opposite.

For example, there's a direct connection between the Holocaust and the Armenian genocide in Turkey in 1915, where around 800,000 of the 1.3 million Armenians in Turkey were murdered.[60] The Nazis were "inspired" by this genocide, and there was a close relationship between the governments of Germany and Turkey. Turkey still doesn't admit responsibility for this genocide and argues that there were "merely" around 300,000 murdered—as if that wasn't already an enormous number—and that, besides, the mass exterminations weren't planned and executed by the government. Turkey's official position is completely false, and it ought to be possible now—nearly a hundred years later—to acknowledge the realities of the event. At the same time, although the persecution of Kurds in present day Turkey can scarcely be described as genocide, it too has claimed around 30,000 lives over the last decades.

Another example would be the gruesome events in the Belgian Congo, modern day Zaïre. Joseph Conrad's *Heart of Darkness* was not simply a fantasy; under Leopold II, the Belgian Congo was very close indeed to the world described by Conrad—only worse. It's difficult to say exactly how many died as a direct result of Belgium's policies, but the most common estimate is that the population was reduced from twenty million to just under ten million during the years (1880–1920) that the land was officially ruled by Belgium.[61] These figures are particularly astonishing because Belgian's involvement in the Congo was almost exclusively economically motivated. That is, Belgium's goal wasn't simply to exterminate the populace, as is the case with most other genocides. The violence in the Belgian Congo was essentially instrumental in nature, based on a concept of how the land could best be ruled with an eye toward turning the maximum profit. At the same time, it's clear that the violence escalated to such an extent that it also undermined its own effectiveness. Much of the valuable work force was either eradicated or disabled. King Leopold II himself recognized the irrationality of cutting off a native's hand—after all, that native could have been put to work. Beyond that, however, he gave no thought to how the natives were treated.[62] Eventually, the terror in the Belgian Congo began to take on a life of its own, divorced from the instrumental considerations that formed its basis. It's clear too that most of those who carried out these "crimes against humanity"[63] were ordinary people without notable sadistic tendencies, although the undertaking did attract a fair number of individuals who took a perverse pleasure in abusing the natives. In brutality and scope, the events in the Belgian Congo are certainly comparable to the Holocaust, though the motivations behind the two genocides were widely different. Indeed, the Nazis' goals could be considered far more idealistic:[64] What makes the

Holocaust especially difficult to understand, perhaps, is that its evil was *not* first and foremost instrumental. The Jews posed no threat to non-Jews, nor had they tried to challenge the government. The Jews were standing in no one's way. In other words: "The Jewish Problem" was in no way a real social, economic, religious, territorial or general political *problem*.

The genocide in Rwanda, in which around 800,000 people were murdered by the Hutus, was more explicitly politically motivated. The victims were mainly Tutsis, but a number of moderate and intellectual Hutus were murdered as well because they were not "radical" enough and therefore were grouped together with the "enemies." The slaughter of the Tutsis was hard work, in part because many of the Hutus were armed only with machetes (which had been imported from China for the occasion), but nonetheless they were able to murder Tutsis at a greater pace than the Nazis' during the Jewish extermination.[65] The violence, however, wasn't "merely" a matter of murder. There was also rape, torture, crippling of victims, etc. And then, similarly, we can also mention Indonesia: In 1966, the Indonesian government accused ethic Chinese of being in league with the communists and murdered hundreds of thousands of people. And when Indonesia invaded East Timor in 1975, around 200,000 East Timorians, or a third of the population, were killed. The list of genocides and similar occurrences is only getting longer.

In the communist regimes, anyone could be a target for aggression, and new groups were always being added to the enemy list. There were as many murders in the largest Gulag camps, like Kolyma, as in the largest concentration camps. In the Nazi camps, prisoners were gassed, while in the communist camps prisoners mainly starved to death. The similarities between the Nazis and the communists is starkly underscored by the fact that a number of former concentration camps, such as Buchenwald and Sachsenhausen, were *reopened* by the Russians after Germany's surrender and filled with Nazis and other political opponents. Some ex-prisoners were even sent to the same camp from which they'd just been released. Even if the prisoner count was significantly lower than when the Nazis managed the camps, there were still around 120,000 prisoners, of which 45,000 died of hunger, sickness, or exhaustion, or else were executed.[66] The Nazis succeeded in murdering around twenty-five million people; over a longer period of time, the communists succeeded in murdering at least a hundred million.[67] Both systems had a remarkable willingness to sacrifice human lives for the sake of a "higher" cause. Mao believed that one in every five people was an enemy; at the time, this meant that thirty of the six hundred million people living in China should be eliminated. He eventually considered letting half the population die in an atomic war, since the country was overpopulated anyway.[68] Any consideration of the *individual* was irrelevant. It's difficult to estimate how many died under Mao, but it was at least thirty-five million people, and presumably this is a conservative estimate. These deaths were regarded as irrelevant, or at least as justified, on the grounds that they served a higher purpose. Then, in Cambodia, the Khmer Rouge murdered approximately two million out of a population of eight million. To murder over a quarter of one's own people for the sake of a political agenda is an example of the totalitarian worldview driven to its most extreme. Still, it's important to underscore that some conception of the *good* lay at the heart of these mass exterminations. That is, it was precisely a concept of the good that led to some of the greatest evils imaginable.

And yet evil—no matter if it's committed on a small scale or a large—always has a multitude of different causes. It's important to keep this complexity in mind, rather than to reduce all evil to a single root cause. As I've mentioned, many theories of evil posit that the root of an evil action is the intent to cause harm—that is, that evil is a goal in and of itself. This is what I will call "demonic" evil, but it's not the dominant form. Theories that reduce all evil to the demonic form cause us to lose sight of the myriad other varieties. Such a one-sided focus on demonic evil also encourages us to regard the problem of evil as irrelevant for an understanding of ourselves, simply because we don't see ourselves as "demons." Evil isn't limited to "demons," however, and most of those who took part in the genocides mentioned above were—and I will continue to stress this—completely normal people without sadistic dispositions. Under certain circumstances, we're all capable of doing unspeakable things to our fellow men. It's therefore essential to pinpoint these exact circumstances. Part II of this book, "The Anthropology of Evil," will be dedicated to this question.

Evil is primarily a moral category and effects a person's every actions. Therefore, it's just as important to understand what we should *do* about evil as to understand *why* we commit evil. It's here we leave the descriptive field and enter into normative ethics and political philosophy. It's also here that the real problem of evil lies. In Part III, then, "The Problem of Evil," I will try to demonstrate that this problem is a *practical* problem, because it's more important to hinder and limit the scope of evil than to explain how it entered into the world. The problem of evil shouldn't be located in theology or the natural sciences, and certainly not in philosophy, but in moral and political discourse. One of this book's most important goals, therefore, is to remove what I've referred to as *theoretical blind spots*—not the least of which are the various theodicies I will discuss in Part I—which direct our attention away from concrete evils and cause us to focus on abstractions instead of the real problem.

I

THE THEOLOGY OF EVIL

Primo Levi writes: "There was Auschwitz, therefore God cannot exist."[69] Levi, who survived several years in Auschwitz, repeated these words a few days before he died in 1987—when he apparently committed suicide. Dostoevsky's romantic figure Ivan Karamasov requires something less radical than Auschwitz to make the same declaration: a single child's tear. We could perhaps say that Levi has an evidential argument against God's existence, while Ivan Karamasov has a logical argument. The evidential argument claims that the *amount* of evil in the world is incompatible with the belief in a good, almighty God,[70] while the logical argument claims that the very existence of evil is incompatible with such a belief.[71] The *logical* argument tries to show that theism is inconsistent, while the evidential tries to show that it is *improbable*.

At the heart of Ivan's great and damning speech is a child's innocence. Ivan believes that the suffering of an innocent child is an unacceptable evil. In a letter, Dostoevsky writes: "my hero has chosen an argument that *in my opinion* is irrefutable—the senselessness of children's suffering—and from it reaches the conclusion that all historical reality is an absurdity."[72] Ivan begins by underscoring the difference between children and adults:

> Although I had originally thought of talking to you about human suffering in general, I have now decided to talk to you only about the suffering of children. [...] I also will not speak of adults at the moment, because,

besides being disgusting and undeserving of love, they have something to compensate them for their suffering: they have eaten their apple of knowledge, they know about good and evil and are like gods themselves. And they keep eating the apple. But little children haven't eaten it. They're not yet guilty of anything. [. . .] Well then, if they suffer here in this world, it's because they're paying for the sins of their fathers who ate the apple. But that is the reasoning of another world and it's incomprehensible to the human heart here on earth. No innocents should be made to suffer for another man's sins, especially innocents such as these![73]

Ivan then produces a number of concrete examples, which Dostoevsky has taken from real life:

People often describe such human cruelty as "bestial," but that's, of course, unfair to animals, for no beast could ever be as cruel as man, I mean as refinedly and artistically cruel. The tiger simply gnaws and tears his victim to pieces because that's all he knows. It would never occur to a tiger to nail people to fences by their ears, even if he were able to do it. Those Turks, by the way, seem to derive a voluptuous pleasure from torturing children—they do everything from cutting unborn babes out of their mothers' wombs with their daggers to tossing infants into the air and catching them on the point of their bayonets while the mothers watch. It's doing this in front of the mothers that particularly arouses their senses. But, of all the things the Bulgarian told me, the following scene particularly caught my attention. Imagine a baby in the arms of his trembling mother, with Turks all around them. The Turks are having a little game: they laugh and tickle the baby to make it laugh too. Finally they succeed and the baby begins to laugh. Then one of the Turks points his pistol at the baby, holding it four inches from the child's face. The little boy chuckles delightedly and tries to catch the shiny pistol in his tiny hands. Suddenly the artist presses the trigger and fires into the baby's face, splitting his little head in half.[74]

Ivan's brother Alyosha asks him where he is going with all this and Ivan answers that "if the devil doesn't exist and is therefore man's creation, man has made him in his own image." Perhaps the most extreme example that Ivan cites takes place on a Russian property. The story is as follows: A little eight year-old boy throws a stone and hits the paw of a dog. Unfortunately, the dog belongs to the property's owner, a retired general. The general grabs the boy and sticks him in a cell over night:

> They brought the boy out of the guardroom. It was a bleak, foggy, raw day—an ideal day for hunting. The general ordered the boy stripped naked. The boy was shivering. He seemed paralyzed with fear. He didn't dare utter a sound. "Off with him now, chase him!" "Hey, you, run, run!" a flunkey yelled, and the boy started to run. "Sic 'im!" the General roared. The whole pack was set on the boy and the hounds tore him to pieces before his mother's eyes.[75]

Ivan believes that such occurrences can under no circumstances be justified as part of divine providence. Because He created a world where such things happen, God is morally responsible. Ivan turns away from God, because God's morals are, to him, unacceptable. He also asks Alyosha to consider the following scenario: "[L]et's assume that you were called upon to build the edifice of human destiny so that men would finally be happy and would find peace and tranquility. If you knew that, in order to attain this, would have to torture just one single creature [. . .] and that on her unavenged tears you could build that edifice, would you agree to do it?"[76] Alyosha is forced admit that he couldn't do such a thing. God's moral stance is one that even Alyosha, his staunch defender, must reject. As a result, his justification of God's morality seems empty.

In the subsequent chapters of *Brothers Karamasov*, Dostoevsky attempts to refute Ivan's world-view through his portrayal of the monk Zosima. However, there are few who will agree that this refutation is successful. Dostoevsky has simply made Ivan's arguments too good. However, successful or not, a number of different theories have been put forward over time in an attempt to demonstrate that all the world's suffering is compatible with the idea of a good, almighty God. These theories don't just belong to the history of ideas, but are also active today—even though "God" is often replaced by other concepts, such as "History." My discussion of these theories is purely negative. That is, I generally consider the theology of evil to be one of the theoretical blind spots that obstruct our understanding of the real problems posed by evil.

THEODICIES

The expression "theodicy" comes from Leibniz and is a combination of the Greek words for God and justice, *teos* and *diké*. A theodicy is a justification of God, an argument for His righteousness. Theodicy is generally associated with Christian thinking, but most of the arguments can already be found in Greek, pre-Christian thought. The basic tenet is articulated in a fragment attributed to Heraclitus, which claims that, for God, everything is beautiful, good, and just. Humans, on the other hand, see some things as just and others as unjust.[77] The basic premise for all later theodicies is likewise that injustice or evil only *appear* as unjust or evil to our limited understanding, while everything—either all parts or the sum of all parts—is good from a divine perspective. The free-will argument, which attributes the presence of evil to our own exercise of choice, can be found in Plato,[78] as well as the claim that this is the best of all possible worlds,[79] while the privation argument—which asserts that evil has no actual existence, but can be understood as an absence—is first systematically formulated by Plotinus, even though this thought also has its roots in Plato. (I should point out, however, that the picture we're painting here is somewhat misleading: ancient Greek philosophy did not, in fact, contain any real concept of "evil," despite the convenient use of the word in translating their texts into contemporary languages; as such, our tracing the above theories back to the Greek philosophers means projecting a later concept back onto them—a problematic undertaking at best. Nevertheless, any history of ideas concerning evil must include the ancient Greeks, because their theories have so strongly influenced later theoretical development.)

Next, the argument that God's omnipotence or divinity is incompatible with the world's suffering goes back to Epicurus and

Sextus Empiricus. However, it receives its classical formulation in *De ira Dei* by Lactantius (in the year 303), who sums up four possible alternatives:[80]

(1) God wants to overcome evil, but cannot.
(2) God can overcome evil, but will not.
(3) God neither can nor will overcome evil.
(4) God can and will overcome evil.

These four alternatives can be further paraphrased as follows: God is either evil or powerless (ultimately evil *and* powerless), or evil does not exist. Therefore, the contradiction presented by opposing a world where suffering exists with the idea of a good and almighty God has two possible resolutions: Either you somehow deny the world's suffering (that is, suffering is eventually shown to belong to a higher order of goodness) or else one or more of God's characteristics (existence, benevolence, omnipotence) are denied. Theists generally choose the first solution and atheists the second.

While the logical and evidential arguments both claim that God cannot exist because evil exists, theodicy takes God's existence for granted and tries to show how God's existence is compatible with the fact that evil is also found in the world. Theodicy tackles many of the same problems as the logical and evidential arguments; it has, however, a different purpose—namely, to show that faith in God is justified. Theodicy may place God on trial, but the verdict has been decided in advance: The accused was declared innocent before the trial even began. Thus, the function of theodicy might be described not as a justification of evil but as a means of explaining how God *can be found innocent* when the world contains so much suffering; theodicy springs from a "cognitive dissonance,"[81] from the seeming paradox created by viewing the world's suffering with the expectation that the world *must* be righteous, since it was created by a righteous God. Theodicy seeks to neutralize this dissonance by showing that the world is "actually" just after all—that suffering is necessary, that God is not responsible for suffering, etc.

I will discuss the strategy of debate adopted by different theodicies. However, most of the thinkers I will mention do not limit themselves to just one strategy, but combine several of them—for example the privation argument, the totality argument, the free will argument, and the aesthetic argument.[82] Augustine is typical in this regard. In the course of his *Confessions*, he works with the privation argument, the totality argument, and the free will argument as well, although he never clearly distinguishes between the three.[83] And, in the course of a single page, Descartes argues first that evil is not a positive existence, but rather an essential lack; second, that evil is caused by free will alone; and third that some things must be less than perfect in order for the world's splendor to shine through. God is of course not to blame in any of this, since he has ordered the universe for the best.[84] This smorgasbord of conflicting arguments confuses the issue much more than is necessary; I myself have chosen to address each argument individually. Of course, some may object that that these arguments form a whole and even support each other—but if each one is implausible, as I will try to demonstrate, then the sum of them must also be implausible; and if I feel that it's important for me to show that these theodicies are implausible, it is because, in my opinion, they have only one function: namely, to justify or explain away all the evil found in the world. But evil should never be justified, should never be explained away—it should be fought.

The Privation Theodicy

The person who first systematically formulates the privation theory is the neo-platonic thinker Plotinus. This primarily takes place in tractate 8 of the First Ennead, which Plotinus devotes to a consideration of "the nature and source of evil."[85] Plotinus claims that the highest form of existence is *The One*. However, we can neither know nor conceive of The One; it possesses neither qualitative nor quantitative characteristics; it's neither active nor at rest; and it's neither in time nor in space. Creation takes place when The One "passes over," as light streams from the sun. This outpouring is called an *emanation* and the emanation shapes a host of creations, from the highest spiritual being to the lowest and most material plane. The first source, The One, is good, but the farther you move from the source, the nearer you come to evil. Therefore, matter itself must be purely evil. From this standpoint, it may seem inexplicable that evil entered the world at all, since all that exists is shaped by emanations from the good, and all emanations are in themselves good. The solution to this quandary is that evil has no actual being. Instead, evil is simply a *lack* of the good. This lack, however, is necessary. In progressing away from the first source, the emanations must necessarily have a "final step," and by the time they have reached this final step, which is material, they contain no trace of the good. Thus, Plotinus's objection to those who complain that evil exists is this: They don't understand that an optimally good world must *necessarily* contain a number of evils. These evils, moreover, are merely a lack of the good, and therefore do not have any actual reality. The world necessarily contains varying degrees of imperfection.

Augustine furthers this privation theory. He likewise asserts that evil is merely a lack of the good and, therefore, that evil has no actual being—a direct continuation of Plotinus's privation theory, minus the idea that all matter is evil.[86] There's nothing evil in nature, he says.[87] Nature is inherently good, and though it can be corrupted, it can never become evil.[88] This theory is further developed by Thomas Aquinas, who asserts that evil can't be understood as a *general* lack: For instance, it's not evil for a person to lack wings, because it isn't in our nature to have wings. On the other hand, it's evil if a bird lacks wings, because this lack directly contradicts the bird's nature. Therefore, it is evil to diverge from the nature God intended us to have; and, according to Aquinas, humanity has chosen to be less than God intended.

A number of other thinkers have also launched versions of the privation theory,[89] and a few proponents are still hanging around,[90] but they've moved from the center to the periphery of the discussion concerning the problem of evil. The privation theory deals solely with evil's ontological status and is logically independent of theories that discuss to what extent everything that exists—that is, to what extent the totality—is good. The primary reason for this independence is that privation can become so all-encompassing that the totality itself comes to seem evil. The privation theory also has no logical relation to the question of guilt: Even if evil is understood as an absence of the good, this absence can be regarded as *willed*, as a willing eradication of the good by God. Augustine and Thomas Aquinas argue that humanity has *chosen* to exist in imperfection and, therefore, has fallen away from God. However, this argument can also be applied to God Himself: God has chosen to create an imperfect world, and, therefore, is responsible for that choice. It could be objected here that the imperfections in creation are necessary, that a certain amount of imperfection cannot be avoided, but this objection can be met with the assertion that a creation that necessarily has such glaring imperfections shouldn't have been undertaken in the first place. As a result, creation begins to seem like a fatal mistake on God's part, a mistake for which we all continue to pay the price. The privation argument, therefore, fails to justify God's benevolence and omnipotence. The argument rests on the idea that everything God has created is good, and that He cannot be blamed for what He didn't create. But a good, almighty God would be responsible for all privations, as well as for all the things that positively exist.

I do agree with privation theoreticians when they say that evil has no actual being, if by "having being" you mean that evil is a *thing*. I regard evil as a *characteristic* of something, not something that exists in its own right. My objections, however, are directed toward a more radical understanding of privation, which persists in denying the obvious. Phenomenologically understood, evil has a positive existence. Suffering is not simply the absence of pleasure, without any actual reality. Ontologically speaking, you can argue that suffering is rooted in human mortality, in the world's imperfections, etc. The question is whether this fundamentally ontological viewpoint helps shed light on the phenomenon of evil. In my opinion, it does not. In the best case, privation theory is irrelevant for an understanding of the phenomenon, and in the worst case it simply *explains away* the phenomenon.

The Free Will Theodicy

The free will theodicy was first suggested by Plato. In book II of *The Republic* he writes that God is innocent of evil, and that we must look elsewhere for evil's source.[91] In book X, he expands on this idea, asserting that *we* are responsible for evil, rather than God, because we are able to *choose*.[92] Plato's argument is, among other things, pragmatic. If people believed that gods did terrible things to humans and to other gods, they'd take their own sins less seriously.[93]

Augustine expands upon this and writes that evil actions stem from an evil will, but that the evil will itself has no root cause.[94] The will doesn't turn toward evil, but turns away from God—only when the will turns toward something base does it become evil. Thus, says Augustine, the will itself is always seeking some form of good—just a good, at times, that is of a lower order. As such, it's the act of turning itself that must be considered evil. If we ask *why* people do this, the answer is found in the doctrine of original sin.[95] This dogma resolves part of evil's conundrum by tracing moral evil back to a choice made by our forefathers, Adam and Eve, who failed to act in accordance with God's will. However, this idea too is extremely contradictory. For example, it was only *after* choosing to eat from the Tree of Knowledge that humanity received knowledge of good and evil: "The man has become like one of us, knowing good and evil"[96] And yet, you have to know what a choice entails before you can exercise free will through choosing it. Humanity cannot be said to have *chosen evil*, because they didn't know what evil was until they transgressed. If the transgression itself gave Adam and Even the knowledge necessary to understand sin, humanity cannot be said to have chosen freely. Even leaving that paradox aside, it's difficult to imagine that sin can be inherited. You can inherit a natural evil—a weak heart, for example—but not a moral evil based on individual choice. The idea that "the result of one trespass was condemnation for all men"[97] doesn't seem logical. There are still a few thinkers who try to defend the doctrine of original sin, but I don't regard it as a subject for rational debate.

Moving on to Thomas Aquinas, we find that moral evil can entirely be ascribed to a person's free will. If this is the case, however, it could be argued that the world would have been a better place without this particular human faculty. However, Thomas insists that the world would have been incomplete if it weren't possible for people to sin.[98] It's important to note that it is simply the *possibility* of sinning, and not sin itself, that's necessary for the world's perfection, and, therefore, that an individual is still responsible for all *actual* sin. Aquinas couples this idea with the belief that God is capable of transforming all evil people into good, but does not, given evil's necessity. But if evil always has a positive effect, then why avoid evil at all? Why not simply do more evil to bring about more good?

Richard Swinburne argues that a good God could create a world of people who have both free will and a sense of responsibility to their fellow man. Even if such a world would lead to evil, it would also contain great goodness.[99] At the same time, the Bible repeatedly insists that nothing is impossible for God.[100] As John Mackie and others point out, God could simply have created a world where people both had free will and always chose to do good.[101] There's nothing in the idea of free will that requires us to choose evil. Therefore, God can be blamed for not having shaped a world where people consequently, consistently choose to do good.

We simply cannot use the existence of evil to derive the value of freedom. There's just no convincing way to do this. For example, would imposing limitations on free will—perhaps by creating human beings in such a way that, in praxis, we always chose to do good—make human life less valuable? The answer is anything but obvious. And even if you accept the argument that free will is the root of all evil, this only explains moral evil, not natural evil. Thomas Aquinas maintains that God is responsible for natural evil, but that it's not actually evil. That is, natural evil only seems evil to us, because our understanding is too limited. In reality, natural evil is a necessary part of a totality that is good. I will return to, and refute, the totality argument below.[102]

I certainly don't disagree with the emphasis that free-will theodicies place on choice, but I do not believe that simply referring to free will resolves this theological problem in a convincing way. Not to mention the fact that the theological dimension still doesn't help us to understand the relationship between freedom and evil.

The Irenaean Theodicy

Named after Irenaeus (130–202), this theodicy maintains that evil can indeed be attributed to God, at least in part. God created human beings in a state of imperfection, and placed them in a world composed of good and evil so that they might be shaped and eventually achieve perfection. This world, with all its suffering and tribulations, is designed to bring about and develop characteristics that will make us ready for and worthy of salvation. The Irenaean theodicy, therefore, stands in sharp contrast to the Augustinian tradition, where humans choose evil of their own free will and—together with fallen angels—are to blame for all the suffering in the world. God, in that scenario, remains guiltless—according to Augustine, humans are created perfect, but fall. According to Irenaeus, humans aren't created perfect, but strive for perfection.

In 1819, John Keats described the world as "the vale of soul-making." The idea is that we're placed in a world full of sorrow so that we can grow and become complete human beings. He writes: "Do you not see how necessary a World of Pains and troubles is to school an Intelligence and make it a Soul?"[103] Thus, suffering is considered necessary to create a real soul.[104] In my opinion, Simone

Weil's defense of suffering's role in human life should be regarded as Irenaean as well. She represents suffering as redemption, because God is present even in extreme evil.[105] Weil bases this idea on the fact that human beings must learn that they are not yet in Paradise.[106] There is no limit to the extremes Weil is willing to go to in order to justify God, such as claiming, for instance, that evil is the expression of God's mercy in this world.[107] She assumes that God is just and therefore interprets every phenomenon as compatible with this idea. Ultimately, for Weil evil only exists because God wills it so.[108] However, this idea is tantamount to abandoning all rational discussion of the subject. To claim that injustice, because it's unjust, is actually just, breaks the rules of meaningful discourse and abandons the subject to irrationality. There's no phenomenon that can oppose Weil's conviction of God's righteousness, because every phenomenon is systematically interpreted as an expression of God's grace. Weil wants to make suffering meaningful, but along the way she manages to refute its character as suffering. According to Weil, suffering should be regarded as a gift from God, but because suffering doesn't have the chance to actually become suffering, in her work, Weil's theory—despite its insistence upon extreme instances of suffering in the world; suffering, moreover, she believes classical theodicies have turned a blind eye to—ends by explaining away suffering itself. Though the Irenaean tradition would like to see itself as the one form of theodicy that preserves suffering's character as suffering, it manages, in reality, to do so the least.[109]

We know that the world's suffering is unjustly dealt and strikes randomly; innocents are often the ones hit hardest. Even if suffering *can* be cathartic, in the long run it often proves destructive. As E. M. Cioran points out, suffering doesn't lead to heaven, but to hell.[110] Usually, good leads to more good, while evil leads to more evil. Suffering isn't something that makes us grow; as a rule, suffering is purely destructive. Intense pain doesn't often make a person stronger; instead, it destroys their worth, their confidence, and their ability to communicate. Martin Amis writes: "There is no language for pain. Except bad language. Except swearing. There's no language for it. Ouch, ow, oof, gah. Jesus. Pain is its own language."[111] Instead of having a language, pain *destroys* language.[112] You can *say* something hurts, but when the pain becomes too intense, you lose the ability to speak and descend into a prelinguistic state. Mental pain can be trumped by physical pain, because physical pain destroys all mental ability.[113] Pain deprives us of experience. It can't be shared with someone else, because there's no room for anything else when pain itself becomes all there is.

What does a child gain by having Lesch-Nyhans syndrome, a disease that gives the child such an intense desire to hurt himself that all his teeth have be pulled as they grow in to prevent him from gnawing his fingers and lips off? As we find in Camus' novel *The Plague*, a child's suffering is "an abomination."[114] Father Paneloux tries to come to terms with the problem:

> Apparently it all came to this: we might try to explain the phenomenon of the plague, but, above all, should learn what it had to teach us. Rieux gathered that, to the Father's thinking, there was really nothing to explain. His interest was again quickened when, in a more emphatic tone, the preacher said that there were some things we could grasp as touching God, and others we could not. There was no doubt as to the existence of good and evil and, as a rule, it was easy to see the difference between them. The difficulty

began when we looked into the nature of evil, and among other things evil he included human suffering. Thus we had apparently needful pain, and apparently needless pain; we had Don Juan cast into hell, and a child's death. For while it is right that a libertine should be struck down, we see no reason for a child's suffering. And, truth to tell, nothing was more important on earth than a child's suffering, the horror it inspires in us, and the reasons we must find to account for it. In other manifestations of life God made things easy for us and, thus far, our religion had no merit. But in this respect He put us, so to speak, with our backs to the wall. Indeed, we were up against the wall that plague had built around us, and in its lethal shadow we must work out our salvation. [. . .] Thus today God had vouchsafed to His creatures an ordeal such that they must acquire and practice the greatest of all virtues: that of All or Nothing.[115]

Paneloux interprets the tragedy as a gift of grace, something that puts faith in God to a test so challenging that lukewarm faith is simply not possible. Instead, a person must either embrace God or reject him completely. Suffering is justified because it provides food for the soul: "[W]e must go straight to the heart of that which is unacceptable, precisely because it is thus that we are constrained to make our choice. The sufferings of children were our bread of affliction, but without this bread our souls would die of spiritual hunger."[116] This is a poor theodicy, because such a test would have no rational basis.

There are a multitude of evils that don't seem to serve any positive function, and this is the foundation for the evidential argument against God's existence.[117] Starving to death, as millions of people do every year, isn't something that leads to personal growth or the like. For one thing, you don't necessarily learn anything from your own suffering—but it's even more irrational to expect others to suffer so that you can learn something from them. Irenaeanists may assert that we can learn generosity from other people's suffering, but in my opinion the argument is untenable. Personal edification cannot justify the suffering of others. John Hick admits that some forms of evil are purely destructive, and perform no useful function for those they strike down. Nonetheless, he includes these evils in his Irenaean theodicy, because these evils give the world an essential quality: mystery.[118] Even if it's true that the world appears more mysterious with such evils in it, Hick's argument is utterly unacceptable. By comparison with what is gained, the price for mystery is far too high—we'd be much better off without it. Speaking generally, the only lesson you can draw from great suffering is that life can be hell . . . and this is a lesson we can all certainly live without.

The Totality Theodicy

Explaining away evil, rather than explaining the phenomenon itself, is a common response to the problem of evil. One assumption that fits into this category is that that which appears to be evil is actually good, if only we consider it in the right light. Plato may have been the first to make the totality argument,[119] but the first thinker who gives it a central place and formulates it systematically is Augustine. Augustine argues that God puts humanity's evil to good use.[120] All that exists may appear to be evil, but in reality it is actually good, since it forms a necessary part of a *totality* that's good.[121] Suffering is generally seen as a punishment for man's sins; since all men are sinners, they all deserve suffering as punishment.[122] And if an individual must ultimately be described as good, suffering is simply a means to make this individual an even better person.[123]

According to Thomas Aquinas, a world without evil must necessarily be less good than the world we actually live in—the world filled with evil. A world without evil would be a world without human beings; without beings, that is, capable of choosing and doing evil; and every creature who has this possibility will indeed choose to do evil from time to time. However, a world without human beings would be less perfect than a world that contains humans, precisely because this world would *lack* humans. Whatever its defects, Thomas's argument only tries to explain why it's necessary that the world contain *moral* evil, and therefore the existence of natural evil cannot, by its lights, be regarded as justified. The answer Thomas gives to this challenge is comparatively cryptic: God could have prevented natural evil, since He did so before the Fall; however, the fact that he allowed natural evil to enter the world after the Fall doesn't make him less good, because natural evils themselves produce great good. It remains unclear how Aquinas imagines this transformation of natural evils into good will occur. On the other hand, it's perfectly clear, from the Thomistic position, that if we could grasp the world as a totality, we would be able to comprehend that everything that exists is good.

Boethius too maintains that all that appears to be evil is actually good, because everything in existence follows God's law. It's simply our limited understanding that makes the world seem otherwise.[124] In Alexander Pope's *Essay on Man*, we find the following: "All Discord, Harmony not understood; / All partial Evil, universal Good."[125] Rousseau also postulates a similar totality argument. He differentiates between the idea that absolutely all parts are good and the idea that the totality itself is good, and writes that the latter point of view does not require *all* evil to be explained away.[126] However, Rousseau's "optimism" is not held to the same burden of proof as the theory he discards: He goes on to argue that the veracity of such optimism cannot be decided by taking examples from the material world, but only by considering God's characteristics. That is, since God is presumed to be good, it follows that the world as a whole is good too. John Milton's explicit ambition with *Paradise Lost* is likewise to "justify the ways of God to men."[127] In this work, justification is again posited through the suggestion that everything that appears to be evil is actually good—a fact that would be obvious if only we could grasp the elusive totality.[128] A plethora of other variations on this argument can be found in philosophy and literature. For Spinoza, evil is something that only exists in our inadequate human understanding, while an adequate understanding would have no conception of evil.[129] Evil is an illusion that no longer appears *as evil* for those capable of seeing the world (God, substance) in the right way. In a letter, Spinoza writes that both good and evil are in God's service; however, while the good man serves God through an understanding of what he does, the evil man becomes God's unwitting tool.[130] Luther, for his part, declares that all evil has its roots in God and the Devil, though the Devil desires evil for its own sake and God desires the good to be found in evil; because God is mightier than the Devil, he uses the Devil to promote the good.[131] In Goethe's *Faust*, we again find that all evil contributes to the good—in replying to Faust's demand that he identify himself, Mephistopheles says: "Part of that force which would / Do evil evermore, and yet creates the good."[132] Therefore, everything is good from a divine perspective that privileges totality over all. In Goethe's time, Romantic thought revolved around the idea that evil is justified, because it serves a higher purpose. Novalis is therefore typical when he suggests that evil is simply a stage to be overcome on the journey toward our union with something higher—the realization of true good takes place through evil's nullification by the good.[133]

However, the thinker who gives the most comprehensive example of the totality theodicy is Leibniz. He imagines that God created the world by conceiving a definite set of possible substances. These substances can be combined in any number of ways, but God chose a definite combination. And because God is a perfect being, He was bound to choose the best possible combination. Our world is, therefore, the best of all possible worlds. Leibniz clearly states, however, that the world isn't perfect. His own philosophy makes this fact unavoidable: In a universe where no two substances are alike, there can only be one perfect substance (God). All other substances have lesser, varying degrees of perfection. Working within these conditions, God has done the best that He can, but not even He can eliminate what Leibniz calls "metaphysical evil."[134] Therefore, Leibniz also regards evil as lack—as a necessary absence of perfection.[135] This idea imposes certain basic limitations on God's act of creation. All God can do is combine all the universe's substances in the best possible way, and since God is perfect and always acts with sufficient reason, he will necessarily have chosen the best possible world from among all the other countless possible worlds.[136] As a necessary part of the best possible totality, then, evil is justified. If a world without moral and natural evil would've been a better world than this one, God would have created such a world. Natural and moral evils therefore exist because they help to realize a greater good or hinder a greater evil.[137] In sum, the world would have been worse than the one we know if God had eliminated even the smallest evil, since then things would be different—that is, it would no longer be the best possible arrangement. As Leibniz concludes: "To permit the evil, as God permits it, is the greatest goodness."[138] In fact, if God had not allowed all the physical and moral evils we have to enter into the world, He would have been guilty of a worse evil still.[139] Ultimately, Leibniz's theodicy forms a perfect circle: Because God is good, he has chosen the best of all possible worlds, and because God has created the best of all possible worlds, he is good.[140]

The totality theodicy is a risky strategy for theists, because it seems to impose serious limitations on God's omnipotence. This brings up an important question: How far does good go in balancing out evil? If we were capable of taking all the good and evil in the world and weighing them against one another, it's conceivable that evil would have a clear majority. However, it's also conceivable that if all of these evils in fact lead to good, then we would be forced to outline the characteristics of first and second orders of good and evil, where an evil of the first order might perhaps lead to a good of the second—for example to generosity. And yet, as John Mackie has pointed out, it's just as likely that an evil of the first order will instead lead to an evil of the second order, or, for the sake of argument, that a good of the first order will finally lead to an evil of the second.[141] In my opinion, the problem with the totality argument is not that it's logically inconsistent, but rather that we have no reason to trust it. The countless instances of suffering in the world don't seem to play any positive role in any totality. The suffering of the child in Ivan Karamasov's complaint—what positive role does that play in the totality? If a recluse is caught in a forest fire and dies a painful death without anyone the wiser, without anyone having learned a single solitary lesson from his suffering—what good does that contribute to the totality? The *sheer number* of evils in the world speak against God's benevolence and omnipotence. Each individual evil does the same. And then there are evils so extreme they make you wonder if it would have been better not to have lived at all.[142] An example from our previous discussion that falls into this category would be a victim of German or Japanese medical experimentation during World War II. The existence of such evils undermines the totality argument: A good, almighty and omniscient God could not allow such evils to strike individuals for the sake of the totality. If a world couldn't be created without such evils, it would have been better to not have created the world. There are, then, two conclusions that can be drawn from the discussion of the totality theodicy: First, we have no real reason to believe in the existence of a totality of good that can justify individual evils; and, second, there are evils so extreme that no totality could ever justify them.

HISTORY AS SECULAR THEODICY

Our contemporary tendency toward secularization has replaced God with History. The belief in progress is something that's deeply rooted in Western thought; nonetheless, time and again, we've had to revise our assumptions. In many people's eyes, for example, the Holocaust undermined the entire concept of historical progress. And yet, no matter how terrible a given occurrence is, we actually have no reason to believe that the world will change for the worse or the better because of it. Yes, it can certainly happen that the world *does* go on to change in one way or the other, but there's never any real basis on which to assume, logically, that the entire world, or any of its parts, will react in any one way to any one event.

We ought to be skeptical, then, of ideas regarding progress and decline—skeptical of optimism as well as pessimism. There's no historical arithmetic, after all, we can use to figure out which is the most reasonable worldview. Certainly we can determine that some relationships have become better and others worse, but we cannot determine if the *totality* has become better or worse: the world's progress or decline cannot be proven in actual terms, because we can never grasp the world as a totality, and therefore cannot compare this totality to different totalities that existed at other stages of history. There isn't one history for optimists and another for pessimists; each worldview deals with the same history, but each interprets it differently, emphasizing whatever aspects they believe to be central. Optimists dismiss negative events as more or less irrelevant. For example, Schelling writes: "[W]hatever is not progressive is not an object for history."[143] Everything that does not aid progress, or might even point in the opposite direction, is dismissed as irrelevant because it does not fit into a totality already defined as progressive. In the same way, Hegel introduces his philosophy of history with the assumption that history is *rational.*[144] And where optimistic theories tend to focus on a totality, pessimistic theories generally single out a few terrifying historical examples to make their point. That is, optimists do not deny that there's evil in the world, but believe there's a higher order that gives this evil meaning;[145] pessimists, however, maintain that no totality is capable of making individual evils meaningful, and instead maintain that the very idea of totality is illusionary—or that if a totality does exist, it only makes things worse. Which is not to say that being a pessimist necessarily implies the conviction that the world's going to hell in a handbasket. Some pessimists believe that the world's always been a pretty terrible place.

The goal of both the optimistic philosophy of history and the theodicies discussed earlier is to invalidate contingence—to order all events, no matter how terrible, into a totality that gives them meaning.[146] The belief in a theory of progress that neutralizes evil by transforming it into a tool for the realization of good is not explicitly limited to visions of historical totality, however, such as those found in Hegelianism or Marxism; we also find it in thinkers like Bernard Mandeville. The idea that agents working to further their own self-interest are also furthering the collective good is clearly formulated in the title of Mandeville's most famous work: *The Fable of the Bees: or, Private Vices, Publick Benefits*. Private vice furthers public good. Mandeville claims that not only is evil the source of all public good, but that evil's existence is necessary for society's existence. To thinkers such as Mandeville, a secularized ideal of providence performs the same function as divine providence does in theodicy—namely, it creates a dialectical turnabout where evil is transformed into good. Evil is the expression—a fragment—of the totality, which is good.

This form of optimism, especially with regard to Leibniz, is parodied in Voltaire's *Candide*. Candide's tutor, Pangloss, outlines the following position with great zeal: "[P]rivate ills make up the general good, so that the greater the sum of private ills the better everything is."[147] This parody demonstrates that simply explaining away all evil by pointing to some common good is an untenable position. In a dark moment, after having been struck by countless misfortunes, Candide also describes this optimism as "the mania for insisting that all is well when all is by no means well."[148]

According to Kant, we are morally obliged to be optimists.[149] Creation's meaning is first revealed in our moral conduct; thus, people are no longer passive observers who watch the divine plan unfold, but are *participants* in history—and the goal of history itself becomes the realization of human freedom. Kant further departs from the idea of an original condition, a natural state where all was good.[150] Instead, he asserts that people simply sense that there's a chasm between how the world *is* and how it *ought to be*, and this idea gave rise to different stories concerning a prehistorical, paradisical natural state. In fact, Kant emphasizes that people have never felt at home in nature. If our natural state were as harmonious as Rousseau, for example, maintains, we would never have abandoned it; instead, this condition was obviously insufficient to provide for human nature or human destiny. People are free, and a realization of *human* nature can only take place if we shape the world in accordance with human reason. Our task is therefore to transform culture in such a way that it can enable us to realize ourselves, our happiness, and our perfection. That is, only human beings can fulfill human needs and find human happiness, and these goals can only be attained if reason is realized in the world. Further, because we have a moral nature, we have the ability to shape rational human societies that correspond to this nature. However, there is an essential ambiguity regarding how this realization of reason and morality will take place. Is it human action that enables the realization of an ethical society? Or does nature itself contain an inherent purposefulness that ensures this goal will be realized independent of people's actions? Kant asserts that progress toward a better world isn't furthered by our quest for the good, but rather by what our nature—or providence—compels us to do.[151] Only providence (nature) can substantially further these goals, and humanity's intentional actions are unfortunately ineffective. In this way, Kant anticipates Hegel's argument that human development takes place with the aid of antagonistic forces in society. In Kant's understanding of society, it is the differences between people that drive development forward—human beings are further characterized by what Kant calls "unsocial sociability" (*ungesellige Geselligkeit*). This results from both our desire to enter into society, since it's there we can feel as though we belong to something greater, as well as our struggle against society, since we also want everything to go our way—and also recognize that everyone else in the world feels the same way.[152] These contrasts result in revolutions, wars, and other violent acts, but war is, according to Kant, also the mother of freedom; he explicitly writes that war is a tool in the hands of progress.[153] Everything negative can be ordered into something higher and positive; even nature's inhospitality and humanity's hunger for wealth and power are necessary to further human development.[154] Suffering too is seen as a useful means to make us better people.[155] All evil either committed or suffered is, therefore, part of a totality progressing toward the realization of the good.[156] According to Kant, moral evil also has the general tendency to work against itself and thereby create room for the good.[157]

The question now becomes whether *individual* reason plays any role in history's progress. Good is the goal of history, and so if all people act in accordance with the good, their actions will result in the end of history—since, if history is understood as being driven by inner conflict, when this conflict ends, history will end as well. Until this utopian vision is realized, however, history will continued to be driven by conflict; and whether we choose good or evil, the result will be the same: history will progress toward a higher world order[158]—and progress progresses with or without our help. Kant underscores that his theory of progress cannot be proven, but that it's *useful* to formulate our actions in keeping with this larger picture.[159]

It is clear, then, that Kant's theory of progress focuses on humanity as a whole, rather than the individual.[160] This is further developed by Hegel, who with even less reservation than Kant orders every horrifying event into a benevolent historical process where every individual is a "means to an ulterior end."[161] Hegel has no problem whatsoever with the fact that his philosophy of history is a theodicy.[162] The *"cunning of reason"* ensures that progress is guaranteed;[163] such progress, however, requires victims. Herder, for example, describes how fortune moves towards its goal over "millions of corpses,"[164] anticipating Hegel's description of history as a "slaughter-bench."[165] All victims on this "slaughter-bench" are reduced to random flotsam watched over by a rational and benevolent totality. Of course, Hegel doesn't really devote himself to evil as an individual problem, but essentially remains within a cosmological framework. "The claim of the World-Spirit" triumphs over all other considerations,[166] and world history exists on a higher plane than morality.[167] Human suffering and the actions that cause it are therefore regarded as means to an end, and that end is progress.

Hegel's theoretical, backward-looking historical viewpoint is transformed in Marxism to a practical, forward-directed *mission*. And just as Hegel believed he could legitimate earlier evils through a consideration of history as a whole, Marxism believed it could legitimate present and future evils. This is clearly stated by Georg Lukács, who claims that the highest duty in communist ethics is to accept the necessity of acting immorally—knowing, however, that the evil which results will be made glorious through the dialectics of historical development.[168] That is, a political ideal will reveal and justify both the historical process and its victims: The end vindicates all actions, and because this ideal was understood to be something of a historical or natural law, it simply had more weight than the individual. It would be up to future generations to rectify the sins of the present day. In many respects, therefore, Marxist communism can be considered a religious ideology. This may seem like an unusual statement, since it would be hard to find a more militantly anti-religious ideology. However, Marxist communism duplicates Christian-apocalyptic patterns of thought: God is simply replaced with history and humanity. Just as Christ's second coming marks the utopian end of days in the one doctrine, communist thought anticipates the end of history when society finally reaches its so-called "highest phase." Of course, we already know how this Marxist teleological suspension of the ethical—that is, the setting aside of morality in favor of a higher purpose—played out: around a hundred million dead, all told. To Lukács's credit, he at least recognized such actions *as* immoral. No such awareness seems to have come into play among the members of the Central Committee under Stalin, for whom historical progress overshadowed all moral considerations. Then again, perhaps it would be more accurate to say that historical progress *was* their sole moral consideration—some followers believed so strongly in this ideal that they even accepted it as necessity when they themselves fell victim to the most egregious injustices.[169] But with the collapse of communism at the end of the 1980s, it became increasingly clear that the movement had finally lost its grand teleological dimension. Of course, there are still countries where religious or nationalistic beliefs give rise to such ideologies, but since human rights has gradually assumed a more central place in the international court, the ideologically motivated persecution of individuals and groups has become less and less acceptable. We no longer accept the validity of the idea that sweeping political goals can take absolute priority over morality—and are no longer so likely to excuse whatever evils happen to be committed in the name of progress, or for the sake of some higher good. On the other hand, it must be admitted that the United States' "war on terror" relies on just such rhetoric, justifying any and all means necessary to defeat terrorism.

The anti-teleological concept of history is nothing new either. This viewpoint was formulated by Schopenhauer, although he doesn't take political ideologies as a point of departure, but instead focuses on the different metaphysical conceptions we discussed earlier. Schopenhauer can be seen as the great-grandfather of the modern pessimist, and modern pessimism—which must be clearly differentiated from antiquity's ideas concerning "decay": ideas that originated in another historical context and that rely on an entirely different historical viewpoint—should perhaps be understood as resulting from the collapse of traditional cosmologies.[170] That is, pessimism arose because optimism no longer seemed trustworthy. For Schopenhauer, the world was a "hell" that never should have existed.[171] He describes optimism as an irresponsible way of thinking, because it doesn't take "the unspeakable sufferings of mankind" enough into account.[172] He further argues that there is no higher providence that gives meaning to an individual's suffering, and that the world's principle—which he calls its Will—is blind. Without a higher providence, individual suffering remains unjustified and cannot be simply "explained away," as it is by Hegel. The "real" world, therefore, stands in terrifying contrast to all "fancied eminence."[173] Schopenhauer further objects to Leibniz and asserts that ours is the *worst* possible of all worlds.[174] For pessimists, the logic of providence is easily the opposite of the optimist's: All good is negated by evil.[175] An invisible hand will ultimately see to it that everything arranged for the worst.[176]

Nietzsche also follows in Schopenhauer's footprints; it's not for nothing that he calls Schopenhauer his "great teacher."[177] Nietzsche explicitly states that the moral interpretation of history, like the religious interpretation of history, must fall by the wayside, because the moral interpretation *is* religious. The one inescapable fact that confronts us is "the meaninglessness of all events," the idea that "the world no longer has any meaning."[178] He also writes that modern man's problem is not suffering itself, but rather the fact that our suffering is meaningless.[179] Nietzsche therefore attempts to overcome this problem by giving our suffering new meaning. According to him, the new man—the superman—doesn't need a justification for evil, nor does he need a God.[180] He says "yes" to life and also to suffering. In keeping with this idea, Nietzsche criticizes those who want to abolish suffering and instead welcomes "great" suffering.[181] Nietzsche's *reevaluation* of all values should not be confused with a simple *reversal* of values, however—where each value is simply transformed into its opposite. Nor does Nietzsche embrace the concept of total chaos. Instead, he wants to establish a *new* morality, and argues for a revision of those values he regards as degenerate. He also opposes the way traditional values are taken for granted and, in a purely polemical way, praises those values we typically disdain. According to Nietzsche, "slave" morality must be discarded. It is a morality without genuine ideals, a morality that may indeed focus upon minimizing "evil," but that cannot conceive of the good as anything other than the absence of evil. For Nietzsche, slave morality is pathetic, incapable of heroism. Therefore, he praises the suffering of self and other, because "profound suffering makes noble."[182] In this way, he fetishizes suffering in what could well be described as a secularized version of the Irenaean theodicy. At the same time, Nietzsche's inverted and secularized theodicy ends exactly as other theodicies do: by simply explaining away the reality of evil.

This inversion of theodicy is formulated in a particularly radical way by the Marquis de Sade. Sade is not simply a belletrist, but also a "philosopher in disguise,"[183] and he can be read as a critic of theodicy. According to Sade, the idea that providence strives for justice is one of "those dangerous sophistries of a false philosophy."[184] His protagonist, Justine, trusts in this concept of justice: that justice will be done, if not in this world, then in the next.[185] Justine's interlocutor, la Dubois, who could be regarded as a mouthpiece of Sade himself, reverses Justine's cosmology and embraces an *evil*, rather than a benevolent providence: "[B]e convinced that as soon as it [providence] places us in a situation where evil becomes necessary, and while at the same time it leaves us the possibility of doing it, this evil harmonizes quite as well with its decrees as does good, and Providence gains as much by the one as by the other. [. . . F]atality [. . .] inevitably saves the criminal by sacrificing the virtuous [. . .]"[186]

It's Sade, rather than Schopenhauer or Nietzsche, who most radically articulates modern pessimism. However, his articulation is so radical that it only refutes itself. Kant writes that the world isn't worth living in if justice does not prevail.[187] The universe Sade describes in his work is indeed uninhabitable. The problem with Sade is that his thought is largely structured by dichotomies: either the world is good *or* it's evil. And since it isn't good, it must be evil. Therefore, he posits as a normative consequence that we ought to act in accordance with evil. However, one obvious possibility that Sade fails to consider is that the world may be a mixture of good *and* evil and that it's our duty—not the duty of God or providence—to make the world a better place. This viewpoint is simple, but decisive. Sade's thoughts are largely structured in the shadow of an absent God; he doesn't recognize that this very absence makes the world man's responsibility. We exist in this world and we're obligated to it. The problem of evil is *our* problem.

JOB'S INSIGHT—BEYOND THEODICY

The Book of Job begins with a bet between God and Satan. Satan insists that Job loves God because God has greatly blessed him. God is confident of Job's faith, and so allows Satan to take away everything Job has. As a result, Job loses his children, servants, herds, and health—in the end, he becomes so sick he nearly dies. Job's wife and friends blame Job himself for his misfortunes: Surely Job must have done something to deserve such punishment. In fact, they're so concerned with the idea of justice that they deny Job human sympathy. Job knows he's done nothing to deserve his misfortunes, and so he blames God; God answers Job's accusation, but emphasizes might rather than justice. As God proceeds to ask: "Would you discredit my justice? Would you condemn me to justify yourself? Do you have an arm like God's and can your voice thunder like his?"[188] In this way, God proceeds directly from the question of justice to the question of raw power. At the same time, even though God is obviously stronger than Job, that fact doesn't necessarily mean that He's more just.[189] In the end, it's difficult to see God, as He's represented in Job, as anything other than an immoral tyrant: On the one hand, God seems to be a kind of natural catastrophe that strikes blindly, without any regard for justice, and yet, on the other, He wants to be loved and worshipped as righteous. There's no compromise between these two aspects, and God doesn't even manage to give a convincing argument for His own righteousness.

"Wisdom is better than strength," writes the Preacher,[190] but in the Book of Job, God never shows wisdom, only raw power. When Job asks: "Where can wisdom be found?"[191] God answers with the following: "The fear of the Lord—that is wisdom."[192] In my opinion, Job doesn't find wisdom in God, but in himself. And this wisdom is based on a simple insight: God, and therefore the world, is unjust.

Toward the end of Job, God praises Job and faults his friends: "After the Lord had said these things to Job, he said to Eliphaz the Temanite, 'I am angry with you and your two friends, because you have not spoken of me what is right, as my servant Job has.'"[193] However, it's unclear why exactly God praises Job and yet blames Job's friends. The only reason He gives is a vague reference to the fact that Job has spoken truly of Him, while his friends have spoken false. But how are we supposed to interpret truth in this context? The main thrust of the friends' conversation is that there is an absolute justice to the world; that Job only *appears* to be innocent of the misfortunes that have struck him; that the injustice of the situation is ultimately illusory, because a God-given cosmic justice is surely behind everything. It's precisely this that Job denies—and because we know about the bet God and Satan made in the first part of the book, turning Job into an innocent pawn in a supernatural game, we know that Job is right. Job has everything and loses it, and he did nothing to deserve this. Moreover, Job clearly has better arguments than God—so much so that we can say that Job gives God a lesson in ethics. In numerous places, the Bible underscores that God doesn't treat men unjustly: "God does not show favoritism."[194] However, it's clear that God *does* treat Job unjustly. He lets Job be struck again and again by suffering and misfortune, and Job never does anything to deserve it. As the Preacher tells us: "In this meaningless life of mine I have seen both of these: a righteous man perishing in his righteousness, and a wicked man living long in his wickedness."[195]

Ultimately, the assertion that the seemingly almighty God is good seems implausible here, insofar as "good" retains its usual meaning. Of course, one solution to this problem would be argue that we cannot apply the human concepts of good and evil to God, because he transcends human understanding. Matthew, Mark, and Luke all state that the only thing that *can* be called "good" is God.[196] With this idea in mind, we might draw a sharp distinction between human goodness (which is not actually "good") and God's goodness, which is the only thing truly deserving of the name. Since our concept of the good is based on human actions, and since this concept forms the basis of our approach to the problem of evil, any basis for approaching evil as a practical issue suddenly disappears. In a certain sense, you could say we've even *solved* the problem by saying this, since we no longer need to justify that God is good according to our understanding of the concept. At the same time, however, we've also abandoned the very thing we set out to prove—namely, that God must be *represented* as good. This is the trap Calvin falls into when he argues that there's no higher standard of righteousness than God's will, and that whatever God wills or does is therefore righteous.[197] We have no access to God's principle of justice, and it's conceivable that God's sense of justice is completely different from ours—in this respect, then, we can hardly state that "God is just" and pretend that this has any meaning. As John Stuart Mill has argued, the rules of logic dictate that we cannot use the same designation for two completely different things—at least not without having outlined the differences—and since we get our notion of justice from human interaction, and since God's "justice" cannot be compared with ours, we cannot identify this apparent characteristic of God's as "justice."[198] If God's characteristics transcend what the human intellect can grasp, therefore, we should not say that God is "good" or "just," but ultimately that God is "X" and "Y," with the addendum that we don't have the vaguest idea as to what "X" and "Y" might signify—but once we've reached this point, we have to admit that the conversation has become totally meaningless.

In my brief remarks concerning theodicy earlier in this chapter, I do not pretend to have proven beyond a shadow of a doubt that all theodicies are inconsistent, untrue, or irrational—only that they are unconvincing. It's possible that it is not logically inconsistent to believe in a good, almighty, and omniscient God—or a historical process that functions as God's equivalent—while at the same time acknowledging the existence of evil. However, consistency itself isn't enough to make conviction either well-founded or rational. Further, I believe that theodicy itself represents a mistaken approach to the problem of evil, because it fails to take suffering into account in any serious way. We must reject theodicies and the like, and see evil for what it is. I say again: Evil shouldn't be justified; it should be stopped.

Let us therefore follow Job and say that the world, seen from a human perspective—and there is no other perspective that allows us to speak meaningfully on the subject—isn't just. This is an important point. *Because* Job's friends lived under the illusion that a cosmic justice exists, they were insensitive to Job's suffering. An abstract, metaphysical principle stood in the way of sympathy. That is their greatest sin. Theodicies aren't so much explanations of God's goodness and justness as they are a *dismissal* of the world's suffering and injustice. As Karl Jaspers writes, the act of denying or dismissing evil is itself evil.[199] Theodicies are evil because they justify and uphold injustice. Justice isn't a natural law; it's a principle instituted by men.

The customary picture we're given of life is this: the world is just, our actions and character have definite meaning, and whether we're rewarded or punished, we'll eventually get what we deserve. Plato believes that one reason poetry is so dangerous is that it contains dramatic examples of unjust people who are happy, and just people who are unhappy.[200] It's essential to uphold the image of a just world where good is rewarded and evil punished: Plato's idea is that even a simple belief in the principle of justice can motivate people to be good. I won't deny that there's something to this. The problem is that this philosophy can also lead us to turn a blind eye to all the injustices that actually do exist.

For those of us living in a world where God is dead, justice no longer has a cosmic anchor. When Job insists that the world is not just, that the world is not ordered according to our concepts of justice, he becomes an existentialist. At the same time, even without a God, people are still inclined to believe that the world is just.[201] This can seem like a harmless conclusion, but it leads to the further conclusion that every victim has in some way earned tyranny or misfortune. The principle of justice, regarded as descriptive rather than normative, can lead to an acceptance of evil. This idea is one step away from blaming the victim, rather than the perpetrator, for the victim's suffering. Before the Second World War, for example, many Dutch Jews believed that the German Jews must have done something seriously wrong to deserve such persecution. The basic problem with this belief was that it took for granted that suffering had to be *earned*. The world is not, however, organized teleologically around human needs and desires. Remember that human beings appeared relatively late on the scene, in the history of our planet, and it's utterly naïve to believe that the world has to conform to our concept of justice. Justice is a duty, not a given.

God's death doesn't mean that man became God,[202] but simply that man must give up believing in his own divinity.[203] It doesn't mean that humanity suddenly became self-sufficient, either. Instead, humanity lost all its ties to that which could have *guaranteed* sufficiency. The death of our almighty God didn't make man almighty; it delivered him up to a world of radical contingence. This means that we're forced to shape our history without any guarantee that our history will unfold in the right direction. Instead of rejecting the concept of evil together with the concept of God, let us say instead that when God vanished, evil became a purely *human* problem. It's *our* problem. Evil plays a role in our lives—and not just moral evil, but also all the natural evils we don't ourselves cause. We can see now that natural phenomena do not have a metaphysical or mystical dimension; they have no higher meaning, are purely destructive, unrelated to anything but suffering and death. And if we were expecting, after the traditional cosmology collapsed, that science would be able to govern our belief in progress, we have found ourselves disappointed. Science has steadily lost its ability to maintain this belief, in part because its own destructive potential was demonstrated time and time again over the course of the twentieth century.

With what is popularly known as "the death of the grand narrative,"[204] thought loses its totalizing characteristic in relation to history. It was this faculty, however, that made the dialectical turnabout possible, positing that evil should be considered part of a good totality. Without this concept of totality, evil at last has the room to show itself *as evil*. Suffering also loses its "why." It can no longer be justified with reference to something higher; there's no authority that halts the flood of questions. Instead of a rational world justly shepherded by an almighty, good God, we have a world shepherded by chance.[205] We aren't rewarded according to our just deserts, but rather by luck—be it good or bad. And there's no moral message to be read in other people's luck, be it good or bad. In a theocentric world, it was possible to trust in life's inherent justice, in the fact that every soul would receive its just reward. Today, it's the world's inherent *unjustness* that greets us every day. Once again it's up to us intervene and do something about it.

II

THE ANTHROPOLOGY OF EVIL

The first part of the book ended with the conclusion that theology is essentially irrelevant for an understanding of the problems posed by evil in the world, and I put theodicies in the category of theoretical blind spots. Evil should only be considered as a human, moral problem. This ethical interpretation of evil implies a demythologization of evil. That is, we no longer ask *quid est malum?* (what is evil?), but instead *unde malum faciamus* (why do we do evil?).[206]

In this section, I will first take up the question of whether people are essentially good or evil. I will then propose a typology of four different kinds of evil—the demonic, the instrumental, the idealistic, and the stupid—and discuss each one in depth. This consideration, in turn, will help to answer the question of why we do evil. This discussion will also help us respond to the real problem: What should we do about evil?

ARE PEOPLE GOOD OR EVIL?

From a Christian perspective, people are essentially evil. In Genesis, it reads: "The Lord saw how great man's wickedness on the earth had become, and that every inclination of the thoughts of his heart was only evil all the time."[207] Furthermore, we find that "every inclination of his heart is evil from childhood."[208] This belief in people's inherent evil is especially developed in Augustine's doctrine of original sin—one of the most influential concepts in Western thought. It has shaped a long tradition and this tradition continues to influence our thinking. This idea can be seen, for example, when theories concerning rational choice take it as a given that a rational person will always seek to maximize their own interests. Both Machiavelli and Hobbes based their philosophies on Augustinian anthropology, and Kant's own attempt to develop a demythologized, rational theory as to why we choose evil also owes much to Augustine.

According to Machiavelli, people will always be evil until necessity forces them to be good.[209] According to Hobbes, all people are *born* evil. We exist in a perpetual state of conflict that has its roots in human nature: The struggle for self-preservation, riches, and fame naturally leads people to live in conflict with one another.[210] Of course, Hobbes also recognizes that humans have an innate ability to sympathize, but this emotion is too weak to prevent these perpetual conflicts. Therefore, anthropology forms the basis of both Machiavelli's and Hobbes's political philosophies, and it shows too that our concept of human "nature" is paramount to the discussion. In Machiavelli's view, however, politics should help prevent human evil, and he tries to pinpoint those strategies that further the cause of evil the least.[211]

In a similar way, Montaigne argues that human nature is predisposed to cruelty.[212] We also find countless examples in literature of individuals who are evil "by nature"; for instance in Lautréamont's *Maldoror*, where Maldoror claims that he was born evil and that he is slave to a force stronger than will. He insists that trying to change his evil disposition would be like trying to change the laws of gravity.[213] The same is true of Herman Melville's character Claggart, who had "the mania of an evil nature, not engendered by vicious training or corrupting books or licentious living, but born with him and innate."[214]

However, there are also theories that take the opposite viewpoint and claim that "by nature" man is good. Perhaps the most famous example is Rousseau. According to Rousseau, man was born free, equal, self-sufficient and without bias, but civilization has transformed him into the opposite of these things. The natural man is savage, happy, and good; civilized man is unhappy and immoral.[215] Since the natural state is evidently a good state, however, we are again compelled to ask why that state was ever abandoned. Rousseau's only answer is a vague gesture in the direction of a "fatal accident,"[216] or the vague promptings of some "natural order."[217] Nature is good, but it was apparently nature too that caused people to enter into the state of civilization that corrupted them. Rousseau doesn't blame God or human nature for the evil in the world, but rather civilization—or, more pointedly, civilized man.[218] Indeed, the category of "natural evil" is not found in Rousseau's thought at all. Instead, evil is understood to be a purely human phenomenon, something that has no actual existence beyond the actions and suffering of civilized man.[219] Within civilization, people do retain a natural goodness, but this goodness can only have a perverted expression in this context. At the same time, it would be misleading to call Rousseau's natural man "good," since he's actually amoral: It's only when civilized man becomes rational that he's able to distinguish between good and evil.[220] Since natural man is completely focused on his own well-being, he ultimately has no desire to compete with or harm others.[221]

In their views on human nature, Rousseau and Machiavelli may appear to be perfect opposites—but, in the end, there's not really much difference between them.[222] When Machiavelli describes man as evil, it's in relation to the *common* good of a civilized society, and in this context Machiavelli considers the natural man to be evil because he's self-centered. For both Rousseau and Machiavelli, therefore, evil is a result of the struggle between what's "natural" and what's "civilized." This struggle can perhaps be illustrated by the following example:

On January 9, 1800, a small figure wandered out of the woods around Saint-Sernin in France and became known as the "the wild boy of Aveyron."[223] The boy, who was around twelve years old, couldn't speak. He refused to be locked up indoors, would become enraged without warning, and tore off his clothes if anyone tried to dress him. Moreover, he bit everyone who came too close to him. The discovery of the boy was widely and enthusiastically discussed. People thought they could finally validate the popular conception of the "noble savage."[224] Victor, as the boy was called, lacked a moral compass: he was neither moral nor immoral, but rather amoral. He "stole" everything he came across, but since he had no concept of thievery, it's better to say he *took* everything he came across. He showed no sign of empathy or any other moral sensitivity that might have helped him modify his behavior in the light of somebody else's moral-determined reactions. Victor simply seemed to see other people as tools to satisfy hunger, thirst, or other primitive desires. If Victor had had a moral conscience, he would've been described as an egotist through and through. On the other hand, he showed no sign of ill-will toward others, and aside from those instances where he felt threatened, he was never aggressive. He demonstrated no desire for dominance, no desire for power and status. In short, Victor was neither good nor evil, but existed in a premoral state. He appeared as the natural man—that is, as man was before he ate from the Tree of Knowledge and learned about good and evil.

What can we learn from Victor's example? In my opinion, very little. Perhaps nothing, besides the fact that ideas regarding "the natural state" do very little to help us understand our moral character. It's a state we're *not* in, and therefore cannot be used to tell us anything about who we "really" are. The natural state is an unknown—perhaps because it never existed in the first place. If we want to discover who people "really" are, we shouldn't focus on a hypothetical primitive state, but rather on what people do and why they do it.

There are only four possible answers to the question of whether our moral "nature" is good or evil:[225]

    (1)   People are good.
    (2)   People are evil.
    (3)   People are neither good nor evil.
    (4)   People are both good and evil.

There's plenty of support for (1) in the form of various good deeds, but just as much support for (2) in the form of evil deeds. However, neither of these answers acknowledges the complexity of our conduct. Now, people arguing for (1) and (2) may assert that nature disposes us to be either good or evil, and that we thereafter fall from grace and become more evil, or else that we struggle against our inherent evil tendencies and become better people—but these assertions lack sufficient evidence. Perhaps you could indeed find a "natural" man somewhere in the world and demonstrate that he has, inherently, good or evil tendencies—though the amount of evidence for both (1) and (2) points toward (3) as being most the likely solution. However, (3) could be interpreted as the belief that we come into the world morally neutral and thereafter *become* good or evil. This idea is certainly reasonable: a newborn baby can hardly be said to have a moral character; since it lacks self-consciousness, it lacks a concept of morality. However, this newborn baby will grow older, and as it grows older, it will, in society, become a moral being—someone who is neither purely good *nor* purely evil, but good *and* evil. Figures who are purely good or purely evil abound in the history of literature, but in the real world, people are good and evil both. Some have more good in them than evil, others more evil than good, but all are a combination of elements.[226] Therefore, alternative (4) is the most plausible, if we're going to speak meaningfully about human beings possessed of moral consciences.

It all boils down to the fact that we're free. This is why we cannot be unambiguously good or evil. Schelling was correct when he said that the root of freedom was the freedom to be both good *and* evil[227] (though when this freedom is operative—when we make choices—our freedom becomes the freedom to be good *or* evil[228]). We're good *and* evil not simply because we sometimes choose good and other times evil, but because both are essential components of our nature. Understanding this is essential to understanding who we are.

TYPOLOGIES OF EVIL

In discussing evil, I believe that it's an error in method to reduce a manifold of phenomena to one basic form. It's more informative to propose a typology of the different forms of evil as they present themselves, and to consider how the different types are related. In C. Fred Alford's consideration of the numerous ways evil is imagined and understood, many of those interviewed said there ought to be more than one word for it, since there are so many different *kinds* of evil.[229] This is a reasonable argument. However, Alford observes that the interviewees primarily wanted to distinguish between different varieties of evil so that they could either excuse themselves or someone else by describing certain actions as examples of a less serious form of evil. Even so, in my opinion, such distinctions have an objective worth that Alford largely overlooks. Of course, he does tentatively distinguish between the evil that's committed and the evil that's suffered, and also in part between an isolated evil act and an evil lifestyle, but he makes evil seem one-sided, as if it's always the same subject and always stems from the same motivation. This mistake leads Alford to miss important distinctions, and ultimately to claim that there's no difference between the desire to squeeze someone's hand until it hurts and the desire to murder millions of people.[230] I will argue the exact opposite: namely, that agents who do evil have an infinite number of motivations, and that these cannot be reduced to a single, basic description.

The different forms of evil can be categorized according to diverse typologies. Starting with Leibniz, we can distinguish between physical, metaphysical, and moral evil: Metaphysical evil is the world's imperfection, physical or natural evil is suffering, and moral evil is sin.[231] Leibniz also refers to moral evil as *malum culpae*, because it's tied to *guilt*. Moral evil can only be attributed to subjects who are able to choose for themselves, and is more shocking than natural evil—it's obviously a tragedy if an avalanche destroys a whole village, but it's far more shocking if the residents of that same village are brutally slaughtered by soldiers.

Nevertheless, it's not so simple to draw a clear line between moral and natural evil. John Hick distinguishes between them by arguing that moral evil is caused by humans, while natural evil has nonhuman causes.[232] In my opinion, this distinction is hardly useful. A large percentage of the evil that people do does not fall under the category of *moral* evil. That is, in many cases an individual might not understand the consequences of his actions, or there might be extenuating circumstances that cause us to absolve an agent of all moral blame. David Griffin distinguishes between moral and natural evil by saying that moral evil must contain the express intent to hurt other people; by contrast, all unintended suffering can be described as natural evil.[233] To my mind, Griffin's distinction is better, but saying that there *must* be a clear intent to hurt others is too strict—this simply excludes too many other forms of evil. Take, for example, an industrialist, trying to earn money, who doesn't stop to reflect on the people who might be affected by his actions. Or a bureaucrat who carries out his appointed tasks without considering the consequences. I would opt, I think, for a more general, tentative definition: A *morally* evil agent is a free agent who inflicts suffering on others against their will and without regard for their human worth. This suffering inflicted on others doesn't need to be intentional, but can be caused by thoughtlessness as well. Further, a thoughtless agent can also be blamed for the evil he commits, because he *should* have thought before he acted.

We can also look at moral evil as a possible determination of human freedom. A world without free agents might still contain evil, but it would only be natural evil, not moral. A world without freedom might contain an infinite amount of suffering, in fact, but only someone who *could have acted otherwise* can be *blamed* for *not* having acted otherwise. Only a free agent can be *guilty* of *moral* evil.

If we limit ourselves to a consideration of moral evil as it pertains to human conduct, and which therefore excludes natural and metaphysical evil, we can distinguish between the following four basic types of evil:

1. *Demonic evil* is the least relevant type. This form of evil—taken for granted by numerous theories—is defined as the activity of doing evil precisely *because* it's evil. I find this conception extremely problematic, and will discuss this idea at length below. In my opinion, furthermore, demonic evil still has a component of good. *Every* desire may have something good about it, if only for the agent himself, and even if the desire itself can be regarded as evil. The fulfillment of a wish is a good, and if for example rape and murder can satisfy a desire, then rape and murder have a good side. Nonetheless, it's obvious that rape and murder should be regarded as evil. Thomas Aquinas, therefore, argues that good can be found in that which is evil.[234]

2. *Instrumental evil* concerns agents who do something evil, well aware that it's evil, in order to accomplish some other goal. The goal can be good, but the means evil. Therefore, instrumental evil exclusively concerns the *means*, not the goal. Evil is instrumental if the agent would have abandoned the action if the goal, for example wealth, could have been achieved in some other way. In this respect, an instrumental evil action does not have value *in and of itself*. Those who carry out instrumental evil do not take pleasure in the action itself so much as in the accomplishment of their goal. And this goal can be good, evil, neutral, or a combination of both.

3. *Idealistic evil* results when agents do something evil in the belief that they're doing something good. Consider, for example, the Christian crusades, or the witch and heretic trials. No doubt most of the participants in these events

considered themselves to be representatives of good. Terrorists can largely be described as idealists who believe they're on the side of good. Consequently, what they do is justified by the struggle against evil. Beyond a shadow of a doubt, many Bolsheviks were idealists—even those who condemned innocent people to death, knowing beforehand that they were innocent. This is demonstrated by the fact that a number of these same people willingly confessed to crimes they weren't guilty of—crimes punishable by death—for the sake of the Party and the revolution.[235] Many Nazis were also idealists driven by an ambition to create a better society, and the SS considered themselves to be a *moral* elite.[236] The fact that their ideology is perverted doesn't make these agents any less idealistic. For idealists—in contrast to those who do instrumental evil—it will often appear not only morally acceptable, but also morally *just* to harm others *for a good cause*.[237] Enemies embody an evil that must be fought. Idealists can recognize that certain actions are deplorable, but will continue to insist that they're justified by a higher mission. Those who do evil often act as if they represent the good, and oftentimes they even believe it. But the conviction that an ideal is good is not enough to guarantee that it really *is* good.

4.   *Stupid evil*, on the other hand, is characterized by an agent who acts without stopping to consider whether his actions are good or evil. Stupid evil is different from idealistic evil, which is characterized by an agent who *thinks* about good and evil, but thinks wrongly. Stupidity can be understood as a form of thoughtlessness, an absence of reflec-

tion. Kant writes at one point that "stupidity is caused by a wicked heart,"[238] but we should reverse this concept and say that stupidity *creates* a wicked heart. It's this form of evil that Hannah Arendt describes as banal.

It can be difficult to decide to which of the four categories a certain agent or action belongs, and a single agent can belong to more than one category (for example, a primarily idealistic motive can be supplemented by a sadistic pleasure in hurting people; I do not believe that any one of us are completely immune to such feelings) . . . An idealist, for instance, can easily become a fanatic. That is, he no longer assumes responsibility for *thinking* a situation through, and begins to follow a given set of directions slavishly: This is how idealistic evil can become stupid evil. Further, a problem with the category of "instrumental evil" is that it threatens to become so broad that it subsumes all other categories—motivated actions *always* have a goal. One thing all four types of evil have in common, however, is the lack of regard for other people's dignity. The four types of evil will therefore serve as a tentative foundation for further discussion.

The problem with many theories of evil is that they assume evil's goal is to cause harm—that is, that evil is autotelic rather than instrumental. In other words, demonic. In reality, however, demonic evil is a marginal phenomenon at best. Theories that reduce all evil to the demonic type lose sight of the other forms; moreover, such a one-sided focus also leads us to lose sight of *ourselves*, because we certainly—as I've said—don't tend think of ourselves as demons. This notion of evil, therefore, seems irrelevant to an understanding of our own conduct. Evil isn't limited to sadists and fanatics, and most of the participants in genocide and the like are no more demonic than you or I. It's a commonplace to say that we all have a dark side, that we all have the capacity to do wrong—I'm certainly not alone in making this assertion. This notion becomes rather unhelpful, however—if not wholly obtuse—if we don't try to identify those things that cause an otherwise normal person to do something truly atrocious. The question we should ask ourselves isn't simply "Is it possible?," but "What would it take for *me* to do something similar?"

DEMONIC EVIL

The real and practical existence of evil becomes quite clear if we define it as anything that, in one way or another, opposes one's living a life both meaningful and worth striving for. The question is whether the extreme, demonic form of evil actually exists—that is, whether evil is ever actively pursued *as* evil. Demonic evil would seem to be self-sufficient, to exist for its own sake. Descriptions of this type of evil tend to appear more often in victims' testimonies than in the confessions of any perpetrators[239]—that is, if we want to understand a perpetrator's motives, we can't take the victim's word as being an authoritative source. To a victim, the only satisfactory explanation for a perpetrator's actions may indeed be pure sadism; but this doesn't mean that the idea has any emotional relevance for the perpetrator. A single action can scar or can even destroy a victim for life, but this same action may seem like a small, meaningless episode to the perpetrator: A professional torturer, for instance, probably doesn't remember each and every victim. Instead, the act of torture is entirely impersonal; after all, he was "only doing his job," despite the fact that his victims will carry this experience with them for the rest of their lives. We often see this enormous gap between the profound negative effect and the insignificant positive effect the same action can have for a victim and perpetrator, respectively.[240] The victim's loss is almost always greater than the perpetrator's gain. The satisfaction we might get from hitting someone who's annoying us will pass, while the victim can suffer serious and lasting damage. This gap is the primary reason conflicts have a tendency to escalate. Even if both sides inflict precisely the same amount of damage on the other, both still feel that they've suffered more harm than they've dealt.

When we think about torture, furthermore, we usually put ourselves in the victim's place, because we can't imagine being torturers ourselves. Torturers seem like monsters, like perverse and inhuman sadists—but the fact is that most torturers are more or less average people without any particular disposition toward sadism. The torturers in the Greek Juntas in 1967–74, for example, have been studied exhaustively, and none of them were found to have obvious sadistic or authoritarian tendencies either before or after their time in the army. Neither was there anything in their family backgrounds or personal histories to distinguish them from the rest of the populace.[241] It's true, however, that some torturers begin to like what they do after a while—the violence starts for one reason and ends up associated with another: the torturer begins to receive a kind of self-validation. During the Vietnam War, for example, it was common American practice to beat Vietnamese soldiers under interrogation. Most times, military intelligence began these interrogations without any real enthusiasm—it was just a part of the ordinary routine. Once they began hitting their prisoner, however, the interrogators found that they began to enjoy it—to enjoy it so much that they had to hold back before the beatings degenerated into more serious forms of torture.[242] Sometimes they were able to restrain themselves, they reported later, sometimes they let the situation deteriorate, and other times they consciously went much farther. War, of course, is a situation in which many people let themselves get carried away.[243] Joanna Bourke's *An Intimate History of Killing* contains countless citations from soldiers claiming that murder is "satisfying," "entertaining" and "attractive."[244] Henry de Man describes how with just a grenade launcher he was able to hit a group of enemies so that their bodies and body parts flew through the air—a description that ends with the words: "I had to confess to myself that it was one of the happiest moments of my life."[245] And Philip Caputo makes a similar confession, stating that going into combat made him "feel happier than he ever had" before. A Soviet veteran of the war in Afghanistan says: "Killing *en masse*, in a group, is exciting, even—and I've seen this myself—fun."[246] Context is all-important: Most people who return from war take up their lives in exactly the same ways as before, and while a number of studies have been made on the relationship between the experience of war—where people are encouraged to act in a brutal manner—and the commission of violent criminal acts in civilian life thereafter, no perceptible increase in the latter has been shown.[247] War and civilian life are so different that there seems to be little transference of the one onto the other. Let us move away, then, from cruelty that appears limited to specific situations, and take up the subject of those people for whom it becomes a mode of conduct.

Popularly, demonic evil is best personified by serial killers. When you read about a particular serial killer, for example about Henry Lee Lucas, the obvious conclusion seems to be that they do what they do because they take extreme satisfaction in inflicting extreme suffering. For example, Lucas would tie up his victim and tell her—most of the victims were women—that she was going to die. After that, he'd sliced her open, beat her, perhaps cut off her fingers and toes, just so she'd know that if she managed to survive, she'd be disfigured for life.[248] Other, more extreme examples don't need to be mentioned here. The point is that there are some actions whose sole motivating factor seems to be inflicting as much harm as possible on another person—actions undertaken solely *for the sake of* inflicting the maximum amount of suffering. If we're going to understand an action, we have to understand its purpose—in these cases, however, it's not clear what the purpose could possibly be. Some murders can't be explained by the fact that the perpetrator was overcome with rage, that he was trying to cover up another crime, or that the victim refused to cooperate with the perpetrator in some way. In other words, there are some murders that can't be explained by any of the usual scenarios; such murders are rare, but they do exist.[249] We can call this autotelic violence: self-justifying, self-sufficient violence. In other words, "demonic."

Evil for Evil's Sake

Montaigne writes:

> If I had not seen it I could hardly have made myself believe that you could find souls so monstrous that they would commit murder for the sheer fun of it; would hack at another man's limbs and lop them off and would cudgel their brains to invent unusual tortures and new forms of murder, not from hatred or for gain but for the one sole purpose of enjoying the pleasant spectacle of the pitiful gestures and twitchings of a man dying in agony, while hearing his screams and groans. For there you have the farthest point that cruelty can reach.[250]

THE ANTHROPOLOGY OF EVIL

Are there people who do evil purely for evil's sake? We know that a person can take pleasure in doing what he thinks is good, precisely because of its goodness; can we imagine there's a person out there who takes a similar pleasure in doing what he thinks is evil *because* it's evil? The idea that people do evil *because* it's evil is a central tenet in much of the existing literature on evil, and many people cite this idea as the paradigmatic example of evil. It's also this form of evil that is dominant in horror films and such.

Schopenhauer defines cruelty as "delight at the suffering of another which has not sprung from egoism, but is disinterested"—where suffering appears to be "an end in itself."[251] In his otherwise excellent book on the holocaust, Berel Lang argues that the Nazis' mass extermination of the Jews was ultimately carried out *because* it was evil.[252] C. Fred Alford makes sadists the paradigm of evil and argues that evil is not just the act of hurting another person, it's also the enjoyment of total control implicit in the ability to inflict harm.[253] For Bataille as well, self-sufficient evil is the true evil. For instance, he doesn't consider crimes for profit to be evil, since they do not provide pleasure independent of whatever material gain may result from them.[254] And the idea that there are people in the world who do evil for its own sake isn't limited to crime, horror films, and speculative metaphysics; it's also present in the work of (presumably) thoughtful, analytical philosophers. John Kekes asserts that there are "moral monsters [who] habitually choose to cause evil" and who "choose to live evil lives."[255] And Colin McGinn defines an evil person as someone who takes pleasure in the pain of others and who does evil for its own sake.[256] He does distinguish between "pure" evil and instrumental evil, but he lets the "pure" form dominate his whole discussion; as such, his definition of evil is synonymous with sadism.[257] John Rawls writes that the motivating factor behind the acts of an "evil person" is love of injustice, and he argues that such a person seeks injustice simply *because* it breaks with the perceived norm of justice.[258]

All these authors write in the tradition of Augustine, who described what might well be the world's most famous instance of pear stealing. Most of us can remember the excitement of indulging in petty thievery when we were children. When I was a boy, for instance, we had a yard full of apple and pear trees—but the apples and pears that fell in other people's yards were far sweeter than anything I could find in my own. Augustine also stole pears as a child, and he transforms this action into a drama between good and evil:

> There was a pear tree near our vineyard laden with fruit, though attractive in neither colour nor taste. To shake the fruit of the tree and carry off the pears, I and a gang of naughty adolescents set off late at night. [. . .] We carried off a huge load of the pears. But they were not for our feasts but merely to throw to the pigs. Even if we ate a few, nevertheless our pleasure lay in doing what was not allowed.[259]

Augustine draws the conclusion that: "I loved my fall, not the object for which I had fallen but my fall itself."[260] I find it difficult, however, to view the young Augustine through the eyes of his elder self: Where he sees a serious sinner, I see a child looking for a thrill. It's far more plausible to assume that the desire for excitement was the motivation for his theft, not the fact that his action itself could be considered evil. This excitement was naturally tied to the fact that stealing pairs is a break with normal behavior, and entails a risk of punishment. Because excitement is the central factor, Augustine's actions have more in common with extreme sport than sadism, and his story about stealing pairs doesn't give us a clue about demonic evil.

What about the man who first originated the idea of "sadism"? Is this an example of doing evil *because* it's evil? Sade challenges Rousseau and other enlightenment thinkers by insisting that nature isn't in fact good, and that criminality and violence are natural laws. Society is simply a continuance of nature and the evil inherent in nature. Sade's agents want to be free and so sever themselves from society's bonds—but in doing so, they simply bind themselves to nature. There's no distinction here between natural and moral evil. Sade's project is, in fact, to make this idea explicit and to take advantage of the resulting possibilities. You can read Sade's work as a parody of philosophical ethics,[261] but it appears Sade's ambitions were greater than caricature. The problem with Sade's philosophy, however, is this: In order to insist that something is evil, something else must be recognized as good—yet the recognition of good is missing from Sade's thought. Ultimately, we can say that Sade rejects every idea of objective good and objective evil and exclusively embraces whatever gives subjective pleasure: For Sade, evil is something that should be *enjoyed* . . . but then that enjoyment cannot be regarded as anything other than a subjective *good*. It's telling that one of Sade's protagonists observes that: "the *evil* I do to others makes me happy, as God is rendered happy by the *evil* he does me."[262] Sade's libertines seek a subjective good, that which gives pleasure, and therefore it's clear that Sade's works cannot be used to develop the idea of a person who does evil solely *because* it's evil. Taking pleasure in the suffering of another is, insofar as it's *pleasurable*, a good, even though this pleasure is caused by something evil.

Can we imagine that an agent might simply invert basic moral norms and *transform* evil into subjective good? In Milton's *Paradise Lost*, Satan declares: "Evil, be thou my good."[263] What we have to ask ourselves is whether this idea is meaningful. What is evil *good for* in Satan's eyes? The answer is nothing other than—freedom. In his pride, Satan revolts against God, because he refuses to be a slave to God and his commandments.[264] "To do aught good never will be our task, / But ever to do ill our sole delight, / As being contrary to his high will, / Whom we resist."[265] Instead of saying that evil is good in and of itself—a statement that would be meaningless—Satan insists that freedom is the greatest of all goods. Satan embraces evil as a means of freeing himself from God. Therefore, for Satan, evil only has an instrumental worth. It's the will to freedom that made Satan such a popular figure with William Blake and other Romantics, an idea that stands in open contrast to Milton's intentions and that he explicitly warns against.[266] In my opinion, Milton's Satan is more like a stubborn child than a freedom fighter. Nonetheless, Satan's goal is freedom, not evil for its own sake.

We find another view in Edgar Allan Poe. In Poe's short story "The Black Cat," the narrator claims that the human heart holds a "spirit of Perverseness," which is the "unfathomable longing of the soul *to vex itself*—to offer violence to its own nature—to do wrong for wrong's sake only."[267] This idea is developed in "The Imp of the Perverse," where perverse actions are described as actions we undertake *because* we know we shouldn't do them.[268] Poe goes on to say that there's no deeper motivation for the perverse action than this—no underlying principle—and that it would be tempting to call such actions the devil's work. As a result, he argues that these actions are based on "a *mobile* without motive, a motive not *motiviert*."[269] It's difficult to know what conclusion we should draw from Poe's short description of perversity. He seems to mean that the fact of something's being evil is reason enough for action. This can hardly be considered a reason, however—it is a non-reason, a non-justification; and when Poe subsequently states that another force seems to be working *through* us, we leave the rational sphere behind and enter into the realm of pathology. Poe has not demonstrated that an action is carried out *because* it's regarded as subjectively or objectively evil; at most, he's merely pointed out that we are capable of carrying out evil actions while fully aware that they're evil, whatever the motivation. This hardly indicates that evil for its own sake is a good basis for action—only that people are sometimes irrational. Even an irrational agent would still have *reasons* for acting—but no reason to prefer a worse alternative to a better.[270] Thus, if we're to imagine a person who does evil for its own sake, we have to assume there's some rational mechanism directing this decision. In my opinion, there are only three possibilities here: aesthetics, pathology, or some combination of the two. Pathology I'm setting aside, because that's a discussion external to the context of freedom—the context, that is, of assuming that someone could have acted otherwise. Let us therefore turn to aesthetics.

Evil's Aesthetic Seduction

An agent can have a reason to do evil, well aware that it's evil, where the reason itself is not based in morality. It can simply be that this action gives the agent a feeling of pleasure.

Colin McGinn ties ethics and aesthetics together and maintains that evil is expressed in repulsive actions, that violence is inherently repulsive, etc.[271] He bases his ideas strictly on a pre-modern concept of aesthetics, and his readers would be justified in asking whether or not he's aware that the Romantic or Modern eras ever occurred. Now, we Romantics—or possibly Post-Romantics—can find beauty in evil and can regard violence as attractive.[272] However, I'm more inclined to call violence and evil *sublime* rather than attractive. According to Kant, the sublime produces a "negative pleasure" in us, and is therefore both attractive and repulsive.[273] Kant calls attention to war, for instance, as something sublime.[274] Consider the confession of an American Vietnam veteran recalling the thoughts that struck him when he stood and looked at the corpses of North Vietnamese soldiers:

> That was another of the times I stood on the edge of my humanity, looked into the pit, and loved what I saw there. I had surrendered to an aesthetics that was divorced from that crucial quality of empathy that lets us feel the sufferings of others. And I saw a terrible beauty there. War is not simply the spirit of ugliness [. . .], it is also an affair of great and seductive beauty.[275]

Through aestheticization—consider war, for example, as it appears in movies—terrible actions can become attractive.[276] You can admire the music of machine guns, the glint of steel on weapons, and the color of napalm. War can even become a comedy, and those wounded and killed can appear to be purely comic figures. By robbing war of its reality, one's individual vulnerability and the suffering of others both become easier to bear. And violence has its own seductions. We can say that violence is repulsive, but we can also say that violence is attractive. This is in no way a contradiction. In both cases, we're talking about taste, and aesthetic taste doesn't follow moral judgment. Aesthetics are often regarded as an autonomous sphere, removed from the demands of morality.

When evil is redefined as an aesthetic object, its moral qualities fall by the wayside.

Plato, therefore, was mostly right in his condemnation of art: The aesthetic object is dangerous because it's irrational. Almost half a century ago, Thorkild Bjørnvig described an "illness of the age" that he termed the "aesthetic idiosyncrasy." The aesthetic idiosyncrasy is the tendency to be "fascinated by details, to burn with infinite passion for those things one finds beautiful, and just as infinite loathing for those things one finds ugly."[277] We can also call this idea an aesthetic irrationality, where aesthetic judgments are deemed sufficient grounds for action and for destroying what we find repulsive. The examples Bjørnvig cites range from Edgar Allan Poe's short story "The Tell-Tale Heart" to the Nazi mass exterminations. If we turn to Poe, we find that the protagonist in Poe's short story murders an old man because he can't stand the sight of the old man's "evil" eye. He admits that occasionally he likes the old man himself, but his hatred for the eye causes him to abstract it from the old man's other qualities.[278] Whenever he encounters the victim, all he can see is his evil eye. We find a similar idiosyncratic action described by Hamsun in "Fra det ubevidste Sjæleliv" ("The Unconscious Life of the Mind"), where a man kills a horse for looking at him wrong:

> I know a man, an upstanding farmer in his thirties, who shot his neighbor's horse three years ago for looking at him askance. The man had no other reason for his action than this: the horse's lopsided glare irritated him to death. Since he couldn't admit the real, ridiculous reason for killing the animal, he held his peace, and every single person put the act down to pure malice[279]

In his description of Claggart, the sadist who plagues Billy Budd in Herman Melville's novel, Melville makes great use of what Bjørnvig calls aesthetic idiosyncrasy.[280] The only thing that motivates Claggart to molest Billy Budd is that he can't stand the sight of Billy's innocence. Bjørnvig dubs Nazism an aesthetic ideology for this same reason, and for Berel Lang, the Jewish extermination is ultimately a modernistic *artwork*.[281] In my opinion, this idea is flawed. Even if morality and aesthetics were closely tied in Nazism, as they are in every totalitarian system,[282] its discourse was focused more on a moral than on an aesthetic project. Furthermore, the aesthetic goal wasn't to create an artwork made up of dead Jews, but rather to remove those people who were deemed to be nothing more than filth: revolting objects, no better than garbage. At the same time, we have to say that it wasn't the dehumanization processes in the camps that created the illusion that Jews were filth, because that idea was already in place before the mass exterminations began. Instead, the dehumanization processes sought to strengthen the extant, ideologically founded belief that Jews were filth—the better to pacify any qualms on the parts of the executioners. If we stick with the art metaphor, we could say that it wasn't the concentration camps themselves that were the artwork, in this case; the artwork would have been the finished product, whatever would remain after all undesirable material had been eliminated from society—like a sculptor removing excess material to reveal a shape. At the same time, I certainly won't exclude the possibility that certain individuals took an aesthetic pleasure in the mass exterminations—however far removed their tastes might be from my own aesthetic preferences.

Nietzsche claims that people in general "enjoy evil" and find "*meaningless evil* the most interesting form."[283] Perhaps Nietzsche has a point: Evil is seductive, and meaningless evil seems to be an especially extreme, and therefore seductive, form of evil. The essential question then becomes, *what type* of seduction does evil present? Jean Genet begins *The Thief's Journal* with the assertion that "for love's sake" he has been driven "[t]oward what is known as evil."[284] He wants to see "a new paradise" where he shall "impose a candid vision of evil."[285] But this becomes Genet's "good," and he describes certain policemen as basking in an atmosphere of "foul infamy."[286] For Genet, the main thing is to create a deviant identity,[287] and to define his own "good" in contrast to the official good he deviates from. What society calls evil, Genet also calls evil, but he considers evil to be good. The important point is that he considers evil to be attractive, and therefore the ethical is subordinate to the aesthetic.[288]

Genet provides a continuation of Baudelaire's thought. Baudelaire holds that evil is harmful as a purely moral category, but as an aesthetic category, he values it. The aesthetic and the ethical evaluations of evil have completely different results. Everything can be made beautiful, but Baudelaire wants more than anything to connect beauty to evil, and he claims for example that murder is one of beauty's most valuable adornments.[289] Morality is subordinate to aesthetics, and good and evil are primarily aesthetic categories: "the things we loathed become the things we loved."[290] Evil can even overcome boredom, the unifying figure in *Les Fleurs du Mal*. It also becomes a kind of good, or rather, a kind of substitute for good—although the good is an *aesthetic* good. When we discuss the desire for demonic evil, however, we must consider evil as a *moral grounds* for action. If the motivations behind evil were purely aesthetic, we would have no difficulty explaining them. The idea of choosing to do *moral* evil *because* it's morally evil does not have a place in the discussion of aesthetic evil; the idea is spoiled by the fact that evil here becomes a source of aesthetic delight.

Sadism

We have yet to establish a clear idea of an agent who does evil simply because it's evil. So far, there has always another motivating factor in the picture. But how about a classical sadist who takes pleasure in the suffering of others?

A common explanation when trying to understand how people can inflict gruesome suffering on other people is that perpetrators reduce their victims to the status of a *thing*, that the victim becomes objectivized to such an extent that the I-you-relationship vanishes. This model of objectivization seems applicable to certain situations, such as the near-mechanical operation of a Nazi death camp, but it contributes little to an understanding of sadistic violence. Sadistic murders have no meaning if the perpetrator has simply reduced another human being to the level of an object. He might as well have kicked a rock down the road, an equally irrelevant action. There's a *reason* the perpetrator would rather kick heads than kick stones. The fact that his victims are conscious beings with their own subjectivity is a *condition* for the action occurring in the first place. A sadistic action presupposes a certain amount of identification with the victim. Otherwise, the action would be utterly meaningless.[291]

I believe that sadism can best be understood in terms of the Hegelian model of recognition. Sadists want to be acknowledged as subjects. In fiction, there's a good representation of this idea in Bret Easton Ellis's novel *American Psycho*. The protagonist, Patrick Batemen, suffers from a lack of personal identity, and therefore tries to compensate by murdering others in extremely sadistic ways.[292] In a famous essay, Hans Morgenthau claims that love and power spring from the same source, namely isolation, but that love tries to dismantle the wall between two people so they become one, while power tries to subordinate another's subjectivity to one's own.[293] Sadists desire power. The screams of the victim prove that the sadist has power over another individual, that the power relationship is authentic. For a sadist, pain isn't the goal. It's simply a means to domination. Of course, suffering can also give pleasure. However, in the I-you-relationship, the goal of pain is subordinate to the goal of domination—that is, to the goal of recognition.

In his struggle for recognition, the sadist utterly subordinates another person's subjectivity to his own, so much so that all autonomy disappears. For this reason, his plan is doomed from the start: Once his goal is reached, and the foreign consciousness is completely beaten and subordinated to his own, the subdued consciousness is no longer capable of giving the recognition he craves. That is, you do not regard a subdued consciousness as an individual. In order to attain true recognition, you must be recognized by an individual that you in turn recognize as an individual. According to the Hegelian model I've used as the basis for this discussion, sadists must necessarily fail; they'll never attain the recognition they strive for.

Colin McGinn interprets sadism in another way, so that sadists do not necessarily fail. He claims that sadists suffer from an "existential envy," a feeling that their lives have less worth than others. It's therefore the sadist's project to reduce the quality of another person's life to an even lower plateau than their own[294]—an interesting hypothesis, precisely because it allows sadists to succeed. The problem, however, is that we have no reason to believe that every sadist suffers from existential envy. We could also claim, for example, that think they're *better* than their victims and, therefore, feel they have the right to treat their victim however they want. Nonetheless, whatever success is provided by McGinn's model will be extremely short-lived. The act will have to be repeated again and again, because the sadists will constantly be meeting people who cause him to feel the same existential envy.

We can imagine other variations as well. Sympathy can be reversed, and I might want another person to feel my pain. I might want to show that my life is hard. I can either express my pain symbolically, in words and pictures, or concretely, by inflicting pain on others.[295] None of these ideas involve doing evil for evil's sake, however: they are simply futile attempts to communicate. I will not pursue this discussion further. My main point is that there's a multitude of possible explanations for sadism that are all *understandable*, in contrast with the idea of doing evil *because* it's evil.

Schadenfreude

What about schadenfreude? Isn't taking pleasure in another's suffering the same thing as taking pleasure in evil *because* it's evil? Plato describes the vicious person as someone who takes pleasure in another person's pain.[296] Most of us fall under this category to some degree; broadly speaking, we've all experienced schadenfreude at one time or another. Colin McGinn distinguishes between active and passive evil: in general, the former is defined as taking pleasure in inflicting suffering on others, and the latter as enjoying suffering when it's inflicted.[297] Schadenfreude, then, would be closely related to "passive evil." Schopenhauer describes schadenfreude as the worst trait in human nature, and as the most demonic of all sins.[298] Kant also condemns schadenfreude as the opposite of the neighborly love we should all feel,[299] and he therefore describes schadenfreude as "inhuman" and "devilish."[300]

There are two clear reasons for schadenfreude: a general delight in another's suffering or a specific delight in seeing justice done.

We cannot exclude, however, the fact that schadenfreude is often a combination of the two. In my opinion, schadenfreude is an acceptable feeling if it's motivated by justice; that is, if it's not the suffering itself, but the sense of justice being done, that produces pleasure. This viewpoint has a long philosophical tradition going back to Augustine.[301] It follows, furthermore, that schadenfreude is harmful when it's not accompanied by the belief that another's suffering is justified. That most of us have experienced both modes could hardly be regarded as a controversial statement. However, the picture becomes more complicated when our sense of justice is confused by a personal entanglement in the matter—for example, if we're jealous. And we should certainly avoid the idea that all who suffer did something to deserve it. Faith in a this kind of just world can be a dangerous concept.

As we've seen time and again, furthermore, violence draws an enthusiastic crowd. There was huge interest in public executions, and if we started showing executions on TV, ratings would surely skyrocket. In France, the guillotine was unpopular at first because executions happened too quickly for the public to see much of anything—there were public protests to reinstate the gallows. The revolutionary government took these protests to heart and instituted a number of changes—higher platforms, displaying of the head afterwards, more executions at once, etc.—in order to meet the public halfway.[302] We can interpret such interest in two ways: (1) A fascination, possibly even a pleasure, in seeing another person suffer and die; and (2) a pleasure in seeing justice done to the fullest. Some will assert that it's naïve to believe that (2) is plausible. But hardly anyone would enjoy seeing an innocent person executed. In order for violence to be pleasurable, therefore, it must appear justified (or fictional). Otherwise, our own sense of justice would protest too strongly. It's no coincidence that those thrown to the lions in the Colosseum were billed as "criminals." Burning Christians for their heresy wasn't always popular with audiences, for the very reason that the audience often—and rightly so—considered the victims to be innocent.

In my opinion, people are not as bad, where schadenfreude is concerned, as—for example—Schopenhauer would have us believe. I trust that schadenfreude is usually motivated by the feeling that suffering has been earned—because the person has done something evil, has done something stupid, etc. Of course, we often laugh at things—when someone trips and falls, for instance—without having any reason to think the person "earned" it. There's just something comical about the situation. But our laughter would quickly die away if the fall was especially hard, or if the person was seriously hurt. Perhaps such laughter should indeed be categorized as a form of schadenfreude, but in any case it's a harmless form. It may seem that I'm trying to put people in a better light than they deserve, where schadenfreude is concerned. However, I really do think that most of us believe that the suffering we enjoy witnessing or hearing about was justified in some way. For example, if someone told me that Ratko Mladić—one of people principally responsible for the massacre in Srebrenica—was suffering from a long-lasting and particularly painful illness, the thought would give me pleasure. At the same time, if I heard the same thing about Nelson Mandela, or a neighbor who had never hurt a fly, my feelings would be exactly the opposite. When we feel schadenfreude, we distinguish between those who deserve to suffer and those who don't. In my opinion, the existence of schadenfreude isn't proof that people in general have a sadistic disposition.

Subjective and Objective Evil

Socrates claims that no one commits evil intentionally. Everyone wants to live the good life, and evil actions hinder that goal.[303] The Socratic argument can be roughly outlined in the following way: (1) No one commits evil intentionally; (2) to act virtuously (with *arête*) is to act knowledgeably; (3) all moral knowledge is knowledge about the good; ergo all evil actions are caused by ignorance of the good.[304] This theory explains how evil actions are possible, but it also goes against our intuition about ourselves as agents: We recognize, in ourselves and other human beings, the tendency to do things we *know* are evil. A more sophisticated variation on Socrates' argument is that those who do good are happier than those who do evil, but that those who do evil aren't aware of this and therefore act in ignorance. It's not that a person is ignorant of an individual action's character as evil, but rather of the relationship between this action and happiness. Seen in this way, there would be no contradiction between knowing an action is immoral and choosing to do it anyway—but while this interpretation of Socrates' account is certainly more in keeping with our experience of ourselves and others as agents, it still denies the possibility that a person could do evil *because* it's evil (and, therefore, it doesn't help us to answer the question of whether or not this is likely). The Platonic variant[305] on the above is more sophisticated still in that desire (*epitumia*) plays an essential role and can vanquish reason (*logos*). But here, too, evil actions are only undertaken involuntarily.

Thus, in any iteration, the Socratic explanation doesn't really seem to match how we normally think of ourselves. The quandary posed by morality is not simply our *knowing* what's right, but *doing* what's right. Most people choose the Platonic variant when explaining their own actions—they don't plead ignorance or irrationality, but instead claim to have been overcome by some form of emotion, and go on to express surprise at just how strong these compulsions can be. While such an explanation is not necessarily irrational, it does contradict the notion that we ourselves are the only ones responsible for our own actions. The logic goes something like this: If you're always letting yourself be overcome by various emotions, you're certainly a pathetic case, but you also aren't morally responsible, since the actions you undertook were unintentional.

Aristotle claims that we can *deliberately* ignore the good.[306] He accepts the Platonic premise that we're led by desire, but claims that submission can be deliberate—that is, that we can choose to allow ourselves to be led. He develops this idea into a sophisticated theory, distinguishing between the weak will and the bad will. The weak will understands what the good is, but fails to act in accordance with it; the bad will acts in accordance with its *interpretation* of the good, but this interpretation is not accurate.[307] According to Aristotle, sin doesn't know itself, but weakness does[308]—as such, there's no way an agent can do evil for the sake of evil. The agent still chooses evil in his pursuit of the good. A foundational premise in Aristotle's ethics is that the good toward which all actions are directed is happiness (*eudaimonia*).[309] An action that doesn't have happiness as a goal is simply unfathomable. The goal of all actions is the good—so exceptions to this rule can only be on account of failing to act in accordance with one's understanding of the good, or else simply being unaware what the good might be. For Aristotle, therefore, all evil actions are either due to weakness or misunderstanding—which, again, fails to match our own experience of ourselves and others as agents, because we know very well that we occasionally do evil things deliberately and with the full understanding that they are evil.

Doing something evil because it's evil, moreover, can't simply be attributed to *akrasia*, the weak will. The weak-willed person does something he shouldn't do because he *gives in*—he doesn't actively choose evil. It's this experience of weak will that Paul describes in Romans: "For what I do is not the good I want to do; no, the evil I do not want to do—this I keep on doing."[310] Doing evil for the sake of evil is an incoherent idea—it means deliberately doing the opposite of what we consider to be good. But is it even possible to desire something we don't consider to be good, in one way or another? As Sartre puts it, you'd have to wish for what you don't want and stop wanting what you wish for.[311] It's a matter of two contrasting intentions; when an agent does something he knows to be evil, he's caught in a self-opposition, caught between the knowledge that he's doing something he shouldn't do and the fact that he's chosen to do it anyway.

Earlier, I discussed a number of thinkers who believe people do evil *because* it's evil, pure and simple, and make this idea into a paradigmatic conception of evil. There are just as many thinkers who claim the opposite, however: that people are always motivated by something that they consider to be good in some way. Thomas Aquinas writes that a man cannot love something evil without also thinking it's good.[312] Leibniz follows this train of thought and maintains that the will can only be motivated by a conception of good, never by evil alone.[313] Hume rejects the concept of "absolute, unprovoked, disinterested malice"[314]—disinterested, autoteleological evil doesn't appear in his works. Rousseau grandly asserts that: "no one does the bad for the sake of the bad."[315] He claims that both good people and evil people try to do good, but evil people seek their good at other people's expense.[316] Kant argues that evil holds no direct attraction for us, only an indirect one[317]—that is, we do evil, but not *because* it's evil. We desire evil things because we interpret them as subjective goods.

Thus, we can say that when someone does something he knows to be evil, evil isn't the primary attraction. The attraction is something else. True demonic evil can only be described as *disinterested*, however, because it has no purpose beyond itself. In my opinion, therefore, disinterested evil simply doesn't exist. Interested evil can spring from envy, jealousy, a sense of injustice, our desires, etc. Interested evils are purpose-driven. They want to maintain or restore a condition or gain something that's lacking. In these cases, evil actions are *motivated*. It's true, of course, that I can also do something without placing a lot of value on it—most of the things I do everyday I do habitually, without reflecting on their moral status. As such, it would be ridiculous to say that *all* my actions are initiated because I'm trying to realize some particular good. Instead, I believe that to the extent to which my actions are caused by reflection—in which case I can identify a *grounds* for action—the grounds for action are somehow related to the realization of a subjective and/or objective good. Every wish is tied to some concept of the "good," even if the good is only good for the agent himself and, in general, can be considered evil. The satisfaction of desire is good—as in the example of rape and murder satisfying a desire, and thus having, subjectively, a good side—though, obviously, rape and murder are certainly evil in and of themselves.

In other words, I would reduce the category of "demonic" evil to being a variant of the instrumental. When evil people do evil, they do so trying to attain some form of good—either for themselves or for a group; demonic evil must be associated with instrumental evil because of the self-awareness implied by the latter category. The difference between instrumental and idealistic evil agents, furthermore, is not that one desires evil and the other good: they both desire good. But the idealistic evil agent desires that which he considers to be objectively good, while the instrumental evil agent pursues what he considers to be subjectively good. The instrumental evil agent, unlike the idealist, knows that what he does is evil, but chooses to subordinate this knowledge to a higher purpose.

KANT AND INSTRUMENTAL EVIL

In my discussion of instrumental evil, I have chosen to use Kant's theory of radical evil in human nature. As mentioned above, the instrumental evil agent knows that what he does is evil, but chooses to subordinate this knowledge to a higher purpose. Kant clarifies this idea by stating that self-love is prioritized over moral law. According to Kant, the assumption that human nature contains radical evil is essential to explaining freedom and moral responsibility.[318] In contrast to theories that stumble blindly toward defining all evil as demonic, the theory of radical evil represents a step in the right direction . . . But it also suffers from some serious weaknesses. Among these is the fact that Kant traces evil back to an inscrutable and unexamined event in human history, something that—contrary to Kant's intentions—threatens to undermine the moral responsibility people have for their own evil actions. However, I will argue that these weaknesses can be addressed satisfactorily, and that Kant's theory—with some modifications—provides a good explanation for the foundational principles of instrumental evil, and further demonstrates why we are wholly responsible for actions that take this form of evil.

The Impossibility of a "Devilish" Will

Kant's answer to the question of why we do what we shouldn't do is that we let moral laws—laws formulated by reason, laws that make us morally responsible beings—become subordinated to sensual appetites. The search for happiness or the satisfaction of desire are not in themselves immoral activities. Evil first occurs when the pursuit of happiness brings about an intentional transgression of moral law. According to Kant, every transgression of moral law is accompanied by a *respect* for moral law. We cannot fully ignore moral law or replace it with another, evil law: radical evil therefore takes place when we recognize the *authority* of moral law, but at the same time ignore its precepts.[319]

Kant believes that agents can only choose what they consider to be good in some way.[320] If I'm going to commit an evil action, it will be because I think the action will help me to satisfy a desire—that is, evil makes possible the realization of a good. The evil, Kantian agent knows what both subjective and objective good and evil are, but chooses subjective good over objective good. A common objection to Kant's theory is that he overlooks the possibility of a thoroughly "devilish" will, that is, a will that takes pleasure in evil for evil's sake—a form of disinterested evil.[321] Kant strongly denies that this type of evil is even possible.[322] According to Kant, we *choose* evil, but we choose it for the sake of something else. Namely, we choose it for the sake of our own self-love.

Kantian evil is not an extravagant form of evil practiced by devilish agents. It's what we might call "everyday evil," or ordinary evil. Radical evil isn't an extreme form of evil; instead, it's the basic foundation of every evil action we commit, even the actions that aren't especially noteworthy. Radical evil is the root (*radix*) of all evil. To talk about radical evil is not to talk about sadistic actions: Radicalism refers to the *depths* of an individual's moral corruptness; that is, when we prioritize self-love over all other considerations. As a result, radical evil is wholly compatible with living what appears to a morally exemplary life. If I live the life of a saint simply to be recognized as a saint by those around me, and not because I think this life is morally correct, I would be evil, as Kant understands the word. It should also be pointed out that this theory of radical evil is also completely compatible with extreme human cruelty. We do not have to postulate the principle of the devilish will in order to explain such actions.[323] They can be explained in the context of a steadily increasing self-love, with the result that an agent becomes more and more morally degenerate. Even the most degenerate agent, therefore, does evil for the sake of something else—namely, for the sake of self-love. There are no limits to the consequences radical evil can have. Indeed, a particularly thought-provoking aspect of Kant's theory of radical evil is that our small, daily offenses spring from the same source as the cruelest actions.

Kant distinguishes between three levels of evil, although there's a gradual transition from the first to the third: (1) Weakness or frailty, where an agent has good intentions but doesn't live up to them; (2) impurity (*Unlauterkeit*), where an agent isn't motivated by morals alone, but where the motivations are mixed; and (3) wickedness or perversity, where an agent tends to choose the greatest evil.[324] The first two types can be described as unintentional evil and the third as intentional evil. The fact that the third is described as intentional evil does not, however, mean the agent chooses evil for its own sake—instead, he chooses evil because he values himself more than he values morality.

A central aspect of Kant's theory of action is what Henry Allison has called "the incorporation thesis."[325] An impulse or desire can determine an agent's ability to choose (*Willkür*) if and only if an agent has chosen to incorporate the desire into his maxims of conduct.[326] Therefore, if the desire leads to an action, the agent must have freely chosen to be guided by their desire. As a result, sensuality can no longer play the villain in evil's drama; moral responsibility presupposes independence from natural causes as determinative sources. Evil ultimately presupposes that a propensity is deliberately included in a maxim of conduct.[327]

Kantian evil, furthermore, belongs neither to psychology nor cosmology, but rather to the metaphysics of freedom. The root of evil may be found in free will, but it's not evil itself (*Böse*) that can be found there, but rather *evils* (*Übel*).[328] Without free will, there would be nothing to blame, because nature cannot be subjected to moral judgments. That is, evil is not external to freedom, but it's a possibility that comes with freedom. For Kant, freedom is not defined as the ability to act in defiance of the moral law;[329] instead, he understands freedom fundamentally as our ability to act *in accordance* with moral law. Which doesn't mean, of course, that freedom isn't also compatible with the ability to defy it.

According to Kant, evil originates in humanity,[330] and every individual is responsible for choosing good or evil.[331] There are no external causes that determine actions or fundamental attitudes. Our innate ability to choose has a single function: to decide on maxims, that is, our codes of action. Every code of action has both sensuous and moral determinates, and therefore evil cannot be said to originate in a maxim of conduct that has sensuous or moral content.[332] Instead, evil originates in the *form* the maxim of conduct takes. Moral evil originates in the subordination of moral law to sensuous inclinations, and radical evil is the choice to follow these inclinations. Therefore, radical evil *precedes* immoral actions.[333] This is the subjective basis for the formation of every immoral maxim of conduct. Moral evil presupposes radical evil, because radical evil is implied in every maxim that intentionally breaks with moral law.

The Paradox of Evil

We have freedom of choice, and this is the origin of evil. Every violation of moral responsibility can only be explained by the fact that we've chosen a maxim whose basis and consequences are known to us. If this were not the case, there would be no such thing as moral evil.[334] Thus, we inflict the propensity toward evil on ourselves,[335] but Kant also maintains that we are "evil *by nature*."[336] The idea of a freely chosen propensity seems to be self-contradictory, and Kant is not very successful in resolving this contradiction—where he otherwise sharply distinguishes between nature and freedom, here he seems to blend the two together. The concept of a freely chosen propensity toward evil is paradoxical, and in order to resolve this paradox the phrase "by nature" must mean something other than it usually does, because here "nature" is not a given, but a *chosen*.[337]

Kant can be understood as describing evil's *dimension*—as it applies to every person—rather than discussing something naturally inherent in every human being. According to Kant, a concept of good is necessary, because moral law is not something we can simply do away with. Evil, on the other hand, is contingent, although people cannot simply eradicate the radical evil inside themselves.[338] In other words, radical evil is both a universal *and* a contingent characteristic of being human, and every individual has a propensity to deviate from moral law. However, Kant gives no evidence for evil's universality aside from a rather unhelpful gesture toward "the multitude of crying examples."[339] Given Kant's assertion that the existence of radical evil cannot be proven empirically, however, this rhetorical strategy is rather strange. Kant gives no empirical evidence to support his claim. The problem here is that our motives are not empirically observable. At best, we can simply draw conclusions concerning the motives that formed the basis for an action, but we can't conclude anything about this motive with absolute certainty.[340] This lack of certainty doesn't simply pertain to other people's motives, but also to our own. What's inside us is no clearer than what's outside us, and the motivation behind an action will always be partially obscure.[341] In a similar way, we cannot observe the maxim for an action, though we can use the action itself to draw conclusions about the maxim and, further, about the agent's disposition (*Gesinnung*).[342] The judgment that an agent is evil cannot be proven experientially with absolute certainty, but only with relative certainty. And even if the relative certainty was high with regard to a number of agents, the fact would still be insufficient to prove that radical evil is *universal*.

Humanity may have chosen its propensity toward evil, but Kant argues we cannot trace this choice back to any one specific point in time; if we could, we would then be implying a causal relationship that would ultimately undermine the freedom necessary to make any subsequent choices. If we are to talk about the origins of evil in choice, he says, we must understand this origin rationally, not temporally.[343] Kant uses this argument to avoid answering the basic question raised by the notion that we have *chosen* our natures: At what stage in our development did this supposed choice take place? However, even focusing on the logical chain of events that such a choice implies, Kant still manages to get himself caught in a number of difficulties.

Radical evil presupposes a consciousness of moral law. If an agent can't understand the requirements of moral law, there's no reason to attribute evil to him.[344] The origin of his or her evil is something an agent must be able to take responsibility for. Therefore, the source of evil cannot be located in the fact that I'm an individual being—that is, the source is not in my physical nature, in my rational nature, or in any combination of the two. The source must be found in *choice*, and this choice must have been an *informed* one. As a result, it must be assumed that when I act, I'm aware of both principles involved in the choice: moral law and self-love. In and of itself, moral law does not motivate an agent's actions. Instead, the *consciousness* of moral law provides a basis for decision. This consciousness is imparted through a *respect* for moral law. But how do we come by this respect? For Kant, the only possible answer is: through the violation of moral law. It's the *violation* itself that gives me insight into my freedom. According to Kant, the disgust that I feel when I act immorally tells me that I'm free and obligated to moral law.

We're acquainted with moral law because it affects our sensibilities, and the respect we feel for moral law is imparted through the feeling of guilt. *Our only access to moral law is through a feeling of guilt.* According to Kant, this idea is applicable to even the most morally degenerate person.[345] I'm guilty, and therefore I'm free. If the question is, what am I guilty of? The answer seems to be: I'm guilty of violating moral law. But how can I be guilty of violating a law I wasn't even aware of? As it is written in Romans: "[W]here there is no law there is no transgression [. . .] for before the law was given, sin was in the world. But sin is not taken into account when there is no law."[346] A person can do something that, considered objectively, they obviously should not have done, even if they have no knowledge of the law. However, without knowing the law, they cannot be considered *guilty*, insofar as ignorance is something they can't be held responsible for. If a person *was* responsible for his or her own ignorance, we could accuse them by saying: "You *should* have known that . . ."; but this accusation is completely illogical if the responsible party was *incapable* of knowing any better—and this is exactly the case with an individual agent before they violate moral law. They could not have known any better. Since consciousness of moral law is only attained *post factum*, after moral law has already been violated and the feeling of guilt sets in, the so-called "original choice" must have taken place *before* we even knew about moral law, says Kant. At this point in the discussion, however, we've lost the ability to use the word *choice* in any meaningful way.

In exercising our ability to choose, we choose maxims that are either moral or immoral. There is no morally neutral maxim or action.[347] We cannot imagine anything that precedes this choice or that motivates it. We want to find an explanation for *why* people choose evil, but Kant only gives a *formal* description without making reference to any concrete rationale. This omission is due to the fact that such reasons would undermine the status of active choice as something spontaneous and autonomous. The problem, however, is that we're now left with the idea of a choice with no reason behind it, and therefore a choice we are in no position to try and understand. We haven't come any closer to explaining why we apparently choose evil. Kant is well aware of the limits of his discourse, and emphasizes the fact that the original choice of evil is characterized by "inscrutability," by the fact that we can find "no conceivable ground" for it.[348] But reference to a given inscrutability is unacceptable in a theory that professes to be rationally acceptable.

Kant, however, points to the inscrutability of the original choice of evil in order to avoid an obvious regress problem. An agent's disposition is the broadest, most general maxim that forms the basis for choosing all other, more specific maxims.[349] However, it's clear that this maxim of disposition will imply earlier maxims that form the basis for the choice of later maxims. In the context of our discussion, this means that there can be no *original* choice of evil, because every choice implies a previous choice: You must be evil in order to become evil. As mentioned above, Kant is aware of this regress problem,[350] but he chooses to solve it in an unsatisfactory way by postulating that the original choice has already taken place and that it cannot be explored further.

Radical evil is paradoxical, because the original choice it implies is only possible in light of presuppositions that have already taken place. It's a choice that presupposes itself. As a result, an individual seems to be both responsible and not responsible for their own evil. Normally, a person chooses to accept such a paradox, without privileging one side over the other; this possibility, however, is not available to Kant. He cannot find any middle position, because then the motivation for evil is indefinite and an agent's status will vacillate between autonomy and heteronomy. In Kant's moral universe, the responsibility is either mine or it isn't. To take an indefinite position with regard to autonomy and heteronomy would be the same thing as choosing heteronomy. The basic question is whether an agent's actions are an expression of his freedom, and this question can only be answered positively if the agent has freely chosen his essential disposition. In the meantime, Kant hasn't been able to convincingly demonstrate the existence of such free choice.

Kant's stubborn belief in an originally chosen evil propensity seems to rely on two premises: (1) We accuse agents of acting according to immoral maxims, and these maxims are the result of an immoral propensity; (2) such accusations are legitimate because agents have chosen their propensity. The first premise is comparatively unproblematic, because it certainly is a fact that we accuse one another. The other premise, however, is extremely suspect, because Kant has in no way provided a clear explanation for how such choice would even be possible.

Moral Rebirth

We've already seen that Kant does not succeed in giving a convincing explanation of how an original choice of evil is possible. However, this does not necessarily imply that he still can't justify the concept of moral responsibility. Even if we can't be held responsible for *being* evil, we can conceivably be accused of *remaining* evil instead of working to become better people. This would be the case if we were capable of choosing a good disposition over an evil one. Unfortunately, this possibility is denied to us, because radical evil corrupts the basis for the formulation of *all* maxims.[351] An individual might want to form a maxim in order to change their disposition, but this does not seem to be feasible, since the basis for formulating all maxims has already been contaminated. That is, if every formulation of a good maxim has already been undermined, there seems to be no possibility of overcoming our propensity to evil.

However, Kant argues that people *do* have the ability to overcome their propensity toward evil, and bases this idea on the logic that, as we have a duty to overcome evil, duty would not demand something of us that we were not capable of giving.[352] *Should* presupposes *can*, and if something is truly our duty, we should be capable of living up to it. Therefore, according to Kant, it should be possible to triumph over evil—yet such a triumph demands nothing less than a *revolution* in an agent's disposition, and this revolution presupposes divine assistance.[353] Kant continues that people must do everything in their power to make themselves *worthy* of such assistance, and thereafter they can only *hope* to receive it: there's no guarantee. In Kant's moral anthropology, it's clear that people are simply unable to overcome evil on their own, and in this respect the duty becomes less burdensome. People should *try* to overcome evil, but they should not be blamed for failing. After all, it's ridiculous to accuse someone for not having received divine assistance. Only by receiving such assistance will agents be *completely* free. Complete freedom is a gift from God, and until this gift is given, agents will only be partially free.

Evil therefore seems unavoidable, and we need more than morality and human will to overcome it. How, then, can morality be as independent of religion as Kant claims? In his preface to the first edition of *Religion*, Kant argues that his moral philosophy is completely independent of religious doctrine and that people don't need a higher power to transform themselves into good, moral agents.[354] However, we have never seen Kant prove this assertion.

In my opinion, there's no doubt that Kant fails in his attempt to explain the possibility of evil and humanity's responsibility for it. He has not given a rationally satisfactory answer for how a person is responsible for choosing a propensity toward evil, since he has not managed to demonstrate that such a choice exists in the first place. Furthermore, he has not explained how this choice would even be possible. He also lacks a rationally acceptable explanation of how the propensity to evil can be overcome—that is, of how we can become better people.

The main problem here is that Kant presupposes a basic choice between good and evil, a choice that all other actions more or less result from, since this choice lays the groundwork for the formulation of all maxims. With that, the focus is shifted from concrete active choice to the *original* choice at the foundation of all active choices. Kant first assumes that we've all chosen our basic propensity toward good or evil, and second that this choice becomes the basis for all further maxim formulation. Both assumptions are, in my opinion, doubtful—or, rather, Kant's first assumption makes the second suspect. Kant only sees two possibilities: a person is either good *or* evil.[355] It's more plausible, however, that all people—both in the depths and on the surface—are good *and* evil, instead of having chosen good *or* evil. A person lives, acts, and is shaped by the life they lead. In being shaped, they develop a character. But at no time can we pinpoint the decisive *choice* of a character that's good *or* evil. Some people lean more towards good, others more towards evil, but all people choose both good and evil. This is an idea that Kant would not necessarily disagree with; he maintains that even the worst person has a kernel of good inside him, but he formulates his theory in such a way that absolute priority is given either to the good or to the evil in every person. It's this absolute prioritizing that I'm skeptical of. Within our own individual situations, we choose between good and evil, and even if a person's disposition guides the choices they make, every person still has the possibility to choose good instead of evil. Freedom, the ability to have acted differently in a given situation, is inherent in every situation where there is choice. It's this freedom that Kant goes a long way towards undermining when he asserts that the supposed original choice of evil undermines all further maxim formulation. In short, Kant creates unnecessary problems for himself. He postulates that we originally chose our propensity to evil in order to say we bear responsibility for this propensity, since, according to his theory, choice alone lays the groundwork for responsibility. But if this propensity is not developed as an either/or, but instead as a both/and, then the principle of responsibility can still be upheld by the fact that a person is always responsible for bettering himself because a person *can* better himself.

Kant's theory has a limited scope. It essentially applies only to agents who know that what they're doing is wrong—or more pointedly, to instrumental evil agents. Therefore, it must be supplemented by other theories, both in the idealistic form—where an agent believes that what he does is good—and in stupid evil, where an agent does not stop to think about whether his activities are good or evil.

THE EVIL IS THE OTHER—IDEALISTIC EVIL

According to Ernest Becker, "man's natural and inevitable urge to deny mortality and achieve a heroic self-image are the root causes of human evil."[356] In my opinion, this idea is extremely speculative and lacks evidence. I do not believe that most people have any real desire to appear "heroic," and instead of denying death, we largely recognize it as an unavoidable fact of our lives. On the other hand, I do believe that Becker comes close to an essential insight in the following passage:

> But men are truly sorry creatures because they have made death conscious. They can see evil in anything that wounds them, causes ill health, or even deprives them of pleasure. Consciousness means too that they have to be preoccupied with evil even in the absence of any immediate danger; their lives become a meditation on evil and a planned venture for controlling it and forestalling it.

The result is one of the greatest tragedies of human existence, what we might call the need to "fetishize evil," to
locate the threat to life in some special place where it can
be controlled. It is tragic precisely because it is sometimes
very arbitrary: men make fantasies about evil, see it in
the wrong places, and destroy themselves and others by
uselessly thrashing about.[357]

In my opinion, *ideas* about evil have caused more evil than just
about anything else. Projects intended to overcome both illusory
and actual evils have brought far more evil into the world than
any straightforward attempt at transgression. Human aggression
is driven more by ideas than by hormones. As human beings,
we struggle to find meaning; in seeking meaning and in creating
meaning, we create ideas that become bases for action. Two of our
most central concepts are "good" and "evil," and these are often
correlated with the difference between "us" and "them." Devils, or
evil people, are always *others*—never oneself.

In a fragment, Novalis argues that people do evil because they
hate evil: that they perceive everything to be evil and subsequently
become destructive,[358] which destructiveness rebounds back on
themselves and strengthens their worldview. In attempting to overcome evil, people introduce evil into the world. Now, I don't mean
to argue here that all evil is imaginary: our actions cause real evils,
and we ourselves suffer real evils. I further believe that we do indeed have a duty to fight these evils—but it's tragic that we so often
introduce more evil into the world by attacking something we have
mistakenly judged to be evil itself.

Throughout history, we have repeatedly seen the catastrophic results of the desire to cleanse the earth of something people consider

to be evil incarnate. As Norman Cohn points out, there's a thought-provoking continuity between the witch and heretic trials of the middle ages and the Renaissance and the Nazi mass exterminations.[359] The innocent people who were condemned for witchcraft and heresy and then burned at the stake were persecuted by people who believed they stood on the side of good—and people who resort to violence often see themselves as representatives of the good: fighting for a just cause. This was undoubtedly the case with many of the Christian crusaders; it's also the case with today's terrorists. From the victim's perspective, however, the situation appears to be quite different. Nietzsche writes that whatever happens because of love happens beyond good and evil.[360] I find it difficult to agree with this idea. An overwhelming amount of the evil in the world happens because of love—love of self, love of family and friends, love of country, love of an abstract ideal, or love of a leader. Nothing that we do, regardless of motivation, is beyond good and evil. And some conceptions of good are themselves, in fact, evil.

"Us" vs. "Them"

We structure the world and define ourselves through opposed ideas such as Christian/heretic, man/woman, Norwegian/foreigner, Aryan/Jew, Greek/barbarian, white/black, Hutu/Tutsi, etc.[361] These concept pairs distinguish first and foremost between "us" and "them," and vary with different historical, geographical, and social contexts. The distinction between "us" and "them" is essential for identity formation. There's nothing inherently wrong with these concept pairs, even if some distinctions are undeniably more arbitrary than others. The problem is that these concept pairs are often interpreted asymmetrically, and form the basis for discrimination.

The German lawyer and philosopher Carl Schmitt writes: "Every religious, moral, economic, ethical, or other antithesis transforms into a political one if it is sufficiently strong to group human beings effectively according to friend and enemy."[362] Schmitt finds that this idea has dramatic consequences: for him, *political* is defined as the separation between friend and foe. A political action originates in the preservation of self and the destruction of whatever threatens the self, and there's little room for overcoming opposition through discussion. Such political action is the right of the state alone, which may, in order to preserve itself, likewise eliminate enemies within—that is, anyone who doesn't fit into its homogeneous whole.

Novalis, in turn, describes evil as isolating, as the principle of separation (*Princip der Trennung*).[363] The word "devil" comes from the Greek verb *diabellein*, which means to distinguish between or divide. Evil takes place when human bonds are broken, when concrete relationships crumble for the sake of abstract identifications. When we divide the world into sheep and goats,[364] into good and evil, the sheep—the self-proclaimed good—have a tendency to subject the goats to the worst imaginable treatment. In doing so, the sheep's group identity is made stronger, something that forms the basis for new and better identification of goats. Violence brings groups together. Philip Gourevitch, for example, describes genocide as an exercise in team building.[365] We have a tendency to "forget" the wrongs that are done to people we've labeled as "evil." After the Second World War there was widespread agreement that the Germans were evil, and the incarceration and forced deportation of around 11.5 million Germans from Czechoslovakia and Poland didn't disturb too many people. They weren't even disturbed by the fact that around 2.5 million of these Germans died under conditions so brutal they bore a striking resemblance to Nazi practice.[366] However, most of the Germans who were forcibly deported had not actively taken part in the war or the persecutions; in fact, most were women and children. Nonetheless, they were German and therefore considered to be "evil." This pattern repeated itself in the summer of 1995 when 250,000 Serbs were driven out of Croatia. The Serbs were considered "evil," and very few tears were shed for their fate.[367]

The fact that the *other* is evil is oftentimes regarded as sufficient reason to use more or less any means necessary to combat him. However, the fact that "the other" is evil doesn't mean that "we" are necessarily good.[368] It's entirely possible that both sides are evil. This is a basic, but essential point. Even if we have good reason to describe "the other" as evil, we cannot use the fact of their evil as a guarantee that whatever means we use to fight them is good. Of course, this latter conclusion is all too common. A famous example from recent history is Osama bin Laden's assertion that he represents a "good terrorism," because he fights the United State's "evil terrorism."[369] For the idealistic evil agent, it's often not only morally permitted, but morally *imperative* to harm the other in the service of good, because the other embodies an evil that must be fought. That bin Laden believes this is perfectly clear. In an interview from May 1998, he said that it was the *duty* of every Muslim to kill American soldiers and civilians, as well as all their allies. He justified this assertion by emphasizing that the United States hadn't distinguished between military and civilian casualties, men and women, adults and children, for example in Hiroshima and Nagasaki. Bin Laden is correct that the United States is guilty of serious war crimes—the United States cannot allow itself to ignore the difference between military and civilian targets—but that doesn't justify the fact that he himself has sacrificed thousands of American lives in protest against the injustices he believes the United States government and lifestyle represent. The brutality of the terrorists' actions on September 11 is irreconcilable with the idea that these actions were motivated by the good. What good could ever come from such means? The result was nothing but destruction. It is natural to believe that anyone who murders thousands of innocent people *must* realize that what they do is evil, but even the most basic moral understanding will crumble in the face of ideological conviction. The world is a complicated place, but in theories about evil, this complexity is often reduced to a single binary opposition—the world becomes little more than a metaphysical drama between good and evil. There's good and there's evil, and no other alternative is possible.

Religion is often polarizing, leading to people of other faiths being demonized as evil. Since evil must be fought, these other faiths seem legitimate objects of persecution. The perpetrator is "good" and the victim is "evil." The Crusades are a clear example of this idea, but we can also cite more recent examples. On February 25, 1994, Baruch Goldstein opened fire on Muslims at prayer in Hebron, killing and wounding 130 people. Goldstein was convinced that he represented the good and that Muslims were evil—and many Jewish settlers supported his actions and hailed him as a hero. Goldstein is only one of countless examples, and I could just as easily have chosen a Muslim perpetrator. There's a clear Biblical precedent for the type of action Goldstein carried out. For example, in Numbers there's an account of the Israelite war against the Midianites. We're told that Moses grew angry when he found out his soldiers had killed the Midianite men, but had let the women and children live. At that, Moses gives the order that every child down to the last newborn baby should be slain, as well as all the women who had ever slept with a man. The rest of the women, however, would be taken as slaves.[370] In Genesis, we find a similar command regarding the treatment of the Amalekites. The only difference is that, in this case, absolutely everyone must be wiped out: "'Now go, attack the Amalekites and totally destroy everything that belongs to them. Do not spare them; put to death men and women, children and infants, cattle and sheep, camels and donkeys.'"[371] The Bible contains many similar episodes.[372]

A notable trait of such exterminations is that the relationship between attacker and victim is reversed in the attacker's eyes, so that the attacker becomes the "actual" victim. The blame rests on the shoulders of the victim, who is represented as and considered to be the aggressor. As Arne Johan Vetlesen points out, this reversal was the case in every genocide in the twentieth century.[373] For the most part, it stems from the inner logic of group thinking: Morally evil traits and practices are often ascribed to "the other," although there's no support for the accusations; a sense of group belonging is created from and based on judgments regarding one's own group in opposition to other groups.[374] To white colonials, the natives often appeared as "evil" savages who, among other things, were cannibalistic—a perception that was seldom accurate—while Africans often mistook the white colonials for the same. Many thought that white men salted and smoked human flesh, made cheese from brains, and red wine from blood. On the slave transport ships, prisoners even died because they refused to eat food made from what they believed to be human flesh.[375] Both sides were in agreement as to the other's corruption.

This tendency toward differentiation can best be explained by taking Benedict Anderson's concept of "imagined community" as a point of departure. The community is *imagined* because most members of a single group have never had contact, nor ever will have contact, with one another. In fact, most members of the group won't even have heard of the others. Nonetheless, they have a feeling of group identity,[376] as a single aspect or trait shared by a number of people has been elevated until it becomes the basis for community. This trait, arbitrarily chosen from a multitude of traits, abruptly constitutes an essential difference, motivating the differentiation between "us" and everyone else on the planet—and the vast number of other traits "we" and "they" might otherwise have in common are summarily set aside. For example, it was precisely the concept of imagined communities that blew up in everyone's face in the former Yugoslavia. Practically speaking, both sides spoke the same language and belonged to the same group of "Slavs." Well might we wonder what trait it could have been that united the groups against one another. The conflict has been blamed on historical and religious differences, yet before 1989, it hadn't occurred to most ordinary Yugoslavians to give those differences much thought. That is to say, the differences were essentially *created* in a rather short period of time—but they were enough to turn friend into foe and drive one group of people to persecute another.[377] One imagined community motivated the persecution of another imagined community.

Characteristics that distinguish "us" from "them" can be as trivial as cheering for different soccer teams. The 1985 tragedy at Heysel Stadium in Brussels, where Juventus faced off against Liverpool and thirty-eight people were killed in the bleachers, showed just how catastrophic the us/them binary can be. There are other examples, such as the war between Honduras and El Salvador in 1969, which was provoked by two qualification matches in the World Championship. The two countries, of course, already had a long history of conflict—nonetheless, the war lasted one hundred hours and cost around six thousand lives.[378] One of the most extreme examples of a sports-based conflict, however, occurred in Constantinople in the seventh century.[379] The large hippodrome in Constantinople was used for chariot races, and the chariots were painted blue and green to distinguish them. Fans quickly began identifying themselves with these colors, and in no time at all two groups had formed: the blue group and the green group. After a while, these divisions became associated with political and religious leanings—in part because Emperor Anastasius, who had been condemned by the Pope as a heretic, supported the greens. As a result, all greens were regarded as heretics. Steadily, the green and blue camps became more and more fanatical, until finally, during a religious festival near the end of Anastasius's reign, the greens murdered three thousand blues. Anastasius was succeeded by Justin, who was succeeded by Justinian, who happened to support the blues. The tension between the greens and the blues continued, and in the year 532 there were huge riots in the hippodrome—riots that ended with the murder of 30,000 greens.

Thus, the perceived difference between "us" and "them" can be based on extremely insignificant details. Often, it's a case of what Freud calls the "narcissism of minor differences."[380] Inspired by Freud, Michael Ignatieff argues that the degree of animosity between two groups is inversely proportional to the degree of difference between them—but this is not strictly true.[381] You can have great differences and a smaller or greater degree of animosity, or small differences and a smaller or greater degree of animosity. Tremendously small differences, differences so small they seem utterly irrelevant to outsiders, *can* create intense hatred, but one does not necessarily follow from the other. Nonetheless, the difference between "us" and "them," which is often based on the most trivial characteristics, can and does lead to systematic discrimination.[382] Even if the quality that forms the basis for categorization is not an *ethically relevant* quality, it results in ethical *consequences*. In the most extreme cases—such as the Jewish persecutions—moral categories were generally considered to be applicable to an individual's own group, while the other group was excluded from the moral arena. The classical, Aristotelian principle that says relevantly equal cases should be treated as equal, and relevantly unequal cases as unequal is systematically undermined by group solidarity.

To use Aristotle's expression, human beings are political animals, and we tend to live in herds.[383] Group solidarity seems to be a basic human necessity, but it becomes dangerous when the group becomes too tightly knit, when individuals in the group stop thinking as individuals and therefore stop reflecting on the group's values, ideals, and actions. When the difference between "us" and "them" is truly established, individuals will often substitute the group's values and judgments for their own. The need for individual reflection disappears, and thinking for yourself can even seem disloyal to the group. Groups are dangerous because a mass does not have a conscience—conscience always belongs to an individual alone—and therefore individuals in a group seem to have broken free of the demands of morality.[384] Emerson describes how the mob deliberately deprives itself of reason and, therefore, becomes like an animal.[385] Group identity triumphs over individual, moral reflection. To surrender individuality means to surrender the capacity for thought, and vice versa. You must consider yourself to be an individual in order to recognize the other as an individual—depersonalization of the self leads to the depersonalization of the other.

William Blake writes: "[N]one can see the man in the enemy [. . .] I cannot love my enemy for my enemy is not man but beast & devil."[386] It's difficult to see an enemy as an individual, because the idea of "enemy" gets in the way of the idea of common humanity. You shouldn't kill another *human being*, but when the other is seen as a monster, it's often considered acceptable to eradicate this threat. Recognizing the humanity of each and every person is therefore essential—or, rather: It's essential not to lose sight of a person's humanity in view of ideologies or group identity. As Tzvetan Todorov writes:

> Someone who sees no resemblance between himself and his enemy, who believes that all the evil is in the other and none in himself, is tragically destined to resemble his enemy. But someone who, recognizing evil in himself, discovers that he is like his enemy is truly different. By refusing to see the resemblance, we reinforce it; by admitting it we diminish it. The more I think I'm different, the more I am the same; the more I think I'm the same, the more I'm different . . .[387]

Violent Individuals

The tendency to separate people into categories of "good" and "evil" is obvious in cases of group violence, but this tendency can also be found among individuals. It is easier to understand group violence than individual violence, because the former can be blamed on pressure in the group, a common goal, or something similar—but how can we explain individual violence? It's not uncommon to blame a perceived threat or low self-esteem for an individual's aggressive tendencies and violent nature,[388] but these are in no way obvious conclusions. There's no proven connection between "low self-esteem" and violent behavior.[389] The typical "badass" who chooses a specific target that they then subject to physical and/or psychological attack is not necessarily compensating for an insecurity complex. Instead, they are often rather confident people with high self-esteem.[390] Perhaps you could say that their self-image is unstable; therefore, they try to bolster it by dominating others. If something threatens their self-image, it can be interpreted as a personal humiliation, and aggression could then be described as an *inverted humiliation*. Instead of suffering the humiliation, the individual targets the person they believe to have caused it.

"Violence" is a notoriously unclear concept. It's difficult to give it an unambiguous definition.[391] Physical violence is at least limited: brutal, painful, and directed at the body. Ted Honderich defines violence as the abnormal use of force.[392] My definition of violence, however, is as follows: the intent to inflict harm or pain on a sensible being against their will. The question then becomes: Why does this occur? We can find an infinite number of reasons to attack another person. Usually self-control holds us back, but sometimes we lose this self-control. I want to underscore, however, that we *choose* to lose control—that is, losing control is an active, rather than a passive action.[393] This idea is illustrated by the fact that most people who "lose" control don't lose it completely, but are able to stop themselves before they seriously harm anyone. Normally, a person loses their self-control when they believe they have suffered some form of injustice. Violence does not only create chaos, it also creates order. In a sense, violence is typically an attempt to create order *out of* chaos: to restore a balance that has been lost.

All actions, furthermore, are situational. That is, they take place in the context of a given situation that has been evaluated beforehand by an agent. One the most informative studies on violent criminality, Lonnie Athens's *Violent Criminal Acts and Actors*, puts "situation" at the center of its analysis. The main point that Athens's study makes is that violent actions should not be understood as resulting from unconscious motives, inner conflicts, sudden passions, or the like, but instead as results of consciously constructed strategies of action formed by individuals who judge their situation to be one where violence is *called for*. In other words, violence isn't something that suddenly *breaks out*, that happens unreflectively. Instead, violence is the result of a decision, of a particular interpretation of events. Athens distinguishes between four different types of interpretation that tend to lead to violence:[394]

(1)   Physically Defensive: Where an individual believes violence is the only thing that will prevent someone from hurting the individual or others.

(2)   Frustrative: The individual believes that the victim is attempting to hinder an action the individual wants to carry out, or possibly that the victim is attempting to force them to do something they don't want to do. The individual sees violence as the only means to make what they want to happen happen. The desired action can be a robbery, a rape, or something similar.

(3)   Malefic: The individual believes that the victim is expressing a malicious intent and that the victim is trying to humiliate or mock them. Violence appears to be an acceptable response to such maliciousness.

(4)   Frustrative-malefic: These types of interpretation are a combination of (2) and (3). The individual believes the victim is attempting to prevent them from acting in a certain way or is forcing them to act in a certain way, and this fact can be attributed to the victim's maliciousness.

Athens gives a number of concrete examples for each of these judgments. In every case, the perpetrator considered himself to be "good" and the victim to be "evil." As a general rule, depictions of unmotivated violence can only be found in the *victim's* descriptions of what took place. A victim will talk about "unprovoked evil," while the perpetrator will usually refer to a specific, previous provocation. In reality, so-called "unprovoked evil" is almost always brought about by mutual aggression, and there is often reason to blame both the victim and the perpetrator for the violent result. A study of 159 murders, where each murder was unconnected to other criminal activity, showed that in most cases the victim had acted aggressively and so contributed to the tragic outcome.[395] The overall picture this study paints is supported by a number of other studies: The descriptions of both victim and perpetrator are biased in the sense that victims tend to describe the situation as worse, and the perpetrator as better, than an objective witness might describe it. It's a rare moment when those who do evil recognize their actions as evil. In other words, evil is almost never found in a perpetrator's self-image, but only in the eyes of victim and witness. Therefore, one's own conscience is not an infallible source of information on the subject.[396] There will often be an enormous difference between the motives the perpetrator thinks he has, and the motives the victim accuses the perpetrator of having. The perpetrator will often find his own motives good, because he has judged his victim to be "evil," while the victim judges the perpetrator's motives to be unconditionally "evil" themselves.

Jack Katz emphasizes that—with the exception of hit-and-runs, as well as of murders committed in connection with robbery and such—the typical murder tends to be motivated by some notion of the *good*.[397] He cites a number of cases where perpetrators, who saw themselves as representatives of the good, murdered people they thought had either challenged or violated the good by being unfaithful, trespassing on personal property, insulting someone or something, etc. At the moment of action, murderers almost always see their own behavior as justified, although afterwards they often realize that what they did was wrong. Some interpretations are better than others, and Athens's study doesn't ever discuss the fact that it's often merely a case of misinterpretation that leads to violence—that sometimes a person attributes motives to another person which they simply didn't have. Interpretations that motivate violent actions often suffer from one of the following weaknesses: (1) Agents interpret all statements and gestures to be directed at them personally, which is only the seldom the case; (2) agents only focus on the aspects of a situation that support their interpretation of the situation, and ignore aspects that contradict it; and (3) their particular interpretation leads to a systematic distortion, where even good intentions appear to be malicious. However, Athens's study does shed light on why such misinterpretations take place. The answer is linked to the perpetrator's self-image: a crucial factor in determining whether a person will resort to violence—and, if so, how far they'll go.[398] Individuals with non-violent self-images typically resort to violence only in the context of interpretation (1), while people with violent self-images tend to resort to violence on the basis of all four of Athens's interpretations. In short, people who consider themselves to be violent are far more likely to decide that a given situation requires a violent response—and people who consider themselves to be violent are generally more likely to judge others to be violent. Even though we would like to think that knowing ourselves allows us to know others, then, the truth is that self-knowledge is ultimately limited to the self.

A weakness with Athens's study is that it generally considers the different interpretations as *honest*, and therefore doesn't allow for cases where a given judgment functions as pure excuse. There are people who just like to mistreat other people. Their attacks don't have any use value: they offer no economic gain, they're not undertaken in self-defense, nor are they a reaction to some humiliation. The action itself is simply "enjoyable."[399] And yet, violence always needs an excuse, a rationale—not just to justify one's actions to other people, but also to oneself. When we accidentally bump into someone on the street, most of us quickly say we're sorry. For some people, however, this is a good excuse to punch someone. The punch is not a reaction to the offence—it was already present as desire; all it lacked was an excuse to legitimate it. The movement from desire to action requires a link, something that will legitimate the action and allow blame to be placed on the shoulders of an opponent. At this point, however, we are again approaching the concept of sadism, as discussed earlier.

ARENDT AND STUPID EVIL

Up until this point, we have limited our discussion to agents who act in keeping with or in struggle against what they perceive as good and evil. The instrumental evil agent knows what evil is, and intentionally does evil because he wishes to achieve some good for himself, whether that be economic gain or the satisfaction of some desire. I have also argued that, in reality, demonic evil is a variation of instrumental evil. In contrast, the idealistic evil actor believes that he represents the good, and that his victims are evil. However, there are still some agents that do not fit the definitions of instrumental or idealistic evil. This was the agent Hannah Arendt saw when she watched the trial of Adolf Eichmann in 1961. She writes:

> I was struck by a manifest shallowness in the doer that made it impossible to trace the uncontestable evil of his deeds to any deeper level of roots or motives. The deeds were monstrous, but the doer—at least the very effective one now on trial—was quite ordinary, commonplace, and neither demonic nor monstrous. There was no sign in him of firm ideological convictions or of specific evil motives, and the only notable characteristic one could detect in his past behavior as well as in his behavior during the trial and throughout the pre-trial police examination was something entirely negative: it was not stupidity but *thoughtlessness*.[400]

> The trouble with Eichmann was precisely that so many were like him, and that the many were neither perverted nor sadistic, that they were, and still are, terribly and terrifyingly normal. From the viewpoint of our legal institutions and of our moral standards of judgment, this normality was much more terrifying than all the atrocities put together, for it implies [. . .] that this new type of criminal [. . .] commits his crimes under circumstances that make it well-nigh impossible for him to know or to feel that he is doing wrong.[401]

The problem with understanding Eichmann was that he did not have the "demonic" traits you would expect to find in a person who was guilty of such terrible crimes. He did not seem like much of a fanatic. He did not have the classic "evil" characteristics you might have assumed he'd have—in fact, he didn't have much character at all. Arendt develops her concept of the banality of evil to try and understand this person without personality.

Arendt's concept of the banality of evil has been much discussed, but the idea itself is nonetheless unclear and for the most part undeveloped. As far as I can tell, the expression only occurs three times in the course of her controversial book on Eichmann, and one of those is in the title.[402] The idea is made somewhat clearer in the introduction to the first volume of *Life of the Mind*, entitled "Thinking,"[403] but is still rather fuzzy. Arendt does emphasize that the idea wasn't meant to make a theoretical contribution to the discourse surrounding the nature of evil,[404] but I don't think this means the idea itself might not be useful for theoretical development. As a result, it's been cited in most philosophical works concerning evil over the last forty-five years—and yet, Arendt's "theory" of evil's banality is still so undeveloped that I've turned to other sources to shed light on it. This section, therefore, is not solely limited to Arendt. And of course, with regard to the banality of evil, she certainly never meant to imply that this is the *only* form of evil that exists; it's only one form, but it's true that it happens to occupy a center stage in modernity. Arendt also emphasizes that though her point of departure was a single individual, Adolf Eichmann, her text is meant to have wider significance and to help us understand "a new type of criminal."[405] In order to form a picture that is more representative of this criminal, we can cite two other central participants in the Jewish exterminations: Rudolf Höss, who commanded Auschwitz, and Franz Stangl, who commanded Sobibor and Treblinka. Eichmann, Höss, and Stangl immediately strike me as three very different personalities, but they functioned in essentially the same way during the Jewish exterminations, and gave many of the same excuses afterward. In addition, as we progress, we'll take a closer look at other examples: foot soldiers who took part in the slaughter in Eastern Europe and American soldiers during Vietnam, among others.

The Evil and the Stupid

Arendt's idea of the banality of evil is a completely secularized conception of the concept. It bears no trace of any transcendent qualities. Her idea is commonly considered to be an innovation in theories of evil, but it's not entirely without precedent. To Socrates and Plato, those who do evil can only be blamed for lacking insight into the good, and to Aristotle, an evil agent is simply someone who has misunderstood what the good is. There are a host of later thinkers with similar viewpoints. In more than one place, François de La Rochefoucauld draws a connection between evil and stupidity,[406] and Pascal describes it as especially evil to be "full of [shortcomings] and unwilling to recognize them, since this entails the further evil of deliberate self-delusion."[407] Baudelaire also ties together evil and stupidity: "There can never be any excuse for being wicked, but there is some merit in knowing that one is being wicked; and the most irreparable of vices consists in doing evil through stupidity."[408] Camus writes: "The evil that is in the world always comes of ignorance, and good intentions may do as much harm as malevolence, if they lack understanding."[409]

The notion of the banality of evil doesn't so much follow the path of thinking wrongly or lacking knowledge as not *thinking* at all. This idea, for example, is more pronounced in Giacomo Leopardi:

He said that negligence and thoughtlessness are the cause
of an infinite number of cruel and evil actions [. . .] He
was of the opinion that in men thoughtlessness is much
more common than cruelty, inhumanity, and the like and
that a substantial part of the behavior and of the actions
of man which are attributed to some innate wickedness
are actually due to thoughtlessness.[410]

In my opinion, however, this viewpoint is best described in Dietrich
Bonhoeffer's letters and memoirs from prison, where he sat until
he was executed just before Germany's surrender for participating in an assassination attempt on Hitler. In his memoirs, there is
a passage entitled "Of Folly," which I have never seen cited in any
of the literature I've read on evil, and which deserves to be cited
(almost) in its entirety:

Folly is a more dangerous enemy to the good than evil.
One can protest against evil; it can be unmasked and,
if need be, prevented by force. Evil always carries the
seeds of its own destruction, as it makes people, at the
least, uncomfortable. Against folly we have no defense.
Neither protests nor force can touch it; reasoning is no
use; facts that contradict personal prejudices can simply
be disbelieved—indeed, the fool can counter by criticizing them, and if they are undeniable, they can just be
pushed aside as trivial exceptions. So the fool, as distinct
from the scoundrel, is completely self-satisfied; in fact,
he can easily become dangerous, as it does not take much
to make him aggressive. A fool must therefore be treated
more cautiously than a scoundrel; we shall never again

try to convince a fool by reason, for it is both useless and dangerous.

If we are to deal adequately with folly, we must try to understand its nature. This much is certain, that it is a moral rather than an intellectual defect. There are people who are mentally agile but foolish, and people who are mentally slow but very far from foolish—a discovery that we make to our surprise as a result of particular situations. We thus get the impression that folly is likely to be, not a congenital defect, but one that is acquired in certain circumstances where people *make* fools of themselves or allow others to make fools of them. We notice further that this defect is less common in the unsociable and solitary than in individuals or groups that are inclined or condemned to sociability. It seems, then, that folly is a sociological rather than a psychological problem, and that it is a special form of the operation of historical circumstances on people, a psychological by-product of definite external factors. If we look more closely, we see that any violent display of power, whether political or religious, produces an outburst of folly in a large part of mankind; indeed, this actually seems to be a psychological and sociological law: the power of some needs the folly of the others. It is not that certain human capacities, intellectual capacities for instance, become stunted or destroyed, but rather that the upsurge of power makes such an overwhelming impression that men are deprived of their independent judgment, and—more or less unconsciously—give up trying to assess the new state of affairs for themselves. The fact that the fool is often stubborn must not mislead us into thinking that he is independent. One feels in fact, when talking to him, that one is dealing, not with the man himself, but with slogans, catchwords, and the like, which have taken hold of him. He is under a spell, he is blinded, his very nature is being misused and exploited. Having thus become a passive instrument, the fool will be capable of any evil and at the same time incapable of seeing that it is evil. Here lies the danger of a diabolical exploitation that can do irreparable damage to human beings.[411]

In this passage on folly, Bonhoeffer describes what Arendt twenty years later would term "the banality of evil." Eichmann was "foolish"—we find the same annihilation of personal judgment and thinking in Arendt's description of Eichmann, the same impersonal embrace of promises and programs, etc. Of course, Bonhoeffer distinguishes between evil and foolishness, but his distinction is the result of a traditional, "demonic" understanding of evil, and he emphasizes that the foolish person commits evil actions. Furthermore, Bonhoeffer seems to understand the evil agent as a type of *victim* of external circumstances, something that's not entirely in keeping with Arendt's idea. Arendt writes about "thoughtlessness," and distinguishes that from "stupidity,"[412] while Bonhoeffer's "foolishness" is synonymous with Arendt's thoughtlessness. I should point out, I use "stupidity" and "thoughtlessness" interchangeably in this book, but I want to underscore that by "stupidity" I do not mean a lack of intelligence, but rather a lack of *judgment*.

Radical and Banal Evil

Arendt's notion of banal evil is a continuation of her concept of radical evil as described in *The Origins of Totalitarianism*. Her concept of radical evil, however, has little in common with Kant's. For Kant, radical evil is something that's exclusively human, while for Arendt it means the annihilation of all humanity, of all individuality, and this annihilation of individuality occurs in both the victim and the perpetrator. For Arendt, totalitarian society is characterized by the fact that all *individuals* have become superfluous and every person can occupy the roll of victim or aggressor respectively.[413] In a totalitarian society, individual uniqueness is irrelevant and everyone is expendable. Totalitarianism ultimately enacts a "transformation of human nature itself."[414]

The process by which an individual becomes superfluous occurs in three stages. First, an individual is eliminated as a juristic person, that is, an individual or a group is singled out and stripped of their civil rights.[415] Next, a person is eliminated as a moral person, because conscience is shown to be in doubt and human solidarity dissolved.[416] Finally, all individuality is completely eradicated.[417] This dehumanization is what Arendt calls radical evil, where "human nature as such is at stake."[418] A large part of what distinguishes Arendtian radical evil from traditional theories is that this radical evil cannot be explained by human motives such as greed, self-interest, ambition, etc.[419]

Instead, victims are chosen according to an almost consistent *arbitrariness*.[420] This was especially evident during the Soviet terror in the 1930s. The Soviet purges had a different character than the Nazi purges, and were driven by a logic of paranoia that assumed the Bolsheviks were under constant threat from subversive forces.[421] Lenin believed that it would not be necessary to use force against masses who were, after all, under the dictatorship of the proletariat, but exclusively against the enemies of the country and the revolution: Ultimately, the regime was there to *serve* the masses. The problem was, the masses were not what Lenin and later Stalin wanted them to be, and therefore violence and excessive force were directed against the very workers and peasants the new regime was supposed to serve. Immediately after the Russian Revolution, a class of people was singled out and stripped of their rights—sometimes even stripped of the right to eat. By 1918, five million people had already fallen into this category—a curious turn of events, to put it mildly, given that the Revolution was founded on a radical egalitarian ideology. After 1932, all Soviet citizens were required to have ID cards on them at all times, and the ID cards categorized people not only by age and gender, but also by social class and ethnicity. Purges under Stalin were more ethnically or racially motivated than is generally understood: This was especially true where groups from the Caucasus or Crimea were concerned, but also included Asians, Jews, etc. Still, ethnicity was only one criterion among many—and as time went on, more and more groups seemed to fit the regime's qualifications.

The terror reached its peak between 1937 and 1938, when it became clear even to Stalin that the violence had spun out of control. The initial purpose of the violence was to give the illusion of political control. The purges could be described as completely irrational, as executioners were given arbitrarily chosen liquidation quotas that changed from week to week, and they could fill these with more or less arbitrarily chosen groups of people. These groups could range anywhere from people of certain nationalities to harmless hobbyists, like students of Esperanto or stamp collectors.[422] Terms like "Trotskyist," which were used to describe particularly dangerous enemies of the Party, state, and Revolution, were constantly changing content as the political situation evolved and alliances shifted, and being a real "Trotskyist" came to mean less and less.[423] However, the fact that the enemy couldn't be described with any accuracy didn't appear to cause too many members of the Central Committee to question whether or not the enemy actually existed—instead, the criteria for selecting "enemies" simply became less and less precise, and therefore applicable to more and more people—not only an individual "enemy," but also his family and friends.

In a totalitarian society, the principles a person should live by are no longer dictated by the individual's reason or conscience, but by the state. Distinguishing between good and evil is no longer a matter for individual conscience, but an affair of state. However, Arendt goes on to say that thoughtlessness is not only found in totalitarian societies, but also characterizes American military advisors, for example, during the Vietnam War.[424] Her reflections, therefore, are meant to have a broader significance than simply the discussion of totalitarian societies, and she emphasizes that those aspects of modernity that made totalitarianism possible do not simply disappear when the totalitarian government in question is overthrown.[425] The depersonalizing aspects of modernity, which can result in a dissolution of politics and morals, also result in apathy; when that happens, personal responsibility and critical thought become threatened, and must somehow be reestablished.

It's difficult to pinpoint the exact relationship between radical and banal evil, and to my knowledge Arendt does not give us a systematic discussion of this idea anywhere in her work. "Banal," in this context, doesn't mean "normal" or "widespread," even though banal evil can certainly be widespread in certain situations. To call a variety of evil banal is to call it superficial. However, when Arendt wrote about banal evil, I do not believe she was trying to describe something that differed in any significant way from what she had earlier described as radical evil. Indeed, the concept of radicalism may be misleading in terms of the phenomena she had originally set out to characterize. "Radical," as I've mentioned, is taken from the Latin word *radix*, which means "root." To say that evil has roots is to say that it has depth—but isn't Arendt trying to character- ize something that *lacks* depth? This is why she places so much emphasis on the fact that Eichmann repeatedly speaks in clichés. Clichés are superficial, and people who rely on them do not strike us as being especially "deep." Thus, Arendt writes that the goal of totalitarian indoctrination is not to create absolute conviction, but instead to destroy the ability to form convictions at all[426]—that is, to destroy the ability to think with depth. In this context, we can also say that people indoctrinated in this way lose the ability to *act*, at least as Arendt understands the concept of action. (She defines the ability to act as the ability to "start again."[427] Seen in this way, her concept of action is very similar to Kant's idea of freedom as spontaneity.) As such, banal evil can certainly be described as an extension of radical evil; it's just that the idea of radical evil seems more relevant to *systems* and banal evil to individual agents. We could perhaps say that Arendt's "radical evil" is a political concept concerning the absence of the *political*, whereas "banal evil" is a moral concept concerning the absence of the *moral*. Banality is not meant to describe an action, but rather a motivation. The problem is, when we talk about a crime, we typically presuppose the exis- tence of an *evil will*, of a definite intent. However, it was difficult to prove that Eichmann had an evil will. The same was true in the cases of Höss and Stangl, commanders of Auschwitz and Treblinka respectively.

Eichmann, Höss, and Stangl

In discussing Eichmann, I will use Arendt's essays documenting the case against him—collected in *Eichmann in Jerusalem*—as a point of departure, and will also refer to the interrogation records kept by the Israeli police force.[428] I will not take up the more juridical aspects of Arendt's book, such as the question of retroactive laws,[429] but am more concerned with Eichmann as an *individual*.[430]

Psychiatrists pronounced Eichmann completely normal.[431] He claimed that, speaking for himself, he was incapable of murder, and that if he'd been forced to command a concentration camp in person, he would've committed suicide.[432] Eichmann complained that the German soldiers were utterly destroyed by what they were forced to do to the Jews—though never that the Jews were made to suffer in the first place.[433] Personally, he said, his nerves "weren't strong enough" to witness what was done to the Jews, and he insists that it was cruel of the officers at Auschwitz to describe to him so directly and so brutally—that is, to a simple, normal office worker—what they were doing in the camps.[434] He repeatedly emphasizes that he wasn't involved in the murders, just in the transport.[435] It's unclear how he sees the question of responsibility. At one point, he admits that he was guilty from a purely *juridical* perspective, but doesn't elaborate on the question of moral responsibility.[436] At another point, he denies bearing any responsibility at all, since he was only following orders.[437] However, at yet another point, he claims that he *was* responsible, precisely *because* he followed orders.[438] It's understandable that for Eichmann the question of responsibility was not a simple one. He was subjected to two contradictory duties: the duty to follow orders and the duty to refuse them. Eichmann chose to follow the false duty, and by obeying his orders, he fulfilled his duty as a bureaucrat, in keeping with Max Weber's description: "[I]t is his honor to carry it [the order] out conscientiously just as if it was in accordance with his own conviction."[439] Eichmann says that his actions didn't involve "a personal decision," but that he was only following orders from higher up.[440] It seems never to have occurred to him to try and change positions. Instead, he truly believed the only possible alternative was to carry out his orders. As Weber observes: "The individual bureaucrat cannot squirm out of the apparatus in which he is harnessed."[441] The fact that bureaucrats fulfill their duties without reference to personal *interests* creates the illusion that personal *morality* is not a factor in their jobs.[442] Not letting personal interests interfere with your job means that an individual shouldn't use their position to further their own interests; this requirement does not, however, negate the personal responsibility every agent has for *all* of what they do, no matter their position. As a private individual, a human being may indeed have a moral perspective that does not coincide with their moral perspective as a civil servant. However, in no case is personal responsibility *nullified*.

Eichmann takes refuge in Kant's moral philosophy in order to explain why he did what he did, and insists that he'd adopted Kant's categorical imperative as his moral norm.[443] Even if we take him at his word, Eichmann does not, however, appear to be a good representative of Kant's moral philosophy. As we know, Kant's ethics are based on a *principle of autonomy*. Nonetheless, in Eichmann's interpretation, Kant's ethics are thoroughly *heteronomous*. To his mind, moral laws don't originate in an individual agent's rational mind, but in the orders handed down by Hitler.[444] A strictly heteronomous ethics—consisting of moral laws that originate *outside* the individual agent, whether they come from another person, an institution, or God—are therefore utterly un-Kantian. Of course,

Kant argues in his philosophy of law that a person has an absolute duty to follow the laws of his land, but this formulation still requires that such laws be grounded in moral principles—something that the laws of the Third Reich certainly were not. Kant explicitly writes, for instance, that an individual should not follow a command that's obviously evil.[445] And Eichmann knew that the Jewish exterminations were evil, because he admits to experiencing an inner conflict when he was told about the "solution to the Jewish problem." However, he soon stopped worrying himself, because he managed to "get out of doing it"—that is, it wasn't *his* hands that would have to shove the Jews into the gas chambers.[446]

In Eichmann's final statement to the court, he insists that he isn't a monster, but, in fact, a victim.[447] His reasoning on this point is still a little unclear. He points to a "fallacy," and apparently we are meant to conclude that he is being blamed for actions he had no direct part in: that is, for concrete murders. This follows the approach he adopted during his police interrogation and then his cross examination in front of the court: admitting he'd had a central role in the transportation of the Jews, but denied murdering anyone with his own hands. During the trial, he appeared most disturbed when a witness (whom the court deemed untrustworthy) swore that they'd seen Eichmann beat a Jew to death for some minor provocation.[448] Eichmann sincerely believed that he'd been unjustly accused of participating in actions that had taken place at a great remove from himself, and which he'd had no direct part in.

When Eichmann described himself as an idealist, he was largely correct.[449] He was idealistic *and* thoughtless. His unconditional obedience of Hitler's orders was idealistic, but his absence of reflection concerning the fact that it's wrong to exterminate Jews was thoughtless. Idealism and stupidity are two sides of the same coin. "I followed my orders without thinking."[450] Because so many prominent people supported the "solution to the Jewish problem," Eichmann assumed that the solution had to be right—therefore, he ceased to have any opinion of his own on the subject, and went on to state: "I felt free of all guilt."[451]

Arendt argues that Eichmann "*never realized what he was doing.*"[452] This is a rather famous assertion—that we know not what we do.[453] It tends, however, to make Arendt's position problematic. On the one hand, she argues that Eichmann didn't know what he was doing; on the other, she supported the decision when he was condemned to death. In contrast, I believe that Eichmann was to a great extent aware of what he was doing, but allowed other considerations—his own career and his faith in the Leader—to get in the way. My objection to Arendt is not that what she writes about Eichmann is wrong—on the contrary, I believe that she uncovers something essential—but that it's too one-dimensional. Of course, Arendt does not go as far as, for example, Zygmunt Bauman in reducing Eichmann to a completely depersonalized bureaucrat. Arendt retains her focus on Eichmann as an individual, however little individuality he may have shown, while Bauman essentially considers him as little more than a passive cog in the wheel.[454] Lack of individuality became a central focus for Arendt, while Bauman hardly raises the question. It's an essential component of Arendt's philosophy that a person reveals who they are, reveals their individuality, through their actions and words. It's precisely this form of individuality that Eichmann *never* demonstrates. In the narrow sense of the word, he doesn't *act*, but simply follows orders. He doesn't *talk*, but simply opens his mouth and lets forth a stream of clichés. He even admits that the only language he knows is the language of the civil servant.[455] The language of the civil servant is a depersonalized language, full of clichés and catchphrases that save individuals from the inconvenient task of having to think for themselves. Nothing requires that the individual resort to reflection; instead, everything can be satisfied with superficial, standard formulae. All particulars—including individual human beings and their individual suffering—disappears in view of such formulae.

And yet, when Arendt argues that Eichmann had no motivation,[456] she overlooks something essential—namely that Eichmann, who had career ambitions, was a Hitlerist to the core. The last thing he did before his execution was to pay homage to Germany, Argentina, and Austria.[457] Arendt mentions this as an example of Eichmann's typical use of catchphrases and clichés, but I believe it confirms something crucial about Eichmann: his self-described idealism. Eichmann wasn't simply an average bureaucrat, but also an average fanatic. In this light, his evil no longer appears quite as banal as Arendt would have us believe; in addition to "stupid" evil, we now have idealistic evil in the equation as well. In either case, his is certainly a form of evil that has something unselfish about it—even if Eichmann was also undeniably driven by selfish motives. As such, the picture Arendt paints of Eichmann as "banal" seems, in my opinion, far too narrow. Even if there was limited anti-Semitism in his personal outlook, he had a strong ideological bent, namely his belief in Führer and Fatherland.

A similar idealism was also present in Rudolf Höss, who was commander at Auschwitz, the largest of the concentration camps. He describes himself as a "fanatic National Socialist" and was a self-proclaimed anti-Semite.[458] When he asserted a year after the war that the mass exterminations were wrong, this wasn't because they were evil or immoral, but because Germany had thereby made itself a target for the world's indignation—which, in reality, had brought the Jews closer to realizing their goal of world domination![459]

When reading the autobiography Höss wrote in prison shortly after the war—a helpless, though fascinating piece of prose—one is struck by the many similarities to Eichmann. Höss was obviously less intelligent than Eichmann, but in terms of stupidity—understood in the context of thoughtlessness—they seem to be peers. Writing his book, Höss didn't seem to have any concept of what he had done. Even though a large number of statements begin with phrases such as "Now I understand. . . ," it's absolutely clear to the reader that such isn't actually the case. As such, strangely enough, he manages to present more of a puzzle than Eichmann. As Primo Levi writes in his introduction to Höss's book, the "commandant" wasn't a monster, but nonetheless his autobiography is "full of malice."[460] Höss declares that he was different from the SS soldiers who took pleasure in torturing the prisoners.[461] He was right about this much, but his declaration shows that he did not understand his own role: He describes these soldiers as evil,[462] but in doing so overlooks his own culpability. Here, as is usually the case, "evil" is an idea that applied to *others*, not to himself. He criticizes these soldiers for failing to regard their prisoners as people,[463] but this is something he too failed to do—otherwise, he wouldn't have been capable of carrying out his job. He claims that he had "too much sympathy" for the prisoners to do his work, that he had a "weakness,"[464] but his "sympathy" and "weakness" never did the prisoners any good. Indeed, these reported emotions hardly seem trustworthy. If Höss recognized his prisoners' humanity at the same time as holding ultimate responsibility for and maintaining oversight of the activities in Auschwitz, he would indeed have been a monster. But I think it's likely that this wasn't the case.

Even as Eichmann claimed he had lived his life according to Kant's categorical imperative, Höss puts great weight on the fact that he was a moral person and tried his best to uphold certain moral distinctions—like the fact that it was perfectly fine to kill Jews, but not for a soldier to steal from them. This concept of morality was not Höss's invention, but came from Himmler, who argued that exterminating the Jews was a moral imperative, but not for the sake of personal profit. Höss also frowned on violent acts such as rape and "unnecessary" brutality, which might occasionally be committed in the process of following Himmler's overriding moral imperative. He underscored the fact that he never *mistreated* the prisoners.[465] What he means by this, apparently, is that he never beat the prisoners with his owns hands, that he never shot them with his own gun, that he never emptied canisters of Zyklon B into the gas chambers. Nonetheless, he commanded the largest concentration camp in history and was absolutely cognizant of the function of this camp. Everything that happened in the camp required his final approval. Höss was not at all a passive figure—in fact, he showed great initiative in commanding his post. He had ample opportunity to make the conditions less harsh for the prisoners, but instead his priority was to create the most "effective" camp possible. He even criticized the prisoners for their immoral behavior toward each other, without taking into consideration the fact that he himself was responsible for forcing them to live in conditions where it was nearly impossible to maintain any sort of moral decency.[466] Naturally, among the prisoners as well as among the guards, there were better people and worse; neither the prisoners nor the guards came from completely homogeneous groups composed of individuals with identical moral qualities. Even if we have a number of examples of prisoners who were able to maintain a sense of moral decency throughout their incarceration in the Nazi concentration camps,[467] it's a fact that morality wasn't a priority there—such extreme conditions typically suspend all moral consideration. It's likewise a fact that some prisoners managed to exceed the guards in their brutal treatment of their fellow prisoners. It's important to remember that just because someone's a victim, they're not necessarily a good person—but it's also indisputable that Höss had no right to judge his prisoners for their behavior. In his detailed description of the six years he sat in prison for politically motivated murder, Höss identifies himself strongly with his own fellow prisoners and criticizes the men guarding him for their excessive brutality. However, he never draws the obvious comparison between his situation and Auschwitz, because he is still unable to see the camp from a prisoner's perspective.

Large portions of his autobiography are devoted to complaints dating back to his time at the camp: limited resources, a lack of qualified labor, disorganized and confusing orders from his superiors—in short, the same complaints you would expect from any bureaucrat. The moral questions posed by the whole operation are completely absent from his remarks. In fact, Höss argues that he was "obsessed" by the task of making Auschwitz as efficient as possible.[468] He considered it very important to be the sort of man who carried out his duties to the letter.[469] This is something else he has in common with Eichmann, but in contrast to Eichmann, Höss puts himself on a par with his underlings by saying that he would not have asked them to do anything he himself was not willing to do.[470] He believed that death by gas was far better for morale than death by gun, since the latter would produce too strong a reaction among the SS soldiers, especially where the execution of women and children was concerned.[471] As with Eichmann, Höss is concerned essentially with his fellow German soldiers, never giving their suffering prisoners a single thought. He asserts, in short, that he only did what he expected his men to do in turn: namely, follow the Leader's orders. It was imperative that he set a good example for his underlings and not show any weakness.[472] In what is perhaps his autobiography's most hair-raising passage, Höss writes:

> When he [Himmler] gave me the order personally in the summer of 1941 to prepare a place for mass killings and then carry it out, I could never have imagined the scale, or what the consequences would be. Of course, this order was something extraordinary, something monstrous. However, the reasoning behind the order of this mass annihilation seemed correct to me. At the time I wasted no thoughts about it. I had received an order; I had to carry it out. I could not allow myself to form an opinion as to whether this mass extermination of the Jews was necessary or not. At the time it was beyond my frame of mind.[473]

This is banal evil at its most extreme: pure thoughtlessness, the unwillingness to even bother with thought. He admits that the order was "monstrous," but nonetheless carried it out, because orders must be followed.

When we come to Franz Stangl, commander of Sobibor and Treblinka, we meet another type of personality—or, rather, we meet a person who actually had a personality. While Höss seems like an emotionally stunted military climber without a single original thought in his brain, and Eichmann like the bureaucrat from hell, Stangl appears relatively well-spoken and sometimes even charming. In 1970, after his trial was over, Gitta Sereny conducted a number of interviews with Stangl in prison. The following comments are based on Sereny's book *Into that Darkness*. Stangl, like Höss and Eichmann, delivers the standard introductory excuses, like the fact that he's never personally harmed another human being, but at certain points in the interviews he seems to fall into what can only be called thoughtfulness . . . before once again giving the impression that he is not aware what he did. It's as if he's always on the verge of questioning his actions, but constantly shies away from this insight. He recognizes his own guilt,[474] but doesn't seem to grasp the extent of what he admits to being guilty of. An admission of guilt is only valid if a person understands what he's guilty *of*; and yet, the murders in Treblinka were so extensive—with hundreds of thousands, perhaps over a million dead—it's hardly possible for any one man to grasp the full scale of the catastrophe. The problem with Stangl's admission of guilt, therefore, is that it's so limited. Even though he doesn't try to hide what actually happened, it's clear he has no idea how far his own responsibility actually reaches. The paradoxical thing is that he admits his guilt *and* asserts that his conscience is clean.[475]

Stangl recalls that when he first arrived at Treblinka, the scene was straight out of Dante's *Inferno*.[476] But he also *chose* to be commander there, a fact that he doesn't deny is roughly the same as choosing to play the role of the devil himself. However, here is another paradox: on the one hand Stangl freely—if a little grudgingly—chose the role of the devil, but on the other hand he has no overtly "devilish" qualities. He doesn't appear to take pleasure in other people's suffering, although it can't be denied that he threw himself into his work with unfeigned zeal. His zeal, however, wasn't driven by a hatred of the Jews, but simply by a strong work ethic.[477] And this work ethic somehow took priority over all other moral considerations.

Treblinka was not a concentration camp, but an extermination camp, and it was the largest of these. The difference between an extermination camp and a concentration camp is often not well understood: Concentration camps were extreme work camps that were far more inhuman than the countless other pure work camps the Nazis constructed for their enemies. In the beginning, concentration camps were institutions for slave labor, but the conditions systematically worsened the longer they existed. At the same time, it should be stressed that even though the prisoners were gassed, shot, starved, exhausted, used in medical experiments, etc., it was *possible* to survive a stint in a concentration camp. Even in Auschwitz, which also had an extermination center (Birkenau), around a fifth of the Jews survived (of the 950,000 Jews sent to Auschwitz, just under 800,000 were murdered), and an even larger portion of non-Jews. By comparison, only eight-seven people—none of them children—survived the five extermination camps in Poland, which ended up claiming around two million human lives.[478] And Franz Stangl commanded the largest of these.

The victims were systematically dehumanized. They were carted around like cattle in cramped train cars without toilets, food, or water, before they arrived in Treblinka. After their arrival, they were separated into groups of men, women, and children, made to strip and subjected to cavity searches—the soldiers were looking for hidden valuables—then were shaved and finally shoved into the gas chambers. According to Stangl, the goal of this humiliating process was to dehumanize the prisoners enough that the soldiers would be capable of carrying out the executions.[479] This dehumanization process had an effect on him as well: the Jews didn't seem like individuals to him, but "cargo" and "a mass of rotting flesh."[480] He avoided talking with those who were sentenced to death,[481] presumably so they wouldn't come to seem again like individuals with some degree of inviolability.

How could Stangl do what he did? He repeatedly says that he was forced to carry out his orders, that it was a matter of self-preservation.[482] This is false—not a single German soldier was executed for being unwilling to take part in the mass exterminations. Stangl says that he should have committed suicide rather than taking part,[483] but there's no reason we can't simply say that he should have *refused* to take part. He asserts that he knew that the treatment of the Jews was a "crime" from the moment the plans for the mass exterminations were first revealed to him,[484] but instead of refusing to take part or actively opposing this crime, he contented himself with requesting a transfer—a request that was subsequently denied. He chose, therefore, to take part in the crime. He tries to explain his actions away a number of times, for instance when he insists that as a young man in the police academy he'd learned that there were four requirements to be met before something was considered a crime: a subject, an object, an action, and an intention. He asserts that he isn't guilty of any crime, because the fourth requirement was never met—presumably because he himself didn't bear any real grudge against the Jews.[485] But it's clear that he knows better, that he is aware of his guilt and complicity. He attempted, at the time, to "limit my own actions to what I—in my own conscience—could answer for."[486] That is, he abstracted thought from deed to such a degree that each of his actions appeared to be justified—essentially for the purpose of absolving himself of seeing the whole picture.[487]

As previously mentioned, Stangl was not an anti-Semite, but he had a deep-seated contempt for his prisoners. This contempt was not due to their "race," but rather to their weakness:

> It had nothing to do with hate. They were so weak; they allowed everything to happen—to be done to them. They were people with whom there was no common ground, no possibility of communication—that is how contempt is born. I could never understand how they could just give in as they did. Quite recently I read a book about lemmings, who every five or six years just wander into the sea and die; that made me think of Treblinka.[488]

Stangl said this in 1971, twenty-seven years after Treblinka was destroyed. It's unbelievable that a person can understand so little after so long a time. As for the assertion that it wasn't possible for him to communicate with his prisoners, he clearly could have proven himself wrong simply by talking to them. And yet, as I've already mentioned, it was insights such as these that Stangl deliberately avoided. Harald Ofstad has suggested that a "contempt for weakness" is central to understanding Nazism,[489] and Stangl provides a clear example of this idea. From Hitler's perspective, the Jews deserved no mercy: "No pity must be shown to beings whom destiny has doomed to disappear."[490] The reasoning is as follows: Fate has dictated that the Jews will perish by making them weak, and *because* they are weak it's perfectly legitimate to set about exterminating them. The weak have no right to life—weakness, and therefore the weak, must be destroyed.

It's obvious that Stangl became more corrupt the longer he remained in service, less able to recognize the fact that he was a central actor in a crime without parallel. After a while, he simply got used to it—as he says.[491] Stangl hardly noticed this personality change—the change from being too weak to refuse to participate to becoming someone who more or less had no conscience. Habituation is a central factor here.[492] Every person has a multitude of habits they're not aware of, simply because they're not conscious of them. Instead, they form a type of "backdrop" for what we *are* conscious of; they determine what we normally look for in a given situation. Viewed in this way, we can say that habits create possibilities for perception, but they also limit our capacity for understanding, because they lead us to dismiss many phenomena as irrelevant. Habits, therefore, become a form of blindness, and in Stangl's case, they obviously led to a progressive loss of moral vision.

One of the most striking aspects of the "confessions" of Eichmann, Höss, and Stangl is that they reveal all three as having been incredibly self-centered. They seem never to have given their victims a thought. Their dedication to their work demonstrated a clear belief in the value of their labors—but we must then ask: What value could anyone possibly find in such monstrosities? For Hitler, the Nazi obligation to purify the races was "the holiest obligation," and this statement was meant to legitimate the exterminations; however, very few of those responsible for the day-to-day work of genocide ever used this idea to explain their actions.[493] In Höss's case (but not in that of Eichmann and Stangl), anti-Semitism is an important motive, but hardly the most important one. All three men certainly had career ambitions—though Stangl less so than the other two—but there remains an enormous disparity between their particular ambitions and the actual work each set about with such efficiency. All three had the utmost faith in Hitler, although Stangl had his reservations, and can therefore be considered idealists.

It's clear as well that Eichmann and Höss didn't just *follow* orders, but actively *supported* the program. What all three have in common, however, is that they seem to lack any basic consciousness of their own personal responsibility—even if Stangl does show glimmerings of this insight. Himmler argues that individual SS soldiers did *not* have any responsibility for their actions, and that the responsibility rested solely on the shoulders of himself and Hitler, but individual responsibility cannot simply be delegated away.

Nonetheless, during the pledge of allegiance, all German soldiers were required to swear allegiance to Hitler *personally*, not to the German constitution, which in any case was synonymous with whatever Hitler decreed. The Führer principle dictates that an individual does not have the right to question the legitimacy of a given order; an order was legitimated by the fact that it came from Hitler. In essence, an order could not possibly come into conflict with some higher norm, because there was no higher norm than the Leader's will. In *Mein Kampf*, we find that not only must the individual set aside his own personal *interests* for the sake of the whole, but also his "personal opinions."[494] To think for yourself is a form of betrayal.[495] From a *juridical* perspective, following orders was the only lawful action. But as Emerson points out: "Good people must not obey the laws too well."[496] To refuse to follow orders is to help undermine them. An order's authority is dependent upon the order being followed, and it's arguable that anyone who refuses to follow orders also refuses to recognize them as legitimate. Therefore, a refusal to follow orders is a potentially powerful weapon. If an order has to be repeated, it's already lost some of its force. Eichmann, Höss, and Stangl seemed to believe that following orders was the only *morally* lawful action. This is especially clear in Eichmann's remarks. However, we can assume that all three also had a moral conscience that operated independent of this conviction. Their immediate reactions when told about the plans for the mass exterminations demonstrate this fact.[497] But this particular moral insight, along with their moral consciences, was discarded for the sake of other considerations.

All three men maintained a normal moral conscience in other aspects of their lives. Robert J. Lifton points to the phenomenon of "doubling," where a person has two distinct selves—a self in the camp and a self outside of the camp.[498] This idea appears plausible, given that both Stangl and Höss maintained relatively normal family lives outside their camps. However, is it not just as plausible to say that every person is a single self, but this self systematically interprets all actions differently inside and outside the camps?

Normal People and Extreme Evil

The most gruesome actions can be carried out by people whose sole focus is on solving a practical problem—people who don't have any sadistic motives.[499] Eichmann, Höss, and Stangl are clear examples of this idea. Again, the stupidity I mention above does not indicate a lack of intelligence. For example, half of the fourteen participants in the Wansee Conference were lawyers, and six of the fifteen *Einsatsgruppenführer*—that is, the leaders of the death squads in the east—had doctoral degrees.[500] And what about the doctors who conducted experiments on the prisoners?[501] It's as if these actions took place in a moral vacuum where ideas of good and evil had no application.

This moral vacuum was intentionally created through a dehumanizing process. Through shaving prisoners, starving them, etc., individuality was minimized and people were made into an undifferentiated mass.[502] An anonymous diary found in Auschwitz reads: "We're not human beings anymore, nor have we become animals; we are just some strange psycho-physical product made in Germany."[503] In the camps, for example, a good deal of trouble was taken to prevent the prisoners from committing suicide. This may seem strange, since their deaths was the obvious goal, but suicide is problematic because it's an action that presupposes individual subjectivity. Suicide reinforces the idea that the victim has human worth, and therefore threatens the intended picture of the prisoners as non-humans. The Nazis, however, had declared that the Jews were not people, an idea that would make it easier for soldiers to exterminate them en masse. It was okay, therefore, to force Jews to wallow in their own filth—in Bergen-Belsen, thirty thousand women shared one latrine—in order to prove that Jews themselves were filth, but there was always the danger that they might start to seem human again. As such, this humanity had to be extinguished in every way possible. In fact, Berel Lang argues that the dehumanization processes that the Jews endured before they were murdered essentially demonstrates that they *were* recognized as fellow human beings by the Nazis.[504] As a result, for Lang, the Nazis should be considered as *consciously* evil, because their crimes were largely committed with intent. He goes even further, and asserts that they did what they did *because* they were evil.[505] As a result, he regards Nazis as representative of demonic evil in its most extreme form— but, as we've seen, this indictment doesn't fit the majority of the perpetrators.

In *Hitler's Willing Executioners*, Daniel Goldhagen criticizes Arendt for representing the Nazis in general as emotionally neutral in relation to Jews.[506] However, Arendt does not mean to speak for *every* participant in the mass exterminations, only for some of them, and she believes that different agents who took part in the exterminations represent different forms of evil. Goldhagen, on the other hand, considers all the agents to be homogeneous. Indeed, for Goldhagen, the central factor is that they were *German*. As Norman G. Finkelstein and Bettina Birn point out, however, there is a definite tension in Goldhagen's remarks between the emphasis on German anti-Semitism on the one hand and individual responsibility on the other.[507] Yet the relationship between these two elements is never clarified by Goldhagen. Goldhagen's insufficient and biased description of German anti-Semitism can ultimately be said to be entirely refuted by Finkelstein and Birn. The documentation indicates that most Germans did *not* share the Nazis' anti-Semitism, not even during the war years. And even though anti-Semitism grew stronger after the Nazis took power, it was not especially strong in the majority of the German people, and for example *Kristallnacht* wasn't necessarily considered a positive development by the ordinary German. See, for example, the following excerpt from an official Nazi report on *Kristallnacht*:

> One knows that anti-Semitism in Germany today is essentially confined to the party and its organizations, and that there is a certain group in the population who have not the slightest understanding for anti-Semitism and in whom every possibility of empathy is lacking.
>
> In the days after *Kristallnacht* these people ran immediately to Jewish businesses . . . This is to a great extent because we are, to be sure, an anti-Semitic people, an anti-Semitic state, but nevertheless in all manifestations of life in the state and the people anti-Semitism is as good as unexpressed . . . There are still groups of *Spiessern* among the German people who talk about the poor Jews and who

have no understanding for the anti-Semitic attitudes of the German people and who interceded for Jews at every opportunity. It should not be that only the leadership and party are anti-Semitic.[508]

Physical violence against Jews was not applauded by average Germans, but the growing limitations on the Jews' civil rights produced few protests, and there was relatively broad support among the populace when the Jews were excluded from certain positions, when their possessions were confiscated, and so on.[509] In the German populace as a whole, it was more a case of apathy and moral indifference than an active hatred for the Jews. In his book, however, Goldhagen resorts to broad generalizations, such as: "Every German was inquisitor, judge, and executioner."[510] In this way, Goldhagen demonizes the German people, and goes on to write about a unique "German culture of cruelty,"[511] a "general [German] propensity to violence,"[512] that Germans "were generally brutal and murderous,"[513] etc. At the same time, Goldhagen has no evidence to support his claims that Germany's culture was a uniquely cruel one that promoted the mass exterminations. A further difficulty Goldhagen falls into is that the emphasis on a unique German culture that's capable of shaping the opinion of every agent stands in a direct contrast to his goal of making individual responsibility a determinant factor in Holocaust studies. If an agent is simply a product of his culture, there can be no discussion of individual responsibility. As a result, Goldhagen's explanation is thoroughly monocausal, despite his claims to the contrary.[514] Everything in his discussion is related back to a specifically German, specifically extreme form of anti-Semitism. As a result, collective guilt replaces individual responsibility. Indeed, if we go by the picture Goldhagen paints of Germany, we have to wonder why the Nazis didn't receive one hundred percent of the vote in the last election, instead of the mere thirty-three percent they actually received. However, there are those, like James M. Glass, who support Goldhagen's viewpoint. He likewise explains the Holocaust monocausally, attributing the mass extermination of the Jews to a culturally propagated anti-Semitism that was scientifically—or, rather, pseudo-scientifically—substantiated, and that spread itself to the German populace as a whole.[515] Like Goldhagen, Glass argues that the German people harbored a deep desire to see the Jewish race annihilated.

An important factor in this discussion, however, is that in contrast to what Goldhagen argues, the average German appears to have been unaware of the full extent of the exterminations. On the other hand, the work camps were so widespread that it's inconceivable the average German wouldn't have been aware that they existed. We must keep in mind, however, that there were significant differences between the work camps, the concentration camps, and the extermination camps. There were over ten thousand work camps, and although most of them were in Eastern Europe, the average citizen *must* have known about them, since for example there were 645 such camps in Berlin and the surrounding areas alone.[516] But if the average German knew about the work camps, the concentration camps were much worse, and there was far less public understanding as to what took place behind their walls . . . and, going one step further, the extermination camps were a closely guarded secret: every one of them was located in Poland, and they only existed for a relatively short period of time. Systematic gassing in the extermination camps first began in the spring and summer of 1942, and most of them were only operational for less than a year and a half. Therefore, there's little reason to suspect that the average German knew about these camps at all. Neither Goldhagen nor Glass makes these distinctions, but simply assume that the average German must have known about all the camps—a claim that is simply not tenable.

For their book *What We Knew: Terror, Mass Murder, and Everyday Life in Nazi Germany*, Eric Johnson and Karl-Heinz Reuband attempted to pin down exactly how much the average citizen knew about the camps by circulating an extensive questionnaire among "normal" Germans and Jews who lived in Germany under Hitler.[517] The investigation revealed that knowledge of the mass exterminations was relatively widespread from the middle of 1942 on; Johnson and Reuband estimate that around a third of the populace knew that mass exterminations were taking place. However, since they too don't distinguish between work camps, concentration camps, and extermination camps in their investigation, this makes it difficult to determine how extensive the knowledge actually was. That is, among those who now believe they were aware of the exterminations, how many were aware at the time?

Regardless, the average German's lack of response to what was going in their country can be attributed more to indifference and a concern for their own well being than any active hatred. The country was in crisis, and during a crisis people have a greater tendency to look after themselves and their own. We must remember that, in the period between the world wars, Germany was afflicted with a depression, inflation, unemployment, an increase in violence and other crime, etc. And most people operate on the basis of what Ervin Staub calls "hedonistic calculus"[518]—that is, when a person compares their own, actual well-being to what they consider normal, to the level of well-being they believe they should have. They then use the results of this equation to estimate how much they should bother to help others. If their own sense of well-being is seen to be substandard, people are far less likely to help others, even when those others have an even lower level of well-being than themselves. When people believe their well-being is sufficient, or better than sufficient, however, helping others seems perfectly reasonable again. Of course, this isn't always the case—especially strong moral considerations are often able to overcome an individual's concern for personal well-being. But seen in the light of this "calculus," it can come as no surprise that—during the period between the two world wars—average Germans would have found their own problems more pressing than the Jews'.

Götz Aly has shed considerable light on this subject with his controversial study *Hitler's Beneficiaries*, where he posits that we can only understand the Third Reich if we regard it as the largest "plunder state" in modern times.[519] He argues that ninety-five percent of the German populace benefited from the Nazis' plundering of both Jews and occupied countries, and this explains the strong support the government had in Germany. The average German may thus be seen as a participant who willingly accepted the trespasses against the Jews in order, explicitly, to secure their own well-being. It's probable, however, that many of the figures Aly cites will have to be revised—for example, it's unlikely that ninety-five percent of the *entire* German populace enjoyed economic benefits during Hitler's time. Even leaving out the Jews themselves, the mentally and physically handicapped, political opponents, etc., it's doubtful that we could reach ninety-five percent. The exact percentages are not what matters, however. The essential point to make is that a clear majority of the German people benefited from what was going on.

The Jewish plunder, the forced labor, not to mention the commerce created by the occupation of other countries—taken together with the inflated value of German currency—all added up to a marked improvement in the standard of living for average Germans. In short, Aly argues that Hitler was popular among most Germans because of the economic improvements his government had made possible. One could perhaps say that the government "bribed" the populace with social goods. As a result, Aly describes Germany in the years between 1933–1945 as having an "accommodating dictatorship," that is, a "considerate dictatorship" with "social warmth." The National Socialists' social politics doubtlessly contained a number of traits that were attractive to many people: No taxes were raised, despite the extensive rearmament, because occupied countries were made to finance their own occupation. Average citizens paid considerably less taxes than the rich. Family allowances were introduced, and newly married couples could receive good loans. Pensions increased dramatically, and pensioners were all given health insurance. Aly doesn't argue that Hitler *invented* the German social state, but developed it quite radically. Seen in this context, Hitler really does look like the *people's* Leader.

This picture stands in sharp contrast to the image presented by what we might call the "totalitarian" school, which was undoubtedly a product of the Cold War, and which was also developed, among other things, in Hannah Arendt's *The Origins of Totalitarianism*. This work is based more on logic than on empiricism, and makes totalitarianism itself the problem, in the sense that a totalitarian regime is supposedly characterized precisely by the terror it inflicts on a people living in chronic fear of secret police, etc. However, new research has modified this picture considerably. For example, it's clear that the Gestapo's resources were much more limited than previously thought, and that the majority of German people went about their daily routine without government interference.

The Nazi government's control of the populace wasn't due to op-pression, but because it had the people's clear support. However, this support did not extend to *everything*. Studies examining what the German people considered to be important factors in the Na-tional Socialist regime found that the fight against unemployment and crime were largely the dominant concerns, while anti-Sem-itism was only mentioned as an especially attractive factor by a small number of people.

Aly's analysis does show that it's impossible to maintain a clear distinction between an oppressive regime and an "innocent" people. At the same time, it's clear that he occupies some of the same ideological territory as Goldhagen, though Aly's assump-tions are considerably more nuanced and plausible, and are better supported than Goldhagen's. A central point Aly's book makes is that more Jewish deportations actually took place after the Allied bombings began, for the simple reason that more homes and fur-niture had to be found for German civilians. These deportations were not kept secret, and the connection between the deportations and "new" apartments couldn't possibly have escaped the German populace. To a certain extent, the same could be said for Ger-many's economy in general: Many people must have realized that *someone* was paying for Germany's prosperity. 1938 is the decisive year in Aly's estimation, because military armament, coupled with tax and social policies, had by then forced Germany to the edge of bankruptcy. Around this time, Nazi economists calculated that the economy could be speedily repaired through the acquisition of Jewish assets. In the beginning, this idea only applied to German Jews, but after a while it was broadened to include new Jews in new territories as well. It's clear that Hitler's government quickly became dependent on a steady stream of slave labor and goods from occupied countries. If the government wanted to support both its armament and social policies, it had to find new territories to plunder, new victims to exploit. In this regard, peace would have meant bankruptcy. Plunder and slave labor was necessary if the German economy was to continue to function.

Nonetheless, Aly's book does not answer, nor does it attempt to answer, the question of why Jews were the first victims. The elements Aly cites function better as explanations for the German populace's support of the Nazi government than as explanations for the Holocaust itself. Aly represents an extreme structural position with all the weaknesses this implies. Even though most Holocaust studies have a tendency to exaggerate anti-Semitism's role as a central motivating factor, one can argue that Aly occupies the opposite extreme and hardly admits its importance at all. In Aly's representation, the Holocaust was more or less an economic operation whose primary motive was to keep the German economy rolling. However, from a purely economic viewpoint, the murders of Eastern European Jews—who formed the majority of the victims—would have been a waste of time. Most of the people were extremely poor and there was little or nothing to be gained from them, economically. Though anti-Semitism wasn't especially strong in the average German—not even among the political supporters and soldiers responsible for the practical side of Nazi social organization—it's still significant that anti-Semitism was an important motivating factor for many of the central agents who planned and ordered that the crimes be carried out.

Obviously, the German people's acceptance of the Jewish persecutions is morally reprehensible. In my opinion, however, the primary focus should fall on those who actively participated in the Jewish exterminations—a matter of several tens of thousands: presumably about a hundred thousand Germans. At the same time, it should be mentioned that not all of these people were aware of full extent of the Holocaust. Naturally, all of the train operators should have refused to take place in the forced deportations . . . and yet, presumably most of them had no idea how unthinkable the conditions were in the worst of the camps. So let us now direct our focus to a group who was directly involved in the murders: Police Battalion 101.

In the literature surrounding the Holocaust, most of the emphasis is given to the gas chambers, but gassing "only" accounted for fifty to sixty percent of the murders. The rest of the victims were murdered in other ways, mainly by shooting. This is an important point, because it causes a number of the usual explanations for the exterminations to fall by the wayside—such as bureaucratization, the separation of labor, technologization, and distancing. The victims were still *people* when they were shot at close range, not "masses" who arrived in a camp like cattle. In order to investigate these murderers, I will take Christopher Browning's study of Police Battalion 101[520] as a departure point. The Battalion itself consisted of around five hundred men who formed a cross-section of the German populace, as was the case with all the task forces stationed in the East. These policemen were not your average soldiers. Nothing was threatening them, no one was shooting back. Yet Police Battalion 101 shot at least 38,000 Jews and deported at least 45,000 Jews to Treblinka in the period between July 1942 and November 1943, and therefore was responsible for the deaths of at least 83,000.[521] On average, this is, every soldier shot seventy-six Jews and was responsible for 166 deaths. Furthermore, hardly any of these men had been in previous conflicts; their actions cannot be explained with reference to a predisposition for brutality.[522] They were average men who were called to duty without being selected according to any special criteria that made them particularly fit for this type of activity.

One of the most thought-provoking aspects of Browning's study is the documentation showing that before their first assignment in Józefow, the men were given the option to *withdraw* if they didn't think they were capable of carrying out their mission.[523] Only a few refused, and that same day 1,500 Jews were murdered in the marketplace. The soldiers' reactions varied. Some didn't seem to have understood what they had agreed to before they stood face to face with their victims, and these asked to be excused. They were subsequently assigned to guard duty away from the marketplace.[524] Others asked to be excused after they'd shot a few Jews, and after a little time had passed, a few hid and tried to avoid the marketplace altogether. A few more consciously missed their targets. But most of the policemen hit what they were shooting at, and *no one* in the whole battalion protested that this slaughter was immoral. Browning estimates that between ten and twenty percent of the men in Police Battalion 101 refused to take part,[525] but Daniel Goldhagen believes this figure is too high.[526] It's difficult to know what the exact figure is, but going by the information both authors cite, it's reasonable to assume that just under ten percent refused. In my opinion, disagreements regarding the exact figures are irrelevant. The important thing is that an overwhelming majority of the men chose to take part in the slaughter, despite the fact that they could have bowed out without suffering any consequences—and indeed were actually offered the opportunity to withdraw. As I've mentioned, there is no evidence that a single German soldier or policeman was executed or put in prison for refusing to kill a Jew. Most soldiers must have realized that they had an opportunity to say "no," but almost all of them chose to say "yes."

It's really one of the most incomprehensible things about Police Battalion 101—that more men didn't refuse to take part in the slaughter, when this choice carried absolutely no consequences for their personal well-being or careers. No one was *forced* to participate. Even more incomprehensible is the fact that those who refused to take part at first later volunteered of their own free will. The men in Police Battalion 101 didn't demonstrate much enthusiasm for or seem to take much pleasure in the slaughter, and many even became acutely depressed after participating[527]—though, certainly, there are also numerous examples of the opposite trend occurring[528]—for the most part suffering strong physical and mental discomfort following the massacre. Why, then, did they do what they did? Browning makes a convincing case that, here too, anti-Semitism was not a decisive motivating factor for the policemen,[529] and, indeed, only twenty-five to thirty percent were members of the NSDAP.[530]

Most people experience extreme discomfort, both physical and mental, when they kill someone for the first time, but we know that this discomfort decreases every time the act is repeated. Many members of Police Battalion 101 felt horrible during and after the massacre in Józefow. This discomfort is tied to a degree of identification with the victims. However, the sheer number of victims—1,500 in Józefow, 1,700 a month later in Lomazy, etc.—helped to transform the victims into a homogeneous mass instead of a group of actual individuals. By the time their second mission in Lomazy rolled around, the policemen were already expressing fewer qualms about their orders.[531] For most of them, any discomfort vanished relatively quickly, presumably because all basis for identification with the victims had begun to disappear. The very act of killing, in fact, made it obvious that there was an enormous gulf between "us" and "them." The policemen were made brutal. It became commonplace for more men to volunteer for a mission than were actually needed, and a competitive culture surrounding the "Jew hunt"[532] developed. They were still somewhat reluctant to kill Jewish women and children, but even this wasn't an insurmountable obstacle. The number of "ardent" murderers increased, while the unwilling few became even fewer. The largest group, however, was composed of men who neither volunteered nor refused, but simply carried out their orders. We can assume that this group generally had more sympathy for themselves—because of being forced to carry out such a mission—than they had for their victims. And, again, each mission only increased their indifference. As unbelievable as it may seem, these men do not appear to have reflected on whether or not what they was doing was evil. For example, one policeman later said: "Truthfully, I must say that at the time we didn't reflect about it at all. Only years later did any of us become truly conscious of what had happened then."[533] This type of thoughtlessness is even more difficult to grasp than Eichmann's. The policemen of Batallion 101 stood face to face with their victims, while Eichmann remained at a remove from the scene of his crime.

The policemen later said that they didn't want to be seen as cowards, that they wanted to be part of the group, etc.,[534] but these excuses seem hopelessly inadequate to explain participation in mass murder. One policeman, however, describes the act of pulling the trigger as being the real act of cowardice here, and this is perhaps closer to the truth: It was easier to take aim than stand out.[535] The men of Battalion 101 rated their relationships with their comrades and the experience of belonging to a group considerably higher than the lives of their victims. This is understandable—though in no way acceptable—since the victims' lives were worth so little to begin with.

It's important for Goldhagen's account that the Germans in Police Battalion 101 *hated* the Jews—but did they? Very few of them express such feelings in interviews. Soldiers in a normal war scenario rarely express hatred for the enemy; group loyalty seems to be far more important to them than hatred.[536] Likewise, loyalty seems to have been more important than anti-Semitism for the men in Police Battalion 101. Furthermore, many of them insist that the root of their behavior was nothing more than the receipt of orders and the determination to follow them. Goldhagen thinks that the actions of the men in Police Battalion 101 can only be explained in terms a unique, German culture. In my opinion, this assumption is false. Take another famous example, namely the massacre in My Lai on March 16, 1968. Lieutenant William L. Calley was commanding officer and was, therefore, principally responsible for this massacre, which lasted around an hour and a half. In that time, 507 innocent people were murdered, among them 173 children and 76 infants. Calley alone killed 102 people. The official report read: "128 enemy resisters killed in battle." However, for one thing, it wasn't 128 people killed, but 507, and for another, they weren't killed in battle, but slaughtered while helpless; finally, they weren't enemy resisters, in the sense of enemy soldiers, but were ordinary civilians. In his own eyes, Calley was simply following orders and was doing what was expected of a good soldier. He couldn't believe his ears when he was accused of mass murder:

> I couldn't understand it. I kept thinking, though. I thought, Could it be I did something wrong? I knew that war's wrong. Killing's wrong: I realized that. I had gone to a war, though. I had killed, but I knew—so did a million others. I sat there, and I couldn't find the key. I pictured the

people of My Lai: the bodies, and they didn't bother me. I had found, I had closed with, I had destroyed the [Viet Cong]: the mission that day. I thought, It couldn't be wrong or I'd have remorse about it.[537]

If we replace "My Lai" with "Józefow" and "Viet Cong" with "Jews," this speech could have been made by any of the soldiers in Police Battalion 101. They also argued that they were just following orders, and that they had "located, confronted, and defeated" the enemy; that it was wrong to kill, but that they were in a war; and last but not least, that they felt no remorse that would have told them they were doing anything wrong. Calley wasn't alone in interpreting the massacre in My Lai this way. Most of the 105 soldiers who participated that day were fine with slaughtering five hundred unarmed civilians, since they were only following orders. Fifteen other officers and nine enlisted men were indicted with Calley. Only Calley was found guilty, however, and even though he was sentenced to life in prison for premeditated murder, he got away with three years of house arrest.

Later examinations showed that My Lai was not a unique event; the difference between Police Battalion 101 and the American company isn't that large. Some American soldiers expressed great satisfaction at having taken part in the slaughter, but others expressed regret or discomfort. One soldier said that he didn't want to participate after looking a Vietnamese woman in the eyes: "Something told me not to [. . .] but when everybody else started firing, I started firing."[538] This was also a common experience in Police Battalion 101. In fact, we find the same patterns in My Lai as in Józefow: A small percentage refused—some even protected civilians and saved numerous lives—while a slightly larger group shot at animals instead of people or intentionally missed altogether, while others hid on the fringes. However, the majority participated without protest. Among the American soldiers, there was no real widespread hatred for the Vietnamese. They only did what they were told. Calley insisted that he hadn't *personally* murdered anyone in My Lai, but that he was only representing the USA.[539] The policemen in Poland could have said the same thing, that they were only carrying out the will of the Leader, and that it wasn't anything personal. But: of course it was personal. And Calley and his men were *personally* responsible for their actions, even if they didn't *feel* this responsibility. When they were put on trial, they didn't feel guilty, but rather saw themselves as victims. Therefore, they obviously had no sympathy with their actual victims. That Calley never recognized his responsibility was one thing, but the fact that it wasn't recognized by others who *knew* what had happened in My Lai is incomprehensible. One of the most shocking things about the trial against Calley is the violent protests it occasioned.[540] These protests were not against the perpetrators, however, but against the fact that a soldier was being put on trial for carrying out his duty. When Calley was condemned, the White House received 100,000 letters of protest in a single day, and a song supporting Calley, "The Battle Hymn of Lieutenant Calley," sold a million copies in a week. In 1970, *Time* conducted an extensive survey, where two-thirds of the Americans questioned said that they *were not* emotionally moved by the massacre in My Lai. Only nine percent of those asked said they thought it was right to indict Calley, while eighty percent of those asked said that it was wrong to indict him. And all these Americans knew exactly what had happened in My Lai: that over five hundred helpless people had been murdered.

Just as the events in My Lai would seem to imply an intense hatred for the Vietnamese, the actions of Police Battalion 101 would seem to imply an intense anti-Semitism, as Goldhagen has asserted.

The public's surprisingly positive opinion of Calley prompted a series of investigations in the years following the trial, where American civilians and soldiers were asked the following question: If you were in the military and received orders to shoot a group of unarmed civilians, among them elderly people, women, and children, would you follow those orders? There is a disconcerting similarity among the different findings: Around thirty percent said they would refuse to shoot, while fifty to sixty percent said they would shoot because they'd been ordered to do so.[541] When we consider that this was a purely hypothetical question, and that it's easier to *say* you'd refuse than actually to do so in a real situation, we come ominously close to the number who participated in Police Battalion 101's slaughter of Jews in Poland.

Let me cite another example, this one from Israel, where Israeli troops carried out a massacre at Kafr Qasim on October 29, 1956.[542] A five o'clock curfew had been imposed that day in the area between the Israeli border and Jordan, and the border patrol received orders to shoot anyone who broke it. The problem was, any Palestinians who commuted to and from work would be coming home after five o'clock, and they hadn't been informed of the curfew. Major Shmuel Malinki of the Israeli border patrol—who had ordered the curfew—had specifically said that no exceptions should be made for such people, and is supposed to have remarked that any casualties would only convince the Palestinians of the seriousness of the situation. Malinski's subordinates carried out his orders without protest. A truck full of women was stopped, and even though the women begged for their lives, they were shot. Fifteen cyclists were ordered off their bicycles and shot, etc. In the course of a couple of hours, the police had shot and killed forty-seven unarmed men, women, and children. Their crime? Returning home from work. Malinki and some of his men were put on trial and sentenced to long jail terms, but their sentences were eventually reduced and they were freed after a relatively short interval. What's the difference between the Israeli border police, Calley's soldiers, and the men in Police Battalion 101? In my opinion, not much. There are differences in the *extent* of their crimes, but with regard to motivation, function, etc. they are disconcertingly similar.

We can go on and draw a further comparison with the genocide in the former Yugoslavia, where Serbian policemen as well as paramilitary and military troops went from town to town, separated the men and boys from the women, herded them into barns, slaughtered them, and destroyed the corpses. These policemen and soldiers were also "normal people." The biggest difference between them and Police Battalion 101 is that some of the Serbian troops knew their victims beforehand. War naturally provides ample opportunities for sadists and people who are ultimately driven to kill *for the sake* of killing, simply because it gives them a "kick," and during the war in Bosnia there were certainly Muslims who, from time to time, would join the Serbian death squad of their own free will. But, again, such people only make up a small percentage of the participants.

What do all these groups have in common? Little more than this very normality. If we look at the agents who participated in the crimes under Hitler's (and Stalin's, Mao's, Pol Pot's, etc.) regime, we find very few out-and-out sadists, very few people who could really be described as representatives of demonic evil. Yes, there were quite a few sadistic guards in the concentration camps—and these sadists even seemed to compete in devising the most extreme and innovative forms of cruelty[543]—but they were a minority, and Himmler actually ordered that such individuals be kept from service.[544]

The majority of the guards in the concentration and extermination camps were stationed in these places because they were unfit for regular military duty. There were few criteria that had to be met to get such an assignment—aside from the requirement that one *not* demonstrate any sadistic tendencies. The majority of the guards were careerists, idealists and, largely, *conformists* who simply did what the others were doing without pausing to reflect on the morality of their actions. The same was true of the guards in the Japanese prison camps in the Second World War.[545] The worst evils are committed not by monsters, but people no different from ourselves.

Conformity is a powerful force. In a famous psychological experiment, groups of six individuals were shown a line and asked to determine which of three other lines was as long as the first. In every group, five people were instructed to choose the wrong line, while the sixth was the subject of the experiment. A large number of experimental subjects gave the same answer as the rest of the group, in spite of the fact that the others had obviously made the wrong choice.[546] What this study doesn't tell us, however, is whether conformity—which leads individuals to endorse an answer they know is false—is merely external, or if it's internalized—that is, if subjects only *say* they agree with the rest of a group, or if they actually *believe* what the rest of the group believes. It's difficult to tell, and perhaps there really isn't much of a transition between *saying* something and *believing* it . . . so that a person who says something often enough will indeed believe it in time.

In 1960, Stanley Milgram conducted a famous experiment that allowed ordinary students to subject—or, rather, to think that they were subjecting—test subjects (hereafter called "victims") to strong electrical shocks when the victim answered a question wrong.[547] In the years that followed, Milgram repeated the experiment in a number of different ways. All the students received a test shock of forty-five volts before the experiment began. The students had nothing personal against their victims, and there were no consequences if a student chose not to participate. They underwent no training, they were not paid for their time, there were no threats, no punishments that could influence their actions—but, nonetheless, the majority of students did what they were told. Sixty percent of the students obeyed all the way up to 450 volts, even though that particular voltage was marked with a warning: "Danger: Severe Shock." When they neither saw nor heard their victims, nearly all of the students cooperated. However, when they could see and hear the victims, only forty percent fully cooperated, and that number sank to thirty percent when the students themselves had to put the test subject's hand on the metal plate. When a non-authoritative person gave the order, there was almost no cooperation. When they did not have to apply the shock, but only had to read the question and judge the answer, over ninety percent participated all the way up to 450 volts. Later, these students justified themselves by saying that they weren't really responsible, because they hadn't actually pressed the button. If a large majority of the group refused to participate, almost ninety percent of the rest would follow suit. There was no obvious difference between the behavior of men and women. Students had diverse methods for dealing with the situation: some focused exclusively on each individual step in the procedure, as if they were trying to avoid the whole picture; some talked extremely loudly to drown out their victim's protests, some turned away so they couldn't see the victim, some insisted that shocks weren't really so bad, and many argued that the victims were so dumb they deserved to be shocked. In the concluding interview, when the students were told that they had been the actual test subjects, many said that they wouldn't have shocked the victims if it had been up to them, that they were only following orders. They overlooked the fact that it was up to them whether or not they followed orders.

In Milgram's experiment, we see only one side of the issue. None of those who thought they were causing someone pain seemed to have any desire to do so. They simply subordinated themselves to a perceived authority. What if some of the test subjects had actually *wanted* to cause pain? Milgram's experiment says nothing about this possibility. An experiment conducted by Robert A. Baron, however, sheds some light on this subject.[548] In this case, the test subjects, male university students, were introduced to a person before the experiment began, and this person deliberately irritated some of the test subjects, while others were treated neutrally. This person, who was employed by the researcher, would be the "victim" in a learning experiment where wrong answers were punished with electric shocks. This experiment differs from Milgram's in that some of the test subjects had been deliberately provoked, and were all personally responsible for controlling the strength of the electric current, which ranged from extremely mild to extremely strong. In addition, half the subjects were stationed in sight of a "pain meter" supposedly showing how much pain their victim was feeling. In the case of test subjects without access to the pain meter, those who had been provoked only gave a slightly stronger shock than neutral subjects; in those cases where the pain meter was visible, however, the difference in behavior was drastic. The neutral subjects—those who weren't provoked beforehand—turned the current down as soon as they received feedback on the victim's pain. The provoked subjects, however, *turned up* the electrical current. They wanted to cause the irritating person pain, and the pain meter telling them that they had succeeded was itself a powerful motivator—despite the fact, as should certainly be mentioned, that the pain the subjects thought they were causing their victim was completely disproportional to the minor provocation they had received before the experiment began. Of course, I do not believe that we can draw many broad conclusions from this experiment, other than the fact that an individual's basis for acting in situations where they are subjected to authority are not as unambiguous as Milgram claims. He concludes, namely, that the deciding factor is not so much who a person is, but in what type of situation they find themselves.[549] However, both factors are clearly quite important, and in foregrounding situation over personality, Milgram seems to underestimate individual responsibility. Yet an individual has the capacity to reflect on and decide about what type of person they want to become, and this capacity implies responsibility.

If, despite this, we focus for a moment on the diverse situations an individual might find themselves in, we can isolate five elements capable of causing people—people who can in no way be described as evil in the classical sense, that is, as sadists—to accept evil:

1. Presentation: It's crucial how a given activity is presented to an agent. There's a big difference between participating in the mass extermination of an innocent and helpless group of people and in defending yourself and those you love against a powerful enemy threatening to destroy you ... and yet, genocide can be described in either way. Presentation was crucial, for instance, in carrying out the extermination of the Jews. The victims were regarded as vermin, garbage. It's true that this image was occasionally difficult to maintain—especially in the case of small children—but certainly not impossible, especially in conjunction with the other elements below.

2. Distancing: The creation of the greatest possible distance between your actions and the people affected by your

actions. For example: Someone makes a decision in an office and the consequences are felt in a completely different location, a place the decision-maker will presumably never visit.

3.   Separation of labor: Where an agent only carries out part of a task, and so doesn't feel responsible for the result of the whole. This was especially evident in the case of the Holocaust, where we can outline the typical murder in the following way: At the Wannsee Conference, the Nazi leadership made plans that were then put into action; a policeman arrests a Jew; Eichmann's division organizes the transport; train engineers and others carry out the transport; the prisoner arrives in a camp directed by Höss or somebody else; this camp has soldiers who each "have their orders"; one prisoner forces another prisoner into the gas chamber—and there you have it. No one has to feel responsible for their actions.

4.   Escalation: Where there's no fundamental alteration in an individual's worldview. Instead, the change happens little by little, every time the individual is faced with a problem that needs solving. In a relatively short period of time, the individual finds himself with a set of values that are radically different from the ones he started out with—and is not even aware that said values have altered so completely.

5.   Socialization: An individual is introduced into a culture where actions that would once have seemed reprehensible are suddenly the norm. Because all agents in the culture accept this norm, the individual's opposition vanishes.

All five of these elements were operative among the participants in the mass exterminations discussed above. And yet, though they can help explain why these men and women did what they did, they cannot, however, be used as excuses. All people, regardless of rank, are free to choose whether they will participate in something or not, and if they choose to participate, they can define *how* they participate. Even in the most extreme of situations, people still maintain the ability to choose. Unfortunately, the choice is often between two evils—and, yes, by choosing the lesser of two evils, an agent may avoid committing a greater. Nonetheless, these agents are still responsible for their lesser evil. The concentration camps had their share of sadistic guards, but likewise had their share of guards who saved prisoners' lives, presumably because they still regarded their prisoners as *people*. For the most part, these humane actions took place in secret, because they directly contradicted the purpose and mentality of a camp. We even know of a number of examples where the most sadistic guards still acted to save the lives of prisoners—as Primo Levi writes, "Compassion and brutality can coexist in the same individual and in the same moment, despite all logic."[550] There were guards too who conducted themselves with relative decency during the entire time they were stationed in the concentration camps. Each guard was an individual with the ability to make individual choices, and they were under no obligation to be vicious. Relative decency, however, does not mitigate the fact *all* the camp guards can still be blamed for having taken part in genocide. It's just that some chose to participate in mass murder in such a way that they could be seen as still retaining a scrap of moral decency at the end of the war.

Thinking as Opposition

Since the particular form of evil under discussion is occasioned by thoughtlessness, it's logical to assume that thought can act as an opposing force. Therefore, Arendt takes it upon herself to investigate the relationship between our capacity to think and our capacity to tell good from evil, and, indeed, whether pausing for thought actually helps to keep us from doing evil. Earlier, I stressed that Eichmann didn't *act*, in the strictest sense of the word, but only followed orders, and likewise didn't *speak*, only spouted an endless stream of clichés. We can go one step further and say that he neither thought nor evaluated his situation. Eichmann demonstrated that thoughtlessness is literally a *lack* of judgment. It's as though Eichmann's capacity for judgment wasn't even operational. Ultimately, such lack of judgment is the epitome of banal evil. All these elements—action, speech, thought, and judgment—are tied together. For Arendt, thought is a positive "destructive" activity that undermines habits and rules, and which therefore is capable of directing action. As she points out: "All thinking demands a *stop*-and-think."[551] Thinking interrupts our activities and tears us out of the frictionless functionality that's so characteristic of our day-to-day lives. We can also call this manner of thought "reflection," and in reflection we can impose a certain distance between our activities and ourselves.

"Thinking deals with invisibles, with representations of things that are absent; judging always concerns particulars and things close at hand. But the two are interrelated, as are consciousness and conscience."[552] Thinking is clearly tied to judgment. It's in making judgments that thinking is first realized in the world, but such judgments can only be made if they are brought about by thought. The goal of thought is to return to the world that was the point of a given thought's departure, and this goal implies that thinking must be *critical*—and being critical is nothing more than exercising the ability to make distinctions. The goal of thought, therefore, is not to produce abstract knowledge, but rather to give us the ability to judge, to make distinctions, such as the distinction between good and evil. Arendt writes that if the ability to make distinctions is linked from the outset to the ability to think—something we have good reason to believe—then we can indeed *demand* that people think.[553]

But what does it really mean to think? In answering this question, Arendt draws closer to Kant, who postulates three maxims for thinking:

> They are: 1. to think for oneself; 2. to put ourselves in thought in the place of everybody else; 3. always to think consistently. The first is the maxim of *unprejudiced* thought; the second of *enlarged* thought; the third of *consecutive* thought. The first is the maxim of a Reason never *passive*. The tendency to such passivity, and therefore to heteronomy of the Reason, is called *prejudice* [. . .] As regards the second maxim of the mind [. . .] it indicates a man of *enlarged thought* if he disregards the subjective private conditions of his own judgment, by which so many others are confined, and reflects upon it from a *universal standpoint* (which he can only determine by placing himself at the standpoint of others). The third maxim, viz. that of *consecutive* thought, is the most difficult to attain, and can only be attained by the combination of both the former, and after the constant observance of them has grown into a habit.[554]

Eichmann, Höss, and Stangl fail in all points: (1) They don't think for themselves, but follow orders; (2) They don't put themselves in anyone else's shoes and they never reflect on how the mass exterminations might have seemed from a prisoner's point of view;

(3) They don't think consequently—and this mistake is a result of the foregoing—because they don't think for themselves. The result is that they can't take the whole picture into account. What they think results directly from what they were ordered to think, and this can change from moment to moment. Where thought is concerned, they all *made themselves guilty* of incompetence. They fail to maintain the ideal Kant proposes for Enlightenment:

> *Enlightenment is the human being's emancipation from its self-incurred immaturity. Immaturity* is the ability to make use of one's intellect without the direction of another. This immaturity is *self-incurred* when its cause does not lie in a lack of intellect, but rather in a lack of resolve and courage to make use of one's intellect without the direction of another. "*Sapere aude*! Have the courage to use your own intellect!" is hence the motto of enlightenment. [555]

Eichmann, Höss, and Stangl are guilty for not having made use of their own understanding, for not having had the courage to think for themselves, simply following orders instead. And they are guilty too for having *chosen* to follow orders. This guilt is not simply Eichmann's, Höss's, and Stangl's, but also belongs to the men in Police Battalion 101, to Calley's troops, and to countless others. It's a guilt we all potentially bear, and therefore the old Enlightenment project is still important and relevant. From the standpoint of the Enlightenment, evil wasn't an independent, active force, but rather a lack of enlightenment; thus, evil could be defeated by overcoming ignorance. This idea bears a certain kinship to the Socratic-Platonic notion that evil stems from ignorance—and if I now return to and support a similar concept, it's because I don't see any other alternative. Adorno argues that the only true oppositional force to the principal introduced by Auschwitz is *autonomy*, "the power of reflection, of self-determination, of not cooperating."[556] This is a view of enlightenment that's as good as any, and perhaps the only opposition to banal evil. The principle of autonomy is a moral principle, which demands the individual think for himself and follow his own conscience instead of simply following orders.

Arendt indicates that there's an important connection between thought and conscience, or rather between thoughtlessness and a lack of conscience[557]—we could find no better illustration of this than the cases of Eichmann, Höss, and Stangl. By conscience, however, I don't just mean the ability to feel guilt. (As far as I know, Euripedes formulated the first conception of conscience, writing: "I know that I have done terrible things."[558]) Guilt is seldom felt while an action is still being carried out, but only afterward, when the individual begins to consider that what they did was wrong; nonetheless, this feeling of guilt can prevent future actions of the same type.[559] The ability to feel remorse is necessary if an individual is going to recognize his own evil. Remorse, therefore, is an expression of moral self-recognition.

Michael Gelven cites three possible reactions to the realization that an individual has done something evil:[560]

1. *How could I have been so stupid?* This reaction doesn't follow an act committed in "honest" ignorance, like pressing an elevator button without knowing a child is in the shaft, or out of carelessness, like running someone over in a car because you didn't check your mirrors. Instead, it's a situation where you *should* have known better and are *guilty* for not thinking your actions through carefully enough.

2.   *Why did I not resist this wrong?* This reaction follows some more-than-typical human weakness. We accept that we are fallible, to a certain extent, but in this case there has been an *unacceptable* form of weakness, leading a person to permit the occurrence of some action or event that is nonetheless recognized as wrong.

3.   *What have I let myself become?* The most serious form of self-condemnation, for here we realize we have let ourselves *degenerate* or *become corrupted* to such an extent that we do not just feel shame, but *disgust* at our moral character.

These reactions are steps to self-recognition. Eichmann, Höss, and Stangl should all have come to (3), but none of them did. Höss didn't even get to (1); Eichmann remained stuck at (1); while Stangl expressed both (1) and (2), and many times, in his testimony, seems on the verge of (3)—one reason he makes a more sympathetic impression than the other two, in my opinion, despite everything. If all three men had reached the third level of self-recognition, there would have been some basis for understanding them, if not forgiving them, because by judging themselves they would have taken a step toward joining the moral community they abandoned by participating in the mass exterminations to begin with. Self-disgust would demonstrate that despite everything, they still belonged among us. Which doesn't mean, of course, that they would not have earned their punishment—but our understanding someone with such terrible crimes on their conscience first requires that they understand themselves. Recognition of one's own moral corruption shows that an individual has retained some sense of his own humanity, that he's not a complete moral wasteland. For instance, to take an example from fiction, a character based on a number of real people, we might cite Kurtz, from Joseph Conrad's *Heart of Darkness*. Kurtz's original goal was to civilize the natives, an ambition not in itself evil. However, he became progressively corrupted over time, and ended by believing the natives should all be destroyed: "Exterminate all the brutes!"[561] It's impossible to know when the change occurred in him, because it doesn't happen at any one specific point in time—rather, it's a gradual habituation and distortion that ends with cruelty becoming habit. Kurtz eventually realizes this, and his last words— "The horror! The horror!"[562]—might be interpreted as an expression of horror at what he's let himself become. With that, Kurtz again joins the moral community before he dies.

EVIL PEOPLE

What can we conclude from our discussion of the different types of human evil? Essentially, just this: that people should be regarded as good *and* evil, rather than good *or* evil. Alexander Solzhenitsyn writes that the line separating good from evil is not drawn between different groups—nations, classes, or political parties—but "right through every human heart."[563] Evil is a possibility found in all of us, because we are all free, moral beings. Evil is part of our common humanity, as is goodness. This is not to say that every person has the *same* mixture of good and evil—it's obvious that this is not the case. Some people are more evil than others. However, it is still possible for each of us to do either good or evil. The most important question is how this possibility is realized in our actions.

What is also clear is that a person can have a number of different motives—or no motive at all—for doing evil. The least plausible motive is the demonic—doing evil simply *because* an action is evil.

However, people do indeed commit evil acts, fully aware of their nature, to reach a subjective good. Despite my reservations about Kant's theory of radical evil, I think that he still gives us the most convincing explanation for instrumental evil. Kant's theory, however, is limited in its applicability to other forms—it can't explain what I've called idealistic or stupid evils, where an agent is either motivated by what he considers to be an objective good, or fails to reflect about good and evil at all.

None of us are immune to evil. We've all committed some variety of evil in one of the aforementioned forms. Most of us have only done so in little ways, but all of us could have committed evil on a much larger scale. Evil people are not just "others," but also ourselves. I'm pretty certain, today, based on what I know of myself, that I would not be capable of doing what Eichmann, Höss, Stangl, or the men in Police Battalion 101 did, but I realize that, in certain situations, I *could* have done what they did. There's nothing in my "nature" that assures me that, in their places, I would not have ended up acting as they did. As Odo Marquard points out, we humans are more accident than intention. It's a mistake to think that people are absolute masters of themselves and their fates. My "self" is largely the result of chance: where and when I was born, what has affected me in the interim, etc. We can see a person's life as thoroughly *determined*, but we must also recognize that we have the ability to change what determines our life: we can describe people as both determined and determining. Human beings can reflect upon who they are and who they ought to be, and they have the ability to choose who they become. We are not strictly determined by our environment, though it does limit our scope of action. People are free, and this means that they could always have acted differently . . . and because they could have acted differently, they can be blamed or praised for their actions, morally speaking. Everyone who took part in the Nazi mass exterminations, for instance, *could have acted differently*—and this is the essential point.

It can be tempting to describe people as inherently evil. Stig Sæterbakken has writen:

> We're all bastards, when it comes right down to it. The only reason we're not all murderers and fascists is that, luckily, the situation's never been right. Under certain circumstances, every single person is capable of torturing another human being. It's a reality we can't ignore. But of course we can ignore it, and we do, every single one of us, every single one of us in our own hypocritical way. If there's any true moral position left to take, it's in admitting that at the critical moment, morality is something we've never even known.[564]

However, even if every single person was indeed *capable* of torturing another human being under certain circumstances, this doesn't mean that every single person would really *do* it. Morality is not something that *all* people are ignorant of in the critical moment, and we aren't all doomed to fail when it counts most. Perhaps the majority do fail, but not *all*. And while there may be no essential difference between those who fail and those who do not, Sæterbakken's assertion is simply too one-dimensional. The problem we face is that our actions, at the critical moment, are as-yet *undetermined*. We can't know what we would do in a given situation—that is, before we actually do it. If we are all doomed to fail, we have nothing to strive for: we may as well give up altogether. But this isn't the case—we can still *hope* that we'd do the right thing, that we'd have the strength to oppose evil. And this hope itself—which is just that, a hope, not something we absolutely *know*—might help us, when the time comes, to make the right choice.

People are fallible. They *fail*. Paul Ricoeur writes: "What is meant by calling man fallible? Essentially this: that the *possibility* of moral evil is inherent in man's constitution."[565] To be human is to have the possibility of doing evil, but since it's only a possibility, not a necessity, this reference to "man's constitution" cannot function as an *excuse*. At most, it can only be part of the *explanation*. Ricoeur goes on to argue that the gap between the possibility and reality of evil is reflected in a similar gap between a purely anthropological description of fallibility and an ethical one.[566] There isn't any contradiction between anthropology and ethics, but the one doesn't follow from the other. Anthropology allows room for ethics to play; it says that we are all *capable* of doing evil, of failing, while ethics *blames* us for our failure—because, despite everything else, we could also have *not* done evil.

All people fail at some point. Pure innocence would be fallibility without failure,[567] but this state of innocence is only an ideal, not something we can actually attain. Only those who can be guilty can also be innocent. Strictly speaking, therefore, an infant cannot be innocent, because—morally—it cannot fail. Innocence is a state that belongs to moral judgment, but that can never be found in its pure form. Pure guilt and pure innocence are idealizations, and we are caught between them. We're all guilty and we're all innocent, if to different degrees. In a religious sense, we can say that we're all sinners.[568] We're all sinners—not because we're victims of original sin, but because we've actually sinned ourselves.

THE PROBLEM OF EVIL

The fact that this chapter is entitled "The Problem of Evil" does not signal a return to theodicy and the question of how evil "came to be." Instead, I will be discussing the problem of evil as a *practical* problem. Neutralizing evil is a far more important task than explaining how it first came into the world. Evil is a challenge to us as *agents*, rather than merely as thinking beings. Therefore, the problem of evil is not a philosophical problem that demands a philosophical solution—our goal shouldn't be to find some subtle line of reasoning that will let us come to terms with the existence of evil. Ultimately, the fact that evil exists is not so much a metaphysical challenge as it is a moral and political one.

THEORY AND PRAXIS

In philosophy, there's a tendency to shy away from praxis, to focus on the world of ideas and neglect the world of action. This disparity is set out in Aristotle's claim that the contemplative life (*bios theoretikos*) is superior to the practical or political life (*bios politicos*).[569] One possible result of this idea is that philosophy loses the opportunity to change the outside world, because now all great ideas—the idea of evil included—belong to the world of inner reflection. This thought is clearly formulated by Marcus Aurelius: "Your evil does not consist [. . .] in any change and alteration of your environment. Where then? Where the part of you which judges about evil is. Let it not frame the judgment, and all is well."[570] Aurelius's ethics are exclusively egocentric, arguing that you should not focus on others' evil, but exclusively on your own.[571]

This stoic ideal turns up repeatedly in the history of philosophy. The "provisional ethics" Descartes suggests in *The Discourse on Method* contains the four following points: (1) To obey the laws and customs of one's country, (2) to be firm in one's actions, (3) to master yourself rather than fortune, and (4) to devote yourself fully to the study and search of truth.[572] In a letter to Princess Elizabeth of Böhmen, he develops this idea further and outlines three rules for the good life, which corresponds to the *three* [sic] moral rules in the *Discourse on Method*: (1) To use reason to discover what we should or should not do, (2) to be resolute in carrying out reason's commandments, and (3) to change ourselves, since external good is beyond our control. He connects these three rules to a fourth, namely that the correct use of reason leads to happiness, and that one should therefore devote oneself to the study of reason.[573] This concept of ethics suggests that the best life is the contemplative life. Since it is not possible to change the world, a person can do nothing more than seek to change within themselves.

Wittgenstein, though an anti-Cartesian, draws the same conclusion. For him, all ethics are directed toward the individual, and Paul Engelmann's remarks in this sense are enlightening:

> In me Wittgenstein unexpectedly met a person who, like many members of the younger generation, suffered acutely under the discrepancy between the world as it is and as it ought to be according to his lights, but who also tended to seek the source of that discrepancy within, rather than outside, himself. [574]

Engelmann further writes that "the person who consistently believes that the discrepancy lies in himself alone must reject the belief that changes in the external facts may be necessary and called for."[575] In keeping this idea, the young Wittgenstein writes that he cannot change the state of the world through will alone, and in this respect is completely powerless: "I can only make myself independent of the world—and so in a certain sense master it—by renouncing any influence on happenings."[576] The solution to life's problems lies in renouncing individual responsibility to change the world. The "ethical reward" for such resignation is happiness, because those who are happy have succeeded in bringing themselves into harmony with the world.[577] The happy life is the contemplative life: "The only life that is happy is the life that can renounce the amenities of the world."[578] Again we find the belief that the purely contemplative life, *bios theoretikos*, is the good life, and represents a type of escape from the vicissitudes of the world. However, this standpoint is not one an individual can simply embrace all at once: it's only in giving up the practical, and devoting oneself purely to the theoretical, that a person can find happiness.[579] Wittgenstein severs philosophy from the world, and therefore from changing the world, again reducing philosophy to a discipline that cannot change the world, only itself. In keeping with this, the older Wittgenstein writes in 1944: "The man will be revolutionary who can revolutionize himself."[580] As we see, the older Wittgenstein's conception of philosophy as a discipline that "leaves everything as it is"[581] had been shaping his work for most of his life: "Thoughts that are at peace. That's what someone who philosophizes yearns for."[582] The younger and the older Wittgenstein seem to share the same basic (and, in this sense, Cartesian) philosophical idea—an idea that is incompatible with the belief that philosophy should help to change the world.

Stoicism does indeed lead to the kind of attitude that Aurelius explicitly recommends—namely, that we should exercise indulgence toward other people's evils.[583] However, it also leads to countless sins of neglect and allows the evil in the world to remain unchecked. Paul places those who *allow* evil on a par with those who *do* evil.[584] However, we might also come to the conclusion that there is no real reason to fight evil. "Such is the self-contrariety of evil," says Pascal, that its "intrinsic malignity" leads it to destroy itself.[585] The example Pascal uses is the lie. A lie is only possible if it is represented as truth, and therefore a lie contains an inherent contradiction—but having an inherent contradiction is not the same as being self-destructive. As long as truth remains an institution—that is, as long as the act of lying is not the rule, but the exception—the lie will continue to function. Therefore, we cannot say that evil destroys itself. Evil must be actively fought and cannot be left to its own self-inflicted ruin.

In my opinion, therefore, philosophical reflection should move from pure reflection to praxis. Kant argues that all interest is ultimately practical;[586] the human race, he says, has a "thoroughly *active* existence,"[587] and he wants to pin down the determining possibilities and goals of this *activeness*. Kant further asserts that "all the operations of our faculties must issue in the practical and unite in it as their goal."[588] Theoretical philosophy, that is, should be subordinate to the practical.[589] But Kant doesn't believe that this principal is limited to philosophy: Ordinary people have faculties enabling them to distinguish between good and evil and to act in accordance with the conclusions they draw. The problem is, this insight is so easily relegated to the sidelines.

Agnes Heller reformulates Kant's categorical imperative to suggest that one should act as though the lessening of everyone else's suffering was dependent on one's own actions.[590] However, we all know that it's possible for us to see a person suffering right in front of our eyes and still remain unmoved. Understanding *how* this is possible can be difficult, since sympathy presupposes some form of immediacy—but sympathy also has a discursive aspect: it is guided by our idea of *who* we feel we can allow ourselves to feel sympathy *for*. Sympathy tears down the walls between others and ourselves—in a certain sense, feeling sympathy for someone implies that we are putting ourselves in their place, "becoming one with them." When we feel for someone, when we're empathetic, we enter into an extremely intimate relationship; the question then becomes, Is this person who's suffering someone I want to get close to? There tends to be a rather large difference of opinion on this point. For some people, sympathy must extend to the entire planet—something I myself am quite incapable of comprehending in its enormity; for others it just extends to animals, leaving humans out of the equation entirely; and for still others sympathy is reserved for a certain group of people only. These "sympathetic groups" don't exist in any kind of hierarchy, so that people who are sympathetic to animals aren't necessarily sympathetic to all people—the Nazis, for instance, who established the first nature preserves and can be considered the founders of the modern environmental movement, certainly lacked sympathy for rather large portions of the human race. But clearly we feel that it's important that the object of our sympathy is considered *worthy* of it. For Aristotle, as well as the typical citizen of ancient Greece, it would have been entirely inappropriate to feel sympathy for a slave, because the slave wasn't worthy of such a response.[591] The same could be said for a white man or woman with regard to an African American during the slave period in the United States. For an SS soldier it would have been wrong to feel sympathy for a Jew or a gypsy, and for a member of Arkan's Tigers it would have been wrong for feel sympathy for a Bosnian Muslim, etc. I won't exclude the possibility that people have a "natural" ability to feel sympathy (as philosophers and others have suggested since antiquity), but I will say that this ability can be effectively blocked by categorization. The difference between "us" and "them" can create walls that sympathy cannot tear down. Höss, Stangl, and others like them naturally knew their prisoners were suffering, but this suffering was dismissed as irrelevant. Suffering had a human face, but they did not allow it to play a corrective roll.

Hume suggests that proximity in time and space plays a role in sympathy,[592] and this is largely accurate. For example, we had much more sympathy for the victims in Bosnia than in Angola in the 1990s, despite the fact that conditions were far worse in Angola. Yet proximity alone isn't always enough. Most people feel little to no sympathy for the homeless men and women they see everyday. Hume writes: "Every human creature resembles ourselves, and by that means has an advantage above any other object, in operating on the imagination."[593] An exercise of the imagination is a requirement for sympathy—That is, I have to think that there's a resemblance between a person suffering and myself before I'm able to sympathize with them. Hume, therefore, argues that we sympathize with the people who most resemble ourselves[594]—yet this is not entirely accurate. Earlier, I called attention to Freud's idea of the "narcissism of minor differences."[595] Take, for example, the relationship between Protestants and Catholics in Northern Ireland. Now, these two groups have more in common with each other than they do with anyone else on the planet, but this similarity is undermined by their sense of belonging to opposing groups—the result being that there is often little to no sympathy between them. What is humanism other than an attempt to tear down such hindrances to human feeling? Sympathy requires individuals to make an essential connection between another person's suffering and their own . . . but this implies that the individual must already identify with the victim.

When some injustice is visited on a group that is already stigmatized or seen as having a lower status—groups that an individual may not identify with very strongly—there is always a great likelihood that it won't remain confined to this group for long, but infect every level of society in time. If a person accepts torture or something like it when it's being inflicted on the bottom rungs of society, this evil will inevitably spread to all social classes. In this respect, a purely egotistical argument for sympathy would be: You shouldn't be so ready to tolerate injustices that will eventually strike you as well. Torture, for example, tends to spread.[596] Roman law first limited torture to slaves who had been accused of a crime, but after a while it was broadened to include slaves who had *witnessed* a crime, until finally it was practiced on free men as well. Ultimately, torture became common, even in criminal cases that weren't especially serious.[597] This pattern repeated itself in the Middle Ages, when Roman law became the norm in most European countries. Around the year 1250, strong restrictions were placed on who one was allowed to torture—for instance, you couldn't torture eyewitnesses, children, the elderly, pregnant women, knights, members of the nobility, kings, and to a large extent the clergy. However, these restrictions had disappeared again a couple of hundred years later, and eventually anyone could in principle be subjected to legal torture.[598] We find the same development in our modern society, but moving at a much greater tempo, so that what begins with "fringe groups" affects virtually all of society in a relatively short period of time. Evil starts small—most genocides didn't begin as extreme acts of violence, but grew to such enormous proportions precisely because the initial stages found little resistance. This was clearly the case, for example, with the Nazi exterminations. The Holocaust could hardly have taken place if the German people had protested against the anti-Jewish laws and the forced deportations that were its predecessors. Even if the German people—in contrast to Goldhagen's argument—were *not* aware that the Jews were being *exterminated* to the extent that they were, they still had a duty to protest against the deportations, which in and of themselves were a severe violation of human rights.

Some small demonstrations did in fact take place, and these demonstrations had consequences: the German people did not simply tolerate everything their leaders did. The Nazis' first euthanasia program, which was directed against the mentally and physically handicapped, produced a strong reaction once the German people realized what was happening. And large protests led to the program's cancellation—admittedly, after 70,000 lives had already been lost. On another occasion, German women demonstrated in Berlin for three days against the imprisonment of their Jewish husbands, and the result was that 6,000 Jewish men were freed.[599] The protests, in other words, produced results. However, there were no large protests in Germany against the deportation of Jews in general. In Bulgaria, on the other hand, there were such large public protests that imprisonment of Jews was severely curtailed. Furthermore, the passivity of other countries in the face of the Jewish exterminations helped strengthen the idea that the exterminations were not so evil after all—and in December of 1942, Himmler wrote that he honestly believed that the English and Americans were onboard with the Jewish genocide.[600] In reality, however, there wasn't all that much the Allies could actually *do* once the war had begun;[601] and yet, even if there were practical hindrances that, for example, made the bombing of Auschwitz impossible before quite late in the war—an alternative that was rejected even by Jewish organizations—the Allies should nonetheless have signaled that they knew what was taking place: that it was completely unacceptable and that the responsible parties would be brought to justice. If this had happened, perhaps nothing would have changed, but perhaps too it might have led to an earlier dismantling of the extermination camps. This is easily imagined, and by extension we can see just how much the German populace itself might have influenced the situation by putting pressure on their government through mass demonstrations. The most obvious explanation for why such demonstrations did not take place is that normal Germans didn't see the deportations as affecting them directly and, therefore, were simply indifferent. This indicates that the average German citizen had already accepted the distinction between "German" and "Jew" dictated by the regime, but it hardly proves that the German people were actively anti-Semitic, as Goldhagen argues. Regardless, it does demonstrate that "normal" Germans felt an indifference to the deportations that can only be described as morally reprehensible.

Witnesses have a duty to intervene. This duty is not necessary a juridical one, but is in any case a moral one. If a person has the opportunity to intercede in an injustice, but fails to, then that person shares part of the blame. However, our high regard for personal comfort—not security, but comfort—has a tendency to overshadow our concern for a victim's welfare, and even existence. Sins of neglect are not the worst type of sin, but they are certainly among the most common. Most murders have witnesses, but it's very rare that these witnesses act to prevent the tragic outcome.[602]

But this leads us to another phenomenon: The more people have an opportunity to intervene, the less personal responsibility each individual feels to do so. This principle of diffused responsibility was introduced by John Darley and Bibb Latané in 1968 to explain why bystanders so often fail to help victims in need.[603] The departure point for their study was a famous case from New York in 1963, when Kitty Genovese was beaten to death for over an hour. None of the forty people who either saw or heard the attack came to her aid or called the police. In contrast to the usual explanation—that people in urban settings are simply indifferent to each other—Darley and Latané suggested that the fact that there were *so many* witnesses led each individual to feel that they had no personal responsibility to step in. Later laboratory experiments strengthened this hypothesis and demonstrated that there is a much greater likelihood that an individual will step in and help a person in need than a member of a group.

Bystanders can do a great deal to influence the outcome of a situation, both in isolated cases of violence and with regard to crimes on a national scale. An example of the latter is Edmund Dene Morel, who fought for years to make the world aware of the crimes taking place in the Belgian Congo. Eventually, he helped bring them to an end.[604] Those of us who live in democracies are *required* to stay vigilant. In a democracy, citizens who keep silent implicitly give their consent. Those who have an opportunity to protest publicly, but refrain, give their assent by failing to protest.[605] Bystanders, that is, can influence a situation concretely by becoming participants. This participation doesn't just mean stepping in physically with violence or sanctions. Helping to define and redefine an event's moral status is just as important as intervention. We must argue that certain actions should be understood in a certain way, and that the agents in question should therefore stop what they're doing. Witnesses who become participants can break the moral consensus and increase awareness that something morally unacceptable is happening. The participant witness can help to awaken our slumbering consciences and thereby incorporate a victim back into the moral community. Most agents, furthermore, feel a need to legitimate their actions—preferably before, but also after they actually do them;[606] as such, it's extremely important to struggle against prejudice at all times, because this helps to de-legitimize prejudice-based justification strategies.

The justification of evil actions usually springs from one of two elements, perhaps from both: (1) A person or a group poses such a serious threat to myself or others that they must be harmed or annihilated or (2) a person or a group has a characteristic, or a weakness, that means they do not need to be regarded as inviolable. In other words, fear and contempt are evil's two primary wellsprings. Witnesses, however, can try and change the picture so that the fear and/or the contempt is revealed to be based on something other than the facts.

The descriptive and the normative, facts and values, are not completely independent of each other. Normative considerations influence how we interpret a situation, and what we consider to be "facts" have consequences for normative evaluations. We seldom *deduce* that a certain type of situation is wrong. For example, we *know* that it's wrong to abuse someone. The concept of abuse goes hand in hand with the knowledge that the act is wrong, but the consciousness that abuse is wrong is only applicable in situations that we recognize as cases of abuse. Bystanders can play a decisive role in helping define how a situation is interpreted. This is especially true, for instance, in the case of genocide. A number of countries avoided calling what happened in Bosnia and Rwanda a "genocide," because that would mean they had the moral, political, and juridical responsibility to intercede. Intervention was considered undesirable, and so these countries had to be pressured to admit that genocide—with all that this implies, as far as the world community's level of responsibility, harking back to the Convention on Genocide in 1948—was taking place. We have a similar responsibility to pressure our own legislators to act.

In my opinion, the primary reason for intervention is this: Victims deserve the recognition that what's been done to them is wrong, and deserve too to see this wrong righted, if at all possible. At the same time, perpetrators deserve to be recognized as members of a moral community, and this membership presupposes that they will be brought to justice for their crimes. I consider this element of punishment, the bringing of a perpetrator to justice, to be far more important than any other possible individual or societal effects punishment might have. In other words, I place the idea of justice above utilitarian considerations.[607]

The purpose of international war crimes tribunals is to hold *individuals* responsible for crimes, rather than demonize a whole people. The tribunals exist to place individual rather than collective guilt.[608] Demonizing an entire group cements the contrast between "us" and "them," and, as discussed earlier, justifies—among other things—further persecution of innocent people. Nonetheless, international war crime tribunals challenge a basic principle of international law, a principle that dates back to the Peace of Westphalia in 1648, namely that international law reflects the interests of sovereign nations who each "manage their own affairs," so long as one nation isn't having its territory violated by another.

By placing another country's soldiers, functionaries, and leaders on trial, the principle of sovereign statehood is violated, because we are, in effect, reducing them to the level of individuals, rather than representatives of a state.

ETHICS OF CONVICTION AND ETHICS OF RESPONSIBILITY

However, it can also be argued that we should do more than simply put perpetrators on trial after they've already committed their crime. It may also be necessary to intervene violently in order to *stop* violations from occurring in the first place. The Prophet Micah writes that people "will beat their swords into plowshares and their spears into pruning hooks,"[609] while the Prophet Joel writes: "Beat your plowshares into swords and your pruning hooks to spears."[610] For the most part, we should follow Micah, but in a world where not everybody follows Micah, we sometimes have to follow Joel. To use Max Weber's distinction between the ethics of ultimate ends and the ethics of responsibility, we can say that the ethics of ultimate ends will generally prompt us to follow Micah, while the ethics of responsibility will sometimes tell us that we should follow Joel. Weber writes that where the ethics of ultimate ends says that evil should not be opposed with force, the ethics of responsibility says: "You *shall* resist evil by force, otherwise you will be responsible for its spread."[611] Weber expands on this idea:

> We have to understand clearly that all ethically oriented action can follow *two* totally different principles that are irreconcilably opposed to each other: an ethic of "ultimate ends" or an ethic of "responsibility." This is not to say that

the ethic of ultimate ends is identical with a lack of re-sponsibility, or that the ethic of responsibility is identi-cal with lack of conviction. There is naturally no question of that. But there is an immeasurably profound contrast between acting according to the maxim of the ethic of ul-timate ends—to speak in religious terms: "The Christian does the right thing and leaves the outcome in God's hands," *and* acting according to the ethic of responsibility: that one must answer for the (foreseeable) *consequences* of one's actions.[612]

A similar ethics of ultimate ends is not only found in the New Tes-tament,[613] but is also well represented in the Old.[614] In short, the idea implies staying your course and leaving the rest up to God. Kant is perhaps the most obvious representative of this viewpoint in modern times. For him, an individual's moral responsibility has such absolute value that, for example, you should not even tell a lie to save another person's life.[615] It seems safest to adopt an exclusive ethics of ultimate ends, because at least you can claim that you've always maintained the proper moral stance—that you were just a victim of circumstances. Oftentimes, the easiest course is sim-ply to follow our conscience, that is, those laws a person develops as they live in order to guide their actions. But the easiest course isn't always the best one. Is it always a good thing to place peace of mind and a clean conscience above the suffering of others? I believe the answer is no. An ethics of ultimate ends and an eth-ics of responsibility are not mutually exclusive, but instead supple-ment each other, and sometimes an ethics of ultimate ends must be suspended for the sake of responsibility. The problem we face, however, is that we are fallible, and do evil by unjustly bringing suffering upon others, suffering that cannot be legitimated. Weber, therefore, goes on to write:

> No ethic in the world can get around the fact that in many cases the achievement of "good" ends is linked with the necessity of accepting ethically dubious, or at least risky means and the possibility or even the probability of evil side effects. And no ethic in the world can predict when and to what extent the ethically good end "justifies" the ethically risky means and side effects.[616]

There is no "moral algorithm"[617] that will tell us infallibly when it is appropriate to suspend an ethics of ultimate ends, and especially not which means are justifiable *when* it is suspended. We have nothing to rely on except our own moral judgment . . . and sometimes this judgment fails—and then a person can become a representative of evil, no matter how good his intentions were at the start. As a general rule, I would argue that an ethics of ultimate ends can only be suspended to prevent further evil, not to realize some ideal of the good. This would limit idealistic evil—as we saw it manifested in the totalitarian regimes during the twentieth century. Furthermore, some evils are of such extreme character that they justify any means. Nonetheless, all other plausible alternatives must be tried first.

An ethics of ultimate ends and an ethics of responsibility can have different values with respect to, for example, the status of human rights. Human rights are not something forced upon an oppressed people against their will. The opposition comes from leaders who defy these rights, while the populace desires them.[618] The concept of human rights has arisen as a normative response to the experience of violence, persecution and oppression. Such rights aren't simply *for* humans, but are also created *by* humans—that is, they are products of history, and ought to be regarded as essentially revisable. Nonetheless, I believe that in everyday praxis, these rights ought to be regarded as absolute—that they should be respected even when they make it more difficult to attain a further good or hinder a prospective evil. They should only be set aside if they come into conflict with other rights that, after an extensive evaluation, we regard as more vital.

An ethics of responsibility should, in my opinion, be developed as a *weak consequentialism*.[619] The difference between a strong and a weak consequentialism is that the strong argues that we have the duty to maximize the total set of best possible consequences in *every* case, while the weak simply argues that there is no case whose consequences are irrelevant for doing what is right.[620] In most cases, weak consequentionalists will agree with an ethics of ultimate ends, but weak consequentionalists will also argue that there *can* be cases where consequences have more weight than, for example, our concern for individual rights.

This largely implies that human rights should be understood as an unrestricted obligation that in principle *can* be deviated from when there's an especially urgent reason to do so—a case where the consequences of upholding human rights would be extremely negative. The question is *when* and *to what extent* human rights can be deviated from. In my opinion, there must be a *specific* threat against a nation's or an individual's security. That means that every single case of departure must be justified individually. There can be no talk of lawful, *general* exceptions to human rights, because this would be the same thing as declaring our rights null and void. Unfortunately, it must be said that the Bush administration's "war on terror" did not fit the bill, and to a great extent resulted in an unjustified nullification of human rights.

In many cases, it will be unclear which course of action will cause the least evil. In these cases, and in cases where the consequences of our actions are wholly unclear, we ought to make a judgment, generally speaking, based on an ethics of conviction. But when we think we have a clear choice between two evils, and one evil is obviously greater than the other, we should choose the lesser evil. Sometimes it *can* be the right decision to infringe on a person's rights if this will prevent a catastrophe. The paradox of "getting our hands dirty" is that sometimes we will find it necessary to do something wrong in order to do something right. To choose the lesser of two evils is not in itself reprehensible—though, at the same time, we must recognize that we will still be morally *responsible* for the lesser evil, and will have to do our utmost to correct things afterwards.

All actions take place on a more or less unsteady ground. We never have a complete overview of all the consequences and circumstances surrounding our actions, and the best of intentions can lead to horrifying results. Without realizing it, and on the basis of choices and circumstances beyond our control, we can end up inflicting terrible evil on another human being. There is no infallible example we can point to that will tell an ethics of ultimate ends what is right in every situation, because, as stated above, there is no moral algorithm. Universalization tests—imagining whether a certain action could be taken up by the entire populace—can point us in good directions, but they aren't infallible, since they necessarily exclude actions that are obviously perfectly acceptable and beneficial and include those that clearly aren't. This point is clearly expressed in Hegel's critique of Kant's categorical imperative—namely, that this degree of abstract formalism has the consequence that any maxim can be transformed into a general law.[621] In addition, universalization can only give us general rules whose relationship to individual cases remains unclear. Hegel therefore argues that because the categorical imperative requires the separation of society and the individual, and only the society can pass moral judgments, this variety of ethics does not have true relevance for our personal conduct, since we are confronted on a daily basis with concrete situations, not generalizations. Because the categorical imperative is not applicable to every individual situation, it is external to every individual situation. As a result, when an individual situation is abstracted to something general, it becomes something unrecognizable.[622] Ethical judgments should take place in the context of general human interaction, and therefore be made on "common ground." In Sophocles' *Antigone*, Kreon is asked by his son Aimon not to *monos fronein*, that is, not to practice what is called practical wisdom without discussing the situation with others.[623] To turn away from *monos fronein* is to hail a proto-democratic principle: Morality and political questions should be addressed in a public forum; in this discussion, we will sometimes decide that violence is necessary to overcome evil.

POLITICS AND VIOLENCE

Where an ethics of ultimate ends normally indicates that a person should not resort to violence, an ethics of responsibility can require it—and violence is never out of the question in any political regime, whether you're talking about a liberal democracy or a dictatorship. Violence is normal. The essential question in the political arena is not between violence and nonviolence, but between legitimate and illegitimate violence. Liberal societies use violence to protect liberal ideas. Their existence presupposes this type of violence. There is, therefore, no contrast—but rather an obvious compatibility—between liberal democracies and violence. As a result, the question is not whether one supports or opposes violence, but rather *what type of violence* one wishes to participate in or support. There are, of course, people who support political violence for its own sake; Georges Sorel, for instance, finds that violence isn't only something *feasible*, morally—an unfortunate alternative one can be forced to resort to once all other choices have been exhausted—but has a high value in and of itself: Violence builds character and brings the proletariat together.[624] Frantz Fanon also believes that, for the oppressed, violence has an essential—in addition to an instrumental—worth, because it's a source of pride and has "positive, formative features."[625] In the foreword to Fanon's book, Sartre supports this view of violence, and even takes it further than Fanon himself. However, I won't dwell here on those theories that consider political violence to have inherent worth, and instead focus exclusively on violence's instrumental aspects.

Pacifism will oftentimes prove a defensible position, and in more cases than is commonly assumed—but violence can prove a moral imperative in cases where it's necessary to check other violence or injustice. Violence is a fact in every society—and if I refuse to use violence, I may still be supporting it indirectly: sharing the blame when violence affects others. The idea that the use of violence can become a moral imperative is absolutely compatible with the desire to minimize violence as much as possible; but this doesn't mean that pacifism doesn't have value. Democracy and pacifism are tied together. Pacifism recognizes that violence is the scourge of a democratic society, because violence is an intentional physical denial of an individual's or a group's right to exist and thrive—and this right is the core of democracy.[626] The problem is that in praxis the very existence of a democracy presupposes violence, as I've said. There are always going to be unjust individuals and groups that subject other people to violence or infringe on their rights in some other way, and if a democracy is going to exist, these people must be persecuted legally and perhaps even subjected to violence themselves, if they oppose their legal persecution.[627] Democracies, furthermore, never achieve a complete balance. They contain individuals and groups with diverse interests who all attempt to define and control society with respect to those interests. There must be a functioning public forum where these differences can play themselves out in nonviolent ways. Disagreement occurs when two or more individuals or groups have diverse opinions and/or interests. If this disagreement is not sustainable, there are only three possibilities: (1) The parties discuss their differences and come to terms, (2) a third party, for example a court, weights the case, decides on a course of action, and implements it, or (3) the parties resort to violence. The problem with idealism—and not the smallest problem, either—is that (1) and (2) so often seem like unacceptable alternatives. Idealists, to their way of thinking, have a monopoly on the good, and anything other than complete, unequivocal victory would be the same thing as allowing a terrible evil to persist. Therefore, only alternative (3) is acceptable to them. In modern, democratic societies, parties are not allowed to solve their differences in such a way: the state itself has a monopoly on violence.[628] As Max Weber writes: "The specific characteristic of the present is that the right to use physical force is only granted to any other associations or individuals to the extent that the *state* itself permits this. The state is seen as the sole source of the 'right' to use force."[629]

If we consider violence as purely instrumental, then the use of force is rational if it fulfills a desired purpose. Having accepted this, however, we still haven't reached an instrumental rationale for violence, and a *substantial* rationale would require that the goal itself be rationalized and legitimated. Arendt observes that violence changes the world, and often only makes the world a more violent place.[630] Therefore, one should only use violence after thoroughly weighing the options and deciding that violence is the best means to attain a given goal—so long as the goal is important enough that it legitimizes the use of violence. In my opinion, political violence is only good if it helps to reduce the amount of violence in the world, if it helps to maintain a free, nonviolent, democratic, and pluralistic society. Political violence is evil when it does the opposite.

All nations have internal laws regulating the use of violence. What's more problematic still is evaluating whether or not to employ violence against *other* countries, especially when it concerns matters within their own borders. This is a problem that's hardly restricted to cases of genocide, though genocide is the obvious test case. We must remember that the concept of "genocide" is relatively new. It was coined by Rafael Lemkin in 1944 to describe the Nazi mass exterminations. At the time, he didn't think the term "mass murder" was adequate to describe what had happened. Since then, the concept has become central to our understanding of evil, and many people will argue that genocide is the greatest of all evils, because it causes the greatest amount of suffering. All other forms of evil seem to be contained in genocide, and an enormous number of people have fallen victim to it. In the 1990s, the expression "ethnic cleansing" also became common, and it's difficult to pinpoint the exact similarities and differences between "genocide" and "ethnic cleansing," especially since the latter expression doesn't have a commonly agreed-upon definition.[631] Regarding "genocide," however, Article II of the Convention on the Prevention and Punishment of the Crime of Genocide says:

> In the present Convention, genocide means any of the following acts committed with intent to destroy, in whole or in part, a national, ethnical, racial or religious group, as such:
>
> (a) Killing members of the group;
> (b) Causing serious bodily or mental harm to members of the group;
> (c) Deliberately inflicting on the group conditions of life calculated to bring about its physical destruction in whole or in part;
> (d) Imposing measures intended to prevent births in the group;
> (e) Forcibly transferring children of the group to another group.[632]

Each of these points qualifies as genocide, but in normal usage, genocide is primarily tied to the activities listed under points a), b), and c). With regard to Article 1 of the Convention, nations are obligated to prevent and punish genocide. Article 2(4) in the UN's charter, however, forbids humanitarian intervention on another country's territory, and Article 2(7) additionally forbids the UN from meddling in a country's internal affairs. The one general exception to these rules is a crime that threatens the freedom and security of the international community. Therefore, one could conclude that the UN's charter forbids what the Convention on Genocide demands, namely intervention when a country is in the process of carrying out genocide on its own territory. But genocide must be interpreted as a crime that threatens the freedom and security of the international community. As I understand it, this means that the UN's charter gives nations *the right* to intervene in another country's internal affairs when they are planning or carrying out a genocide, while the Convention on Genocide imposes a *duty* on nations to carry out such an intervention.

If current trends are any indication, the need for humanitarian intervention will only increase as time goes on, especially since so many of the larger armed conflicts today are civil wars. Edmund Burke writes: "Civil wars strike deepest of all into the manners of the people. They vitiate their politics; they corrupt their morals; they pervert even the natural taste and relish of equity and justice."[633] "Normal" wars are gruesome enough, but the sides tend to conform—at least to some extent—to a given set of rules, especially those set down by the Geneva Convention, which are meant to limit the worst aspects of the process. Today, however, wars play out far less often *between* countries than *within* countries—and, in internal conflicts, the rules of war are not necessarily followed to any appreciable degree.[634] The UN and traditional international law has been built around conflicts between nations, and as Sadako Ogata argues, we haven't yet developed adequate, international tools for intervening in internal conflicts.[635] In many cases, however, such conflicts can only be stopped by international intervention, and we should all feel we have this duty to intervene—even if neither of the participating sides want this—out of concern for the civilian population. All wars affect civilian populations far more than the actual combatants, but this happens to an even greater degree in internal conflicts. Although additional protocols to the 1977 Geneva Convention explicitly forbid attacks on any civilian population, this rule is constantly broken.

Since World War I, however, more civilians than soldiers have lost their lives in war. UNICEF estimates that ninety percent of those killed in war since 1945 have been civilians, and expects that in the future, one hundred civilians will die for every single soldier.[636] Seen in this way, war is not something that plays out primarily between soldiers, but between *soldiers and civilians*. This can perhaps shed some light on the extensive use of rape in war.[637] In Bosnia, it's estimated that around 60,000 women were raped. However, this was not a purely Serbian activity. *All* the various sides in Yugoslavia—Serbs, Croatians, Muslims—indulged in rape to a startling extent. In the media, these rapes were represented as a new development in such conflicts. However, rape can be described as a common military praxis. Just to mention a few figures: When the Japanese took Nanking in 1937, around 20,000 women were raped, and in Korea during World War II, between 100,000 and 200,000 women were captured by the Japanese and sent to camps, where they were repeatedly subjected to rape and other sexual torture. Around 200,000 women were raped in Bangladesh in 1971. In just Berlin and the surrounding areas alone, possibly up to a million women were raped as the Russians approached the city in 1945. Around 5,000 women were raped by Iraqi troops during the occupation of Kuwait. Rape is not a marginal phenomenon, and should be regarded as a systematic characteristic of war. Carl von Clausewitz underscores, however, that the purpose of an invasion is not to conquer the invaded land, nor to win the struggle against the enemy army, but instead to inflict general harm.[638] War is not so much about the destruction of an army as it is about the destruction of a culture.[639] The extensive rape of women fits into this picture, because in wartime it is largely women who hold families and society together.

Massive assaults on women destabilize the whole culture and aid in its dissolution; rape of women is a symbolic rape of an entire society.[640] Rape is used to "contaminate" the culture—that was an expression used by both the Serbians in Bosnia and the Russians when they approached Berlin in 1945. In Yugoslavia, rape camps were set up and received logistical and economical support from Bosnian and Serbian leaders, something that plainly demonstrates that the action was a national initiative, rather than individual soldiers simply running amok—a typical representation of rape in war. As we saw in Bosnia, a typical course of action when troops enter a city is first the destruction of cultural objects, for example historical monuments, churches, and mosques—something explicitly forbidden by Article 53 of the 1977 Geneva Convention's additional protocols—then to arrest and often execute intellectuals, for example priests and teachers who also serve to unite the local culture, and finally to subject women to sexual assault. Rape is a crime against humanity when it's carried out on political grounds. Earlier, this fact did not receive enough attention, and it was a real breakthrough when a war-crimes tribunal in The Hague on February 22, 2001 found three Bosnian Serbs guilty of crimes against humanity. They were charged with a number of sexual assaults, among others the rape of a twelve-year-old girl.

Globalization is changing the moral world, and our responsibility extends further than ever. There is no longer any place on earth external to our sphere of responsibility. Should we, therefore, embrace what Thomas Mann called a "militant humanism"?[641] I believe so. At the same time, politics often creates greater evils in the attempt to overcome lesser—that should be especially clear to us after the twentieth century and the recent "war on terror."

Adorno's assertion that acts of overcoming are always worse than what's being overcome, therefore, is not entirely unreasonable.[642] If taken literally, however, the statement is extremely exaggerated and is politically and morally indefensible. If Adorno's idea held true, our only strategy would be to simply make peace with all the evil in the world. Instead, we must attempt to defeat evil—well aware of the fact that each defeat is a potential catastrophe. Evil is something we cannot remain neutral to; we have a duty to step in—perhaps even to use military force—when circumstances require it.

Classical realism, as it emerges in theories surrounding international politics, argues that nations, not individuals, are the only meaningful agents, that foreign policies must be driven by national interest and that ethical considerations are improper, unacceptable, or even directly harmful in international relations.[643] In modern times—after the Westphalia peace accord in 1648, that is—such realism has become almost universal, although a gradual thaw has taken place since World War II. That is, from the Nuremberg Trials on, international relations have placed increasing importance on individual and moral considerations, and equally we find steadily stronger limitations placed on the principle of an individual nation's inner autonomy or sovereignty. I regard this development as positive. Of course, the weakening of an individual nation's sovereignty should not result in nations being replaced by one world government, for as Kant has already pointed out, that could lead to the development of a global despot or else a single world nation constantly torn apart by inner strife.[644] Nations must retain their sovereignty, but boundaries must be established as to how far that sovereignty may extend, where the individuals living in a given nation are concerned. These limitations are partially imposed by the concept of human rights, which in the last fifty years has become more and more central to international law and has largely set the principle boundaries for how a war may be conducted, as well as how far a nation's inner autonomy extends.[645] Human rights are considered to be universally relevant, whether or not they have local support. Any infringement of human rights must be condemned—in more serious cases with sanctions, and in worst cases with intervention.

Modern "humanitarian" war is, in reality, a return to the Christian teaching regarding *just war*. This is a tradition extending from Augustine to Michael Walzer,[646] with Hugo Grotius emerging as perhaps the foremost, classical theoretician.[647] For Augustine, war is fought for the sake of peace.[648] Just war concerns *negative* justice: that is, it is conducted to limit an evil instead of to attain a good. This is especially clear in Grotius. This tradition recognizes that war is an evil that should be prevented, and therefore maintains strict requirements for calling a war "just." These requirements can be separated into three main points:

(1) *Jus ad bellum*—legitimacy of going to war.
(2) *Jus in bello*—legitimacy of the means.
(3) *Jus post bellum*—legitimacy of the war's conclusion.

I will only discuss (1) and (2) in this context. The requirements of (1) are traditionally as follows:

(1.1) Lawful grounds: A nation can enter into war only if it has lawful grounds, for example self-defense, the protection of the innocent, or the punishment of violations of international law.

(1.2) Correct intentions: Not only must a nation have lawful grounds, they must go to war on these grounds alone—

> that is, these grounds must prove the essential motivating factor.
>
> (1.3) War must be publicly declared by the nation's lawful authorities.
>
> (1.4) War must be the last resort after all (plausible) peaceful alternatives are exhausted.
>
> (1.5) It must be reasonable to assume that war will lead to the attainment of the legitimate goal.
>
> (1.6) War must not inflict greater suffering or loss of life than can be prevented.

The requirements for (2) are traditionally that one must distinguish between targets, so that only the targets directly involved in the war are attacked; that one cannot use more violence than is strictly necessary to attain a goal; and that one cannot use means that are inherently evil themselves, such as rape, torture, weapons of mass destruction, biological and chemical weapons, etc. Today, the requirements for *jus in bello* are specified in the four Geneva Conventions of 1949 and the two additional protocols from 1977.

Classical theories concerning just war demand that all the above requirements be met, and thus that a war which does not meet *all* of them is evil. Most wars, however, seem to fall tragically short of most of these requirements. If we look, for example, at the U.S.'s war in Vietnam, there is reason to believe that *not a single* requirement of *jus ad bellum* and *jus in bello* was met. A more problematic example, however, is NATO's war in Kosovo. As far as I can judge, NATO met the requirements for *jus in bello*, since no open transgression of the Geneva Conventions has been proved as far as its methodology—even though a strategy of bombing from 15,000 feet resulted in far more civilian suffering than was necessary.[649] At the same time, it's doubtful that the initial requirements for *jus ad bellum* were met.

We can demand that humanitarian intervention meets the criteria for just wars—but I will, regardless, continue to insist that there *are* just wars, and that, when the circumstances are right, it can be immoral *not* to go to war. For example, Rwanda is a sin of neglect of enormous proportions. It was obvious before it even began that genocide was going to take place. Nonetheless, it took months of slaughter before the U.S. and other nations condemned these actions as genocide. They hesitated, as I've said, because calling the events by their proper name would have forced the world community to act in accordance with the Genocide Convention of 1948. As a result, 800,000 people were slaughtered in the course of a hundred days—a faster pace than in any previous genocide. Not stepping in to prevent this was a crime in and of itself. There have been many cases where the UN has been so concerned with remaining neutral that they have neglected to intervene in genocide, because such intervention would imply partiality. However, one cannot afford to be impartial when one group is trying to drive out or exterminate another group, an entire people.

There is no formal, juridical definition for "humanitarian intervention," but the main line of thought is that a nation or a society of nations has a right and perhaps even a duty to intervene to protect the people of another nation, whether or not these are threatened with what might be described as a purely internal conflict. In an important speech in Chicago on April 22, 1999, Great Britain's then Prime Minister, Tony Blair, said that NATO troops in Kosovo had altered the balance between human rights and sovereign statehood.[650] The intervention set a precedent for NATO, dictating that humanitarian concerns must have a higher priority than national sovereignty. A week later, Jürgen Habermas wrote that the intervention in Kosovo represented a step away from classical international law, as it had continued since the Peace of Westphalia in 1648, and toward a cosmopolitan law for a world conceived of as one large community[651]—and he was right. But when one goes to war for humanitarian reasons, there are even stricter requirements regarding the way the war should be conducted. Even if the strategy of bombing from 15,000 feet, with all the suffering it entails for the civilian population, is not necessarily in direct conflict with *jus in bello*, it is still highly questionable. NATO's goal of a risk-free war here operated on the assumption that the lives of NATO soldiers were more valuable than the lives of the people they were trying to save—a problematic stance where human rights are the reason for the intervention, given that human rights are meant to imply that all human lives are of equal value.[652] If a humanitarian intervention is to be honorable, it must be conducted according to humanitarian principles—among other things this same principle of universal equality. Jean Baudrillard writes that the unwillingness to risk life is *worse* than the wish to destroy life, because such unwillingness implies that nothing *means enough* to justify the possible sacrifice.[653] If we are not willing to risk anything, we cannot be said to have an authentic relationship with our values.

The urgent question we must ask ourselves is whether individuals have rights that are important enough for national sovereignty to be set aside. In my opinion, the answer is yes. The international community must be willing to send troops in when the situation demands it, and these troops must oppose acts of tyranny. There should never be a repetition of Srebrenica in June 1995, when UN troops stood passively by and watched as seven to eight thousand men and boys were murdered, and 23,000 women, children, and elderly people were deported. One cannot remain neutral in the face of a massacre, and one must be prepared for soldiers to die in the attempt to stop such atrocities. A pure non-intervention strategy implies that evil is allowed to occur unhindered.

Globalization has ethical consequences, and our responsibility does not stop at any one border. As we have seen, this responsibility can require that we resort to violence, despite our thereby running the risk of introducing even more evil into the world.

EVIL AS A CONCRETE PROBLEM

In my opinion, morality is *sui generis*: that is, we cannot define "good," "evil," and other moral ideas in terms of facts that are not themselves moral. We also don't actually require such a definition, but can take morality as a given. Our task in examining the problem of evil is not to create a new system of morals—where would we even begin?—but rather to insist on the relevance and worth of the morals we already have. These morals place us under clear obligations, and no matter what theoretical standpoint we take, it's indisputable that we have a duty to respect human worth, prevent suffering, etc. We can argue about the basis for human rights, but how many reasons do we really need before we realize that people shouldn't be murdered, maimed, tortured, etc.? We've all experienced pain and we can—at least partially—imagine what other human beings might be feeling. I agree with John Rawls that the practice and realization of the concept of rights is more a practical and social task than an epistemological or metaphysical problem.[654] It is less important whether the concept of rights are "true" than whether such a concept can form the basis for a logical discussion about how our social and political institutions can best serve human freedom and well-being.

In the political arena, therefore, pragmatists are better than idealists and we can regard politics as a form of social engineering. Karl Popper, for example, distinguishes between utopian and piecemeal social engineering as the model of social development.[655] According to his definition, a utopian social engineer wants to see society change all at once—existing society is seen as being in such miserable shape that gradual improvements won't save it. The old must be destroyed to make way for the new.

However, utopias and paradises are places for angels and saints—and we humans don't fall into either category. People are, as previously mentioned, fallible—they *fail*. In addition to fallibility, human life is characterized by a pluralism of values, by the pursuit of goals that are not only dissimilar, but that are also often incompatible. Because people have different values and ideals, every society will contain a mixture of these. In light of this, a true utopia can only be realized through mass oppression. Utopia presupposes that all conflicts cease to exist, because the entire society is organized according to the conception of a good life shared by absolutely everyone.

Utopias, therefore, can't survive if they contain either fallibility or pluralism. Instead of trying to realize a version of utopia, we should try to encourage a peaceful shared existence for groups and individuals with different and possibly incompatible concepts of the good life, so long as it is presupposed that certain moral requirements are met. I give Popper my full support when he writes:

"Work for the elimination of concrete evils rather than for the realization of abstract goods. Do not aim at establishing happiness by political means. Rather aim at the elimination of concrete miseries."[656]

Those who embrace the opposite of utopian social engineering, namely piecemeal social engineering, can also have ideals, but they will always be prepared to revise their ideals, to make compromises when they see that the human cost for realizing their ideals is too high. There's no room for compromises among utopian engineers. That is, the goal of advancing a society where people can flourish is so attractive that no price seems too high for its realization. As Popper also asserts, however: Those who try to realize heaven on earth will only succeed in making earth into hell.

In other words, we should proceed negatively, rather than try to realize grand positive visions. Much concrete good can be done to work against poverty, sickness, discrimination, torture, war, etc. In fact, there are far fewer differences of opinion between people regarding what's evil than what's good; ethics has a far greater consensus on its negative, rather than on its positive side. Therefore, the identification of evil and the agreement that evil must be fought can largely be attained no matter what ethical and meta-ethical position one takes. As Stuart Hampshire argues: "There is nothing mysterious or 'subjective' or culture-bound in the great evils of human experience, re-affirmed in every age and in every written history and in every tragedy and fiction: murder and the destruction of life, imprisonment, enslavement, starvation, poverty, physical pain and torture, homelessness, friendlessness."[657] We don't need a theory to tell us that these evils are evil—and every theory that concludes that these evils are not in fact evil will be wrong. As I've said time and again, such evils must be fought. This is the basic presupposition behind every known moral stance, and ought to be one for all political stances as well. Though different concepts of the good can lead to different priorities in the struggle against evil, all people agree on one thing: these evils, and others like them, must be opposed. What matters now is finally doing it.

CONCLUSION

Evil is not merely a theoretical problem: it's a highly practical one. All our countless theoretical blind spots serve only to prevent us from arriving at one simple insight: Evil is not primarily a subject for theology, the natural or social sciences, or even philosophy, but a concrete problem that must be addressed in the moral and political arena. We cannot understand and fight evil as long as we consider it to be an abstract concept external to ourselves.

Theology, and especially theodicies, attempt to salvage the idea of a good, almighty God, but this attempt mostly results in a failure to recognize the reality of evil. Since everything from a divine perspective is "actually" good, or will be transformed into good, evil's reality is *explained away*. However, our task is not merely *to come to terms* with evil. Instead, we're actively called upon to do something about it. This, among other things, is the reason I believe that theodicies are themselves evil. They lead us to accept evil's existence passively.

The most important question is not, "What is evil?" but rather: "Why do we do it?" The answer is that we do evil for a number of different reasons, and we all have a variety of motives—but one reason we can be certain is *not* among these is *because* it's evil. This "pure" form of evil, "demonic" evil, should be dismissed as a myth. And yet, demonic evil is often regarded as evil's fundamental form. The problem with considering evil in this light, however, is that it makes the phenomenon appear external to ourselves: do you see yourself as a demon? The problem, then, with focusing on demonic evil is not theoretical, but practical. It hinders the realization that every single one of us has the capacity to do evil.

More to the point, we often do evil, well aware that it's evil, because we want to realize a subjective good. The instrumental evil agent understands the difference between good and evil, but sets good aside in favor of their own self interest. However, instrumental evil can only explain some of our evil actions. We must also take idealistic and stupid evil into account, where agents are either motivated by the *idea* of an objective good or else fail to reflect on whether their actions are good or evil in the first place. But, without exception, we are all evil. We have all done evil in one of the aforementioned forms, even if we don't always recognize our actions as evil. Most of us have only done evil on a small scale, but all of us could have done evil on a much larger scale. It's not only "others" who are evil. It's *we* who are evil.

Our basic problem isn't a surplus of aggression. Instead, it's a lack of reflection. This lack leads people to accept and even participate in the most lunatic transgressions imaginable against their fellow men. Pure egotism is a motivating factor in far fewer murders and assaults than an unreflective, unselfish surrender to a "higher" purpose. However, simple indifference results in even more victims—and not just the ones who are out of sight and, therefore, out of mind. Indifference, furthermore, is not just a factor in violent crimes, but is also a contributing factor to the reality that 1.2 billion people continue to live in extreme conditions of poverty, and likewise that several million people die of starvation every year. The evil in the world is not simply the sum of unjust actions committed by individuals against individuals, along with whatever natural catastrophes happen to be taken place. Evil can also be found in social institutions. Indeed, from this perspective, we could begin to talk about structural evil. John Rawls's "norm of justice" suggests that economic and social differences should be organized so that the worst situated receive the greatest advantage.[658] In my opinion, this should apply not only to the organization of individual societies, but globally as well. Rawls stops short of making a similar statement,[659] but he does agree that a just society should do far more to help other societies than Western politics allows for today. Evil is not simply one overarching problem, but rather a multitude of concrete problems—all those situations where our identity as free, active beings capable of reason and reflection is put to the test. Ultimately, it all comes down to what we decide to *do*.

Can we imagine a human world without evil? Since evil is *human*, I seriously doubt such a thing is conceivable. In this world, we may all be victims of evil, but we also inflict evil on others. There are many reasons for this, not least being that we are moral creatures, and therefore tend to divide everything we see in the world into good and evil—whatever threatens or harms us is labeled evil. We want to make the earth a habitable place, and therefore reflect on how to can gain *control* of evil. We're always on the lookout for evil, and when there's no immediate threat, we often try to go out and get a jump on it. We localize evil so that we can fight it, and often imagine that we must be good since we're fighting the good fight.

Humanism was founded on the idea that people should overcome their animal nature. In short, that *homo humanus* should overcome *homo barbarus*. But is *homo humanus* any less barbaric than *homo barbarus*? It seems to me that *homo humanus* has never quite overcome his animal nature, and has simply invented new outlets for barbarism.

Perhaps we can say finally say that humanity itself is the root of all evil. Animals can't be evil—only us. Despite the attempts of the Enlightenment and humanism to find a different culprit, the short answer to the question concerning the origins of evil remains this: evil exists because people are free. To be free, moral agents necessarily implies that we are both good *and* evil. This does not imply, however, that we are all good and evil to the same degree. And it certainly does not imply that the *amount* of evil in the world will always be the same.

So what is the solution? The most dangerous response is the belief that if only we localize and exterminate the world's "forces of evil," evil might be eradicated once and for all. In that case, however, we overlook Alexander Solzhenitsyn's observation that the line dividing good and evil doesn't run through different groups—nations, classes, or political parties—but "right through every human heart." Personally, the only solution I see to the problem of evil is a continuation of a humanist project, of Enlightenment thinking. This won't eradicate the evil in the world, but at least offers us the hope that it might be limited.

NOTES

1   Cf. Schuller and Rahden (eds.): *Die andere Kraft: Zur Renaissance des Bösen*. In these notes, the sources are cited by the author's last name, the work's title and the page number. For a more complete citation, see the biography at the end of the book.

2   This is a notable trend in the titles of several anthologies that have come out in the last few years. For instance, Häring and Tracy (eds.): *The Fascination of Evil* and Liessmann (ed.): *Faszination des Bösen: Über die Abgründe des Menschlichen*.

3   This is obviously nothing new, and our present fascination with evil clearly has its roots in the Romantic. For more on this subject, see Davenport: *Gothic: 400 Years of Excess, Horror, Evil and Ruin*; Gillespie: *Nihilism Before Nietzsche*, especially chapter 4; Russell: *Mephistopheles*, especially chap. 5; Bohrer: *Nach der Natur*.

4   Weil: *Gravity and Grace*, p. 70.

5   Oscar Wilde writes about how art expresses reality—that is, life—but in a tame form that prevents us from hurting ourselves. Therefore we must turn to art—not life—for all our adventures and experiences: "Because Art does not hurt us. The tears we shed at a play are a type of the exquisite sterile emotions that it is the function of Art to awaken. We weep, but we are not wounded . . . But the sorrow with which Art fills us both purifies and initiates . . . [It] is through Art, and through Art only, that we can shield ourselves from the sordid perils of actual existence" (Wilde: *Complete Works*, p. 173). Art, therefore, becomes a defense against life's burdens, and

aestheticism becomes *escapism*. In my opinion, this describes *all* aestheticism—and Wilde himself develops a critique against such aestheticism in his later works, especially *The Picture of Dorian Gray* and *De profundis*.

6   The term "sadism" is used in this book in association with abuse, not consensual sexual intercourse.

7   Cited in Masters: *The Evil That Men Do*, p. 179.

8   For example, I was unable to cover Schelling's speculative theory about evil in his work *Philosophical Inquiries into the Nature of Human Freedom* from 1809. In my opinion, Schelling's discussion is one of the most difficult works in the history of philosophy, and even a short paraphrase would have taken up too much space. Nor I have devoted much space to psychoanalytical theory. (For an excellent study of evil within a psychoanalytical framework, see Alford: *What Evil Means to Us*.) The main reason for this is that I'm skeptical of psychoanalytical theories in general—but this is not the place for a systematic outline of what I perceive to be the weaker points of the field.

9   For those who are interested in an overview of representations of the Devil from antiquity until today, I suggest Jeffrey Burton Russell's four volume work *The Devil: Perceptions of Evil from Antiquity to Primitive Christianity*; *Satan: The Early Christian Tradition*; *Lucifer: The Devil in the Middle Ages*; and *Mephistopheles: The Devil in the Modern World*. Russell has also published a more popular discussion of the four volumes' main thesis in *The Prince of Darkness: Radical Evil and Power of Good in History*. However, Russell's study is strongly influenced by the fact that he himself seems to believe in the Devil (see especially *Mephistopheles*, p. 251, 296–301). Still, the study mainly restricts itself to a reiteration of the historical changes that have taken place in the representation

of the Devil over time. For an excellent discussion of the history of the Antichrist, see McGinn: *Antichrist.*

10   Cf. Kittsteiner: "Die Abschaffung des Teufels im 18. Jahrhundert."

11   Ricoeur: *Fallible Man*, p. xlvi.

12   For an overview of how evil is understood in different cultures, see Parkin (ed.): *The Anthropology of Evil.* For a discussion of the way evil appears in different world religions, see Cenkner (ed.): *Evil and the Response of World Religion.*

13   Blake: "A Divine Image," in *The Complete Poetry and Prose of William Blake*, p. 32.

14   Mann: "The Problem of Freedom."

15   Cioran: *Drawn and Quartered*, p. 110.

16   Delbanco: *The Death of Satan*, p. 3.

17   Baudrillard: *The Transparency of Evil*, p. 81.

18   Andersen: "The Snow Queen," pp. 175–206. The similarity between Baudrillard's world-view and Andersen's "The Snow Queen" is only a partial one. In the fairy tale, those who get a splinter of the devil's mirror in their eye only *perceive* everything that is good and beautiful as evil and corrupt. According to Andersen, that is, it is only *as if* evil and corruption were found everywhere. On the other hand, Baudrillard believes that evil really *is* found everywhere.

19   Baudrillard: *The Transparency of Evil*, p. 81, 85.

20   Baudrillard: *Fatal Strategies*, p. 7.

21   Ibid., p. 77.

22   Delbanco: *The Death of Satan*, p. 9.

23   Ricoeur: *The Symbolism of Evil.*

24   Ibid., p. 350.

25   Rosenbaum: *Explaining Hitler*, p. xxi.

26   Ibid., p. 87.

27   Gauchet: *The Disenchantment of the World*, p. 168.

28   Wright: *The Moral Animal*, p. 368.

29   Watson: *Dark Nature*, p. 86.

30   Dostoevsky: "Environment," p. 136.

31   Harris: *The Silence of the Lambs*, p. 19.

32   Cf. Midgley: *Wickedness: A Philosophical Essay*, p. 49.

33   Morris: "The Plot of Suffering: AIDS and Evil." Morris points to Levinas as an example of this idea, and some of Levinas's works do support this interpretation (cf. Levinas: "Useless Suffering"), but Levinas also describes evil as a responsibility persisting despite its refusal of responsibility to the Other (Levinas: *Humanism of the Other*, p. 56). In general, Morris's observation is true, but it's not necessarily correct to use Levinas as a typical representative of this conception of evil, since Levinas also upholds the dimension of personal responsibility.

34   For an example of this viewpoint, see Plack: *Die Gesellschaft und das Böse*.

35   Marquard: *Apologie des Zufälligens*, pp. 21ff.

36   See Rosenbaum: *Exploring Hitler* for a critical overview of the different explanations.

37   Shakespeare: *Hamlet*, II.ii.

38   The central reactions from intellectuals alive at the time (Voltaire, Rousseau, Kant etc.) to the earthquake in Lisbon are collected in Breidert (ed.): *Die Erschütterung der vollkommenen Welt*.

39   Novalis: *Pollen*, in *The Early Political Writings of the German Romantics*, p. 9.

40   Gaita: *A Common Humanity*, p. 39.

41   Ricoeur: *The Conflict of Interpretations*, p. 303.

42   Levinas: *Of God Who Comes to Mind*, p. 128.

43   Cf. Ricoeur: *Fallible Man*, p. 4.

44   Heidegger's remarks on evil are nowhere assembled in his works into a systematic presentation, but he repeatedly returns to a statement of the problem. As far as I know, the one comprehensive account of Heidegger's reflections on evil is Irlenborn: *Der Ingrimm des Aufruhrs: Heidegger und das Problem des Bösen*. This study is marked by the same incomprehensibility that characterizes so much of the commentary on Heidegger, and so is not recommended for readers who do not have a comparatively solid knowledge of both Heidegger's earlier and later philosophy.

45   Cf. Heidegger: *Being and Time*, p. 331f; *Hölderlins Hymne, "Andenken,"* p. 102; *Hölderlin's Hymn "The Ister,"* pp. 78f.

46   Cf. Heidegger: *Contributions to Philosophy (From Enowing)*, pp. 81f.

47   See especially Heidegger's reflections on evil in Heidegger: *Feldweg-Gespräche*.

48   My discussion of Heidegger in *The Philosophy of Boredom*, pp. 131f., should provide a glimpse of the direction such a critique would take, namely criticizing Heidegger for a false ontologicalization of evil that causes him to overlook all concrete evils in favor of an essential force, Being, which he is not able to convincingly legitimate.

49   A representative selection of articles from this tradition can be found in Adams and Adams (eds.): *The Problem of Evil*.

50   Cf. Robertson: *Crimes Against Humanity*, p. 454.

51   Cf. Glover: *Humanity*, p. 47.

52   Leyhausen: *Krieg oder Frieden*, p. 61.

53   Watson: *Dark Nature*, p. 160.

54   Hobbes: *De Cive*, pp. 58f.

55   Augustine: *City of God*, book XIX. 4.

56   Trevor-Roper: *The European Witch-Craze of the Sixteenth and Seventeenth Centuries*, pp. 38f.

57   For an excellent discussion of the arguments for and against the thesis of uniqueness, see Brecher: "Understanding the Holocaust: The Uniqueness Debate."

58   Adorno: *Negative Dialectics*, p. 365.

59   Adorno: *Minima Moralia*, p. 65.

60   Cf. Naimark: *Fires of Hatred*, pp. 40f, 57f.

61   Cf. Hochschild: *King Leopold's Ghost*, p. 233.

62   Ibid., p. 224.

63   Sixty years before it assumed a central place in the Nürnberg Process, this expression was used by the historian George Washington Williams to describe the situation in the Congo.

64   Seen in this way, Belgium's actions in the Congo are more reminiscent of the German slaughter of the African Hereros: When the Hereros revolted against Germany in 1904, Lieutenant General Lothar von Trotha gave the order that *every* Herero found on German territory should be shot. Over a couple of years, seventy-five percent of the Hereros—that is, about 60,000 people—on Germany territory had been exterminated (cf. Pakenham: *The Scramble for Africa*, p. 611). In both of these cases, evil can primarily be considered to be *instrumental.*

65   Cf. Gourevitch: *We Wish to Inform You That Tomorrow We Will Be Killed With Our Families*, p. 3. Gourevitch's book is exceptionally well written, but also rather journalistic. A more solid and well-documented work on the genocide in Rwanda is des Forges: *Leave None to Tell the Story.*

66   Tzvetan Todorov: *Facing the Extreme*, p. 134.

67   Courtois et. al.: *The Black Book of Communism.*

68   Cf. Glover: *Humanity*, p. 297.

69   Cited in Anissimov: *Primo Levi*, p. 1, 181.

70   For an overview of different variations on the evidential argument, see Howard-Snyder (ed.): *The Evidential Argument from Evil*.

71   In my opinion, the most convincing statement of the logical argument is put forth by John Mackie in the article "Evil and Omnipotence" (Mackie's article appears in a number of anthologies, among others in Adams and Adams (eds.): *The Problem of Evil*). For a more comprehensive thematisation, see also Mackie: *The Miracle of Theism*.

72   A letter to Nikojaj Aleksejevitsj Ljubimov May 10, 1879, in Dostoevsky: *Selected Letters*, p. 465.

73   Dostoevsky: *The Brothers Karamazov*, pp. 315f.

74   Ibid., p. 317.

75   Ibid., p. 323.

76   Ibid p. 326. Dostoevsky also uses this example in "Pushkin (a Sketch)," p. 1287.

77   Heraclitus: *Fragments*, p. 39.

78   Plato: *The Republic*, 617e.

79   Plato: *Timaeus*, 29–30.

80   Lactantius: *The Wrath of God*.

81   Cf. Blumenthal: "Theodicy: Dissonance in Theory and Practice."

82   I do not discuss the so-called aesthetic argument here, because it's hardly convincing. The argument claims that good becomes more valuable when contrasted with evil. For example, Augustine (*City of God*, book XI.18) writes that the world's splendor would be diminished if good were not contrasted with evil. This thought is later found in Descartes (*Meditations*, fourth meditation) and Leibniz (*Theodicy*, § 214), but does not play a central role in either of them. The aesthetic argument fails because an *aesthetic* effect is not a good *moral* reason to allow suffering. This

claim is a categorical fallacy. The aesthetic argument is also untenable if we judge God as an individual. If God can inflict suffering on humanity for the sake of beautifying the world, we should be able do the same. In contrast, if it's not permissible for an individual to use aesthetics to justify inflicting suffering on another, it certainly should not be permissible for God.

83   Augustine: *Confessions*, VII.12–16.

84   Descartes: *Meditations on First Philosophy*, fourth meditation, pp. 45f.

85   Plotinus: *The Enneads*, p. 76.

86   See Augustine: *The Nature of the Good*, chap. 17 in *The Essential Augustine*, p. 49.

87   Augustine: *City of God*, book XI. 22.

88   Augustine: *The Nature of the Good*, chap. 4.

89   Pseudo-Dionysius has perhaps given the theory its most radical formulation in *On the Divine Names*. He writes that evil is neither being, nor *of* being, nor *in* being. In other words, evil has no existence whatsoever. For Pseudo-Dionysius, evil can only be described negatively, as non-being, non-beautiful, non-living, non-reasoning, etc. The privation theory can hardly find a more extreme representation that it does in Pseudo-Dionysius.

90   For example, Ralph Waldo Emerson was still insisting on the privation theory in an address from 1838 ("An Address," in *The Essential Writings of Ralph Waldo Emerson*, p. 65), though in Emerson's time its role was already diminishing. Emerson argues in a classical way that evil reduces itself, and this is the punishment for evil. (This justification is further developed by Emerson in "Compensation," in *The Essential Writings of Ralph Waldo Emerson*, pp. 154ff.) There are also a few later privation theorists. For example, in *Wickedness*, Mary Midgley explicitly locates her discussion of

evil in a privation theoretical framework, describing evil as purely negative, stripped of its own positivity.

91   Plato, *The Republic*, 397c.

92   Ibid., 617e.

93   Ibid., 391e, 619c.

94   Augustine: *City of God*, book XII. 6.

95   Augustine bases his doctrine of original sin on *Romans* 5:12, but today there is widespread agreement that the doctrine hinges on a mistake in translation that is not found in the original Greek text.

96   Genesis, 3:22.

97   Romans, 5:18.

98   Aquinas: *Summa Theologica*, I, 48, 2, 3.

99   Swinburne: *The Existence of God*, p. 200.

100   Mark 10:27, Luke 1:37, Genesis 18:14, Jeremiah 32:17, 27, Job 42:2.

101   Cf. Mackie: "Evil and Omnipotence."

102   There are other suggested solutions to the problem of natural evil. According to Swinburne, the free-will argument not only functions as a justification for the existence of moral evil, but also for natural (Swinburne: "Natural Evil"). The reason he gives is that natural evil must exist to give human beings the knowledge necessary to bring about moral evil. Here we could object that, in the first place, an almighty God could simply have given man the necessary knowledge without forcing him to take lessons from natural evil, and, in the second place, that man can learn more than enough from the moral evil he himself causes (cf. Stump: "Knowledge, Freedom, and the Problem of Evil"). Swinburne's argument further postulates that the free-will argument is a valid explanation of moral evil, but this is, as I've said, doubtful. On the other

hand, Alvin Plantinga argues that fallen angels rather than God are responsible for natural evil (Plantinga: *The Nature of Necessity*, p. 192). This is an argument that could well have been relevant in a historical epoch other than our own. However, as John Mackie makes clear, this idea is an arbitrary *ad hoc* solution, since we have no knowledge of such beings. In the best case, fallen angels form part of the religious hypothesis under discussion, and there's no independent reason to allude to them (Mackie: *The Miracle of Theism*, pp. 126f.).

103   John Keats: "To George and Georgina Keats, February 14 to May 8, 1819," p. 249.

104   Keat's phrase has become the slogan for the modern version of Irenaean theology, represented among others by John Hick. See especially Hick: *Evil and the God of Love*.

105   Weil: *Gravity and Grace*, p. 27.

106   Ibid., p. 81.

107   Ibid., p. 145.

108   Ibid., pp. 75f.

109   Marilyn McCord Adams later developed a concept of suffering very similar to that of Weil's, where suffering enables a mystical unity with God, whether or not the sufferer acknowledges it (Adams: *Horrendous Evils and the Goodness of God*, see especially chap. 8.)

110   Cioran: *On the Heights of Despair*, p. 109.

111   Amis: *London Fields*, p. 348.

112   Cf. Scarry: *The Body in Pain*.

113   Ibid., p. 34.

114   Camus: *The Plague*, p. 214.

115   Ibid., pp. 223ff.

116   Ibid., p. 226.

117 For a convincing formulation of this argument, see Rowe: "The Problem of Evil and Some Varieties of Atheism."

118 Hick: *Evil and the God of Love*, p. 330.

119 Plato: *Timaeus*, 29–30.

120 Augustine: *Confessions*, book 5.8.

121 Ibid., book 7.12–13. See Augustine: *Enchiridion*, chap. 10, in *The Essential Augustine*, p. 65.

122 Augustine: *City of God*, book XII.8.

123 Ibid., book I.29. There is no limit to the extremes Augustine will go in order to explain that absolutely everything must ultimately be regarded as good. One of his examples is: If a virgin is raped, it helps to destroy her actual or possible pride or arrogance, and therefore the act has an element of good in it (ibid., book 1. 28). And if a christened baby, the most innocent thing in the whole Augustinian universe, suffers greatly, it helps to teach us something about earthly life and makes us to long for God in His Heavenly kingdom (ibid., book XXII.22).

124 Boethius: *Consolation of Philosophy*, book IV.6.

125 Pope: *An Essay on Man*, book I, line 291f.

126 Rousseau: "Letter from J.-J. Rousseau to Mr. de Voltaire, August 18, 1756," p. 213.

127 Milton: *Paradise Lost*, book I, line 26, p. 3.

128 Ibid., book XII, line 469–73, p. 283.

129 Spinoza: *The Ethics*, 4P64.

130 Spinoza: *Letter to William Blyenbergh*, January 1665, pp. 238f.

131 Cf. Russell: *Mephistopheles*, pp. 37ff.

132 Goethe: *Faust*, p. 159, verse 1336f.

133 Correspondingly, Novalis sees suffering and sickness as means toward "a higher synthesis" (Novalis: *Notes for a Romantic Encyclopaedia*).

134   Leibniz: *Theodicy*, § 21.

135   Ibid., § 20, 153.

136   Ibid., § 8, 9.

137   Ibid., § 9, 23, 24.

138   Ibid., § 121.

139   Ibid., § 130.

140   Leibniz also has other arguments. Among these is the assertion that there is not as much evil in the world as people suppose (ibid., § 220), and that God couldn't have shaped human beings as creatures of reason without allowing physical and moral evil (ibid., § 52, 119). The ultimate source of all evil is metaphysical evil, but man's free will is the direct cause of moral evil and therefore man is to blame for all of it (ibid., § 273, 288, 319). At the same time, the world is completely justified; therefore, we can trust that every unjust evil inflicted upon us by other people will be followed by at least the same amount of good (ibid., § 241).

141   Mackie: "Evil and Omnipotence."

142   See Marilyn McCord Adams's discussion of "horrendous evils" that inflict such suffering they transform a whole human life into something that's not worth living (Adams: *Horrendous Evils and the Goodness of God*, p. 26).

143   Cited in Rapp: *Fortschritt*, p. 159.

144   Hegel: *The Philosophy of History*, p. 15, 25.

145   Cf. Pauen: *Pessimismus*, p. 11.

146   Cf. Rapp: *Fortschritt*, p. 144.

147   Voltaire: *Candide*, p. 12.

148   Ibid., p. 52.

149   It may seen strange that I cite Kant in a discussion concerning theodicy, especially because he claims in a famous article that all philosophical theodicies must necessarily fail (Kant: "On

the Miscarriage of All Philosophical Trials in Theodicy"), but this is only true, he implies, of theodicies that are strictly theoretical. In fact, Kant develops a form of theodicy in both his moral philosophy—for example in the postulates on practical reason (Kant: *Critique of Practical Reason*) and in his philosophy of history. I limit my discussion here to the philosophy of history, but it should be noted that the subject is closely tied to Kant's moral philosophy, since theodicy in Kant changes from "natural theology" to "ethical theology" (cf. Kant: *Critique of Judgment* pp. 219–227).

150   Kant: "Conjectural Beginning of Human History," in *Toward Perpetual Peace and Other Writings*, p. 36.

151   Kant: "On the Common Saying: 'This May Be True in Theory, But It Does Not Apply in Praxis,'" in *Political Writings*, p. 90.

152   Kant: "Idea for a Universal History from a Cosmopolitan Perspective," in *Toward Perpetual Peace and Other Writings*, pp. 6f.

153   Kant: *Critique of Judgment*, p. 211.

154   Kant: "Idea for a Universal History from a Cosmopolitan Perspective," in *Toward Perpetual Peace and Other Writings*, pp. 7f.

155   Kant: *Anthropology from a Pragmatic Point of View* in *Anthropology, History and Education*, p. 338.

156   Kant: "Conjectural Beginning of Human History," in *Toward Perpetual Peace and Other Writings*, pp. 29f.

157   Kant: *Toward Perpetual Peace*, in *Toward Perpetual Peace and Other Writings*, pp. 102f.

158   A problem with the whole *tendency* in Kant's thought comes from his idea that it is through humanity's enlightenment and autonomy that the good will be realized, while, at the same time, Kant denies that man's intentions will play any substantial role in the realization of this goal on a global scale, and instead leaves this

task to nature's design. We can imagine three possibilities with regard to the relationship between man's intentional actions and history's progress: (1) the two function completely independent of the other, (2) history is driven by its own engine and human enlightenment is a product of history, or (3) human enlightenment propels history toward a realization of the ideal life. The whole tendency in Kant's thinking speaks for (3), but it's nonetheless (2) that Kant embraces. Humanity is placed in a situation whose outcome was established beforehand, independent of what you and I might choose to do. In *Critique of Judgment* (§83), however, we find a slightly different viewpoint. Instead of regarding the progress of history as something originating in a more or less mechanically functioning natural law, the perspective changes. Progress is now understood as a byproduct of humanity. Of course, nature still plays an essential role, but the understanding of nature has evolved away from what we might call natural history, resituating it as an element somewhere between the natural world and freedom. Nature "acts" to stimulate progress toward an ever more cultivated and civilized (though not necessarily moral) world order. However, in being thus stimulated, man is perfected along the way; he becomes capable, to a larger and larger degree, of taking destiny into his own hands. We can perhaps sum up this idea in the following way: Nature drives humanity toward enlightenment, and after that we're in a position to take control. Nature has a plan for humanity, but the enlightened individual understands this plan and aids in its realization.

159   Kant: "Reviews of Herder's Ideas on the Philosophy of the History of Mankind," in *Political Writings*, p. 220; cf. Kant: "Conjectural Beginnings of Human History," in *Toward Perpetual Peace and Other Writings*, p. 36; Kant: *Toward Perpetual Peace* p. 92.

160   Cf. Kant: "Idea for a Universal History from a Cosmopolitan Perspective," in *Perpetual Peace and Other Writings*, pp. 122f.

161   Hegel: *The Philosophy of History*, p. 33.

162   Ibid., p. 15. Hegel concludes the essay on the philosophy of history by repeating the idea that the recognition of world history as the spirit's actualization is the only true theodicy (ibid., p. 457).

163   Ibid., p. 33.

164   Herder: *Another Philosophy of History for the Education of Mankind*, p. 88.

165   Hegel: *The Philosophy of History*, p. 21.

166   Ibid., p. 37.

167   Ibid., pp. 66f.

168   Cf. Hollander: "Revisiting the Banality of Evil: Political Violence in Communist Systems," p. 56.

169   Cf. Getty and Naumov: *The Road to Terror*.

170   Cf. Pauen: *Pessimismus*, p. 31.

171   Schopenhauer: *The World as Will and Representation*, p. 325; *Parerga and Paralipomena II*, p. 368.

172   Schopenhauer: *The World as Will and Representation*, p. 326.

173   Ibid., *The World as Will and Representation: Volume 2*, p. 643.

174   Ibid., p. 583.

175   Cf. Lacroix: *Das Böse*, p. 77.

176   This inverted theodicy receives a clear expression in Giacomo Leopardi, who claims that all happiness is either deceitful or illusionary (Leopardi: *The Canti*, p. 65). In reality, everything is rooted in evil, even though at times it can seem otherwise. Existence itself is evil, and true happiness can only be found in nonexistence.

177   Nietzsche: *On the Genealogy of Morals*, p. 19.

178   Nietzsche, *Nachgelassene Fragmente* 1884–1885, pp. 625f.

179   Nietzsche, *On the Genealogy of Morals*, p. 49.

180   Nietzsche, *Writings from the Late Notebooks*, p. 180.

181   Nietzsche, *Beyond Good and Evil*, § 225.

182   Nietzsche: *Beyond Good and Evil*, § 270.

183   Airaksinen: *The Philosophy of the Marquis de Sade*, p. 5.

184   Sade: *Justine*, p. 458.

185   Ibid., p. 481.

186   Ibid., pp. 481f, cf. pp. 128ff. This espousal of an evil providence is purely rhetorical, for there is no place for a metaphysical concept such as providence in Sade's worldview. His universe is a cold machine where all bodies are mechanical, in keeping with La Mettrie's *Man a Machine*—a Cartesian concept without any *res cogitans*. Everything can be quantified. Because every qualitative difference disappears, all moral difference disappears as well. The fact that a human being has qualities that an insect lacks is irrelevant: mass is mass. The essential quality of action is the size of the organs, the number of sexual acts, partners, and orifices, the amount of sperm and blood and the number of victims. Quantity is the same as intensity and therefore also as quality. For Sade, quantity is the only quality. The human body, both your own and that of another, is raw material that should be used, and its pleasure is directly proportional to its consumption.

187   Kant: *Metaphysics of Morals* in *Practical Philosophy*, p. 473.

188   Job 40:8f.

189   Of course, Hobbes agrees with God and says that God is just precisely *because* he's so powerful. (Hobbes: *Leviathan*, chap. 31, p. 246.)

190   Ecclesiastes 9:16.

191   Job 28:12.

192   Job 28:28.

193   Job 42:7.

194   Cf. Acts 10:34, Romans 2:11; Galatians 2:6.

195   Ecclesiastes 7:15.

196   Mark 10:18, Matthew 19:17, Luke 18:19.

197   Calvin: *The Institutes of the Christian Religion*, p. 141.

198   Mill: *An Examination of Sir William Hamilton's Philosophy*, pp. 273f.

199   Jaspers: *Von der Wahrheit*, p. 533.

200   Plato, *The Republic*, 392b.

201   Cf. Lerner: *The Belief in a Just World: A Fundamental Delusion*.

202   Cf. Ferry: *Man made God*.

203   Cf. Gauchet: *The Disenchantment of the World*, p. 199.

204   Lyotard: *The Postmodern Condition*.

205   Delbanco: *The Death of Satan*, p. 143.

206   Ricoeur: *The Conflict of Interpretations*, p. 301.

207   Genesis 6:5; cf. Ecclesiastes 9:3.

208   Genesis 8:21.

209   Machiavelli: *Discourses*, book 1, chap. 3.

210   Hobbes: *Leviathan*, chap. 13.

211   Machiavelli wants to cancel out evil with evil. Instead of being a victim of evil, he decides to actually do evil. According to Machiavelli, the weakest position is somewhere between good and evil, and a person should choose to be wholly good or wholly evil (*Discourses*, book I, chap. 26). However, because people are essentially evil, goodness will ultimately result in self-annihilation. The only true alternative is to opt for the greatest evil possible, because paradoxically this choice will limit evil. This idea is not relevant to all spheres of life, of course, but a prince must be ready to exercise maximum brutality when the situation requires it. Machiavelli's whole political philosophy can be summed up in the cliché

that violence is always the best answer. It's also worth noting that Machiavelli's whole political philosophy is structured around his anthropology.

212 Montaigne: "On Cruelty," p. 182.

213 Lautréamont: *Maldoror*, p. 31.

214 Melville: *Billy Budd*, p. 326. See also the following description of Claggart: "With no power to annul the elemental evil in him, tho' readily enough he could hide it; a nature like Claggart's surcharged with energy as such natures almost invariably are, what recourse is left to it but to recoil upon itself and [. . .] act out to the end the part allotted it." Ibid., p. 328.

215 Rousseau: *Emile*, pp. 39f.

216 Rousseau: *On the Origin of Inequality*, p. 115.

217 Ibid., p. 109.

218 Rousseau: *Emile*, p. 67.

219 Ibid., p. 282.

220 Ibid., p. 67.

221 Ibid., pp. 104f.

222 Cf. Grant: *Hypocrisy and Integrity* and Bloom: "Introduction," pp. 12f.

223 The following story about the wild boy of Aveyron is taken from Masters: *The Evil That Men Do*, pp. 4ff., 31f., 67, 203.

224 Rousseau, for that matter, knew about several cases of children who grew up without human contact, who were fostered by wolves or the like, but he didn't explicitly use these examples in his discussion of the natural man. (Cf. Rousseau: *A Discourse on Inequality*, p. 140n.)

225 Cf. Gelven: *The Risk of Being*, pp. 162f.

226 No one only does good or only does evil. Dennis Nilsen, one of Great Britain's worst serial killers, helped some of the young men he lured to his home, who were often destitute—feeding

them and sending them on their way. Others, however, he murdered. In 1970, Ted Bundy saved a three year-old from drowning (cf. Masters: *The Evil That Men Do*, pp. 10f.) In this context, we can also mention Quisling, who helped to save thousands of Ukranian Jews from starvation in the 1920s. Nonetheless, he was responsible for the deportation of a third of the Norwegian Jews in 1942 and 1943.

227 Schelling: *Philosophical Investigations into the Essence of Human Freedom*, p. 23.

228 Cf. Nancy: *The Experience of Freedom*, p. 135.

229 Alford: *What Evil Means to Us*, p. 32.

230 Ibid., p. 142.

231 Leibniz: *Theodicy*, § 21.

232 Hick: *Evil and the God of Love*, p. 21.

233 Griffin: *God, Power and Evil*, pp. 27f.

234 Aquinas: *Summa Theologica*, I–II, 92.

235 See the documents collected in Getty and Naumov: *The Road to Terror*.

236 In my opinion, Hitler represented an extreme form of this type of evil, because he was convinced that his ideology, and the actions legitimated by his ideology, was entirely just. In Hitler's eyes, the National Socialist movement represented the good.

237 Cf. Baumeister: *Evil: Inside Human Violence and Cruelty*, chap. 6.

238 Kant: *Reflexion* 6900.

239 Cf. Baumeister: *Evil: Inside Human Violence and Cruelty*, chaps. 1 and 2.

240 For more on this gap, see ibid., pp. 18f.

241 Conroy: *Unspeakable Acts, Ordinary People*, p. 88.

242 Cf. Katz: *Seductions of Crime*, pp. 5ff. Also see Sofsky: *Traktat über die Gewalt*, chaps. 5 and 10.

243   Though it should be noted here that most soldiers do *not* shoot at the enemy. Only as high as between fifteen and twenty-five percent of American troops shot at enemy positions or personnel during the Second World War, even though around eighty percent of them had the opportunity to do so (Bourke: *An Intimate History of Killing*, p. 75). There's reason to believe that the corresponding figures for soldiers during the First World War are even lower. Such ineffectiveness was considered unacceptable, so the United States revised its military training methods in an effort to create more efficient killing machines. The marines especially upped the brutality of their training process—employing, among other things, depersonalization, destruction of all privacy, unilateral induction into a group mentality at the cost of individuality, extreme physical stress, harsh punishments, forced lack of sleep, strict emphasis on the absolute necessity of following orders no matter how absurd they might seem, etc. That the same men who went on to receive this kind of "education" turned around and carried out the massacre in My Lai shouldn't have come as a surprise to anyone. We should mention too that bayonet training is still included in such training, not because bayonets are an especially common weapon—they made up only one percent of all the weapons used in both world wars, and today only form about a thousandth of a percentile—but because they desensitize soldiers (ibid., pp. 89–93, 153). People capable of killing other people with a bayonet will presumably have fewer qualms about killing a person from a greater distance.

244   Bourke: *An Intimate History of Killing*, chap. 1.

245   Cited in ibid., p. 31.

246   Cited in Glover: *Humanity*, pp. 54f.

247   Bourke: *An Intimate History of Killing*, pp. 356f.

248   Cf. Norris: *Serial Killers*, p. 32.

249   Jack Katz lists a number of such cases in *Seductions of Crime*, chap. 8.

250   Montaigne: "On Cruelty," p. 181.

251   Schopenhauer: *The World as Will and Representation I*, p. 363.

252   Lang: *Act and Idea in the Nazi Genocide*, p. 29, 56.

253   Alford: *What Evil Means to Us*, p. 21.

254   Bataille: *Literature and Evil*, pp. 17f.

255   Kekes: *Facing Evil*, p. 126, 131.

256   McGinn: *Ethics, Evil and Fiction*, pp. 62ff., 82.

257   Ibid., pp. 65ff.

258   Rawls: *A Theory of Justice*, p. 439.

259   Augustine: *Confessions*, book 2.4 and 2.6.

260   Ibid., book 2.4.

261   Cf. Airaksinen: *The Philosophy of the Marquis de Sade*, p. 103.

262   Cited in ibid., p. 150.

263   Milton: *Paradise Lost*, book 4, line 111.

264   This idea is also found in Isaiah 14:12ff.

265   Milton: *Paradise Lost*, book 1, lines 159–162.

266   Ibid., book 4, line 957.

267   Poe: "The Black Cat," in *The Complete Illustrated Stories and Poems*, p. 237.

268   Poe: "The Imp of the Perverse," in *The Complete Illustrated Stories and Poems*, p. 441.

269   Ibid., p. 440.

270   Cf. Davidson: "How is Weakness of the Will Possible?," p. 42.

271   McGinn: *Ethics, Evil and Fiction*, p. 101.

272   In contrast to his mentor Hegel (cf. Hegel: *Hegel's Aesthetics: Lectures on Fine Art, Volume I*, pp. 221ff.). Karl Rosenkranz pointed out that the most evil can do is evoke aesthetic interest

(Rosenkranz: *Ästhetik des Häßlichen*, pp. 260–309) and this idea strongly influenced modernism.

273 Kant: *Critique of Judgment*, § 23, p. 62.

274 Ibid § 28, p. 76.

275 Cited in Oppenheimer: *Evil and the Demonic*, p. 79.

276 Soldiers' perception of the wars they take part in are shaped by the movies they've seen. Many express disappointment that war doesn't live up to the expectations created by the movies, while others claim they experienced the whole war as if it were a film. (Bourke: *An Intimate History of Killing*, pp. 26ff.)

277 Bjørnvig: *Den æstetiske idiosynkrasi*, p. 41. Translated by Kerri A. Pierce.

278 Poe: "The Tell-Tale Heart" in *The Complete Illustrated Stories and Poems*, p. 244.

279 Hamsun: "Fra det ubevidste Sjæleliv."

280 Melville: *Billy Budd*, see especially p. 327.

281 Lang: *Act and Idea in the Nazi Genocide*, p. 29, 56.

282 Cf. Walter Benjamin's remark that fascists aestheticize politics, while communists politicize art ("The Work of Art in the Age of Mechanical Reproduction," p. 242).

283 Nietzsche: *Writings from the Late Notebooks*, p. 180.

284 Genet: *The Thief's Journal*, p. 5.

285 Ibid., p. 162.

286 Ibid., p. 154.

287 Ibid., pp. 64, 174ff.

288 Ibid., pp. 14f.

289 Baudelaire: "Hymn to Beauty," in *Baudelaire*, p. 42.

290 Baudelaire: "To the Reader," in ibid., p. 13.

291 Cf. Alford: *What Evil Means to Us*, p. 32, 126.

292 I have analyzed *American Psycho* comparatively exhaustively in another context and shall not repeat my findings here. Instead,

I'll content myself with saying that we find the acknowledgment motivation well represented there. (Svendsen: *Philosophy of Boredom*, pp. 69–80.)

293   Morgenthau: "Love and Power."

294   McGinn: *Ethics, Evil and Fiction*, p. 80.

295   For a discussion of symbolic representations of evil, see Alford: *What Evil Means to Us*, pp. 12f., 44f., 113ff., 146f.

296   Plato: *Philebus*, 48b7.

297   McGinn: *Ethics, Evil and Fiction*, p. 66.

298   Arthur Schopenhauer: *The World as Will and Representation II*, p. 693; *Parerga and Paralipomena II*, p. 215; *On the Basis of Morality*, p. 156, 158.

299   Kant: *Metaphysics of Morals* in *Practical Philosophy*, p. 577.

300   Kant: *Lectures on Ethics*, pp. 197f., 420f.

301   For a broad philosophical thematisation of schadenfreude and its history, see Portmann: *When Bad Things Happen to Other People*.

302   Cf. Sofsky: *Traktat über die Gewalt*, pp. 119f.

303   Plato: *Protagoras*, 352a; cf. Plato: *Meno*, 88d, *Gorgias* 460b., 509e, Xenophon: *The Memorabilia*, book 3.9.

304   Plato *Protagoras* 352a–358d.

305   Plato: *The Republic* 439a–441c.

306   Aristotle: *The Nicomachean Ethics*, 1110b17.

307   Ibid., 1152a.

308   Ibid., book 7.8.

309   Ibid., 1079b.

310   Romans 7:19.

311   Sartre: *Baudelaire*, p. 71.

312   Aquinas: *Summa Theologica*, I, II, 27, 1.

313   Leibniz: *Theodicy*, § 45, 154.

314   Hume: *Enquiries Concerning Human Understanding and Concerning the Principles of Morals*, p. 277.

315   Rousseau: *Emile*, p. 243.

316   Ibid., p. 105.

317   Kant: *Lectures on Ethics*, p. 198.

318   Kant: *Vorarbeiten zur Religion innherhalb der Grenzen der bloßen Vernunft*, p. 101.

319   Cf. Kant: *Fundamental Principles of the Metaphysics of Morals* in *Basic Writings of Kant*, pp. 181f.

320   Cf. Kant: *Critique of Practical Reason* in *Practical Philosophy*, pp. 195ff.

321   Cf. Kant: "Reflexionen zur Anthropologie," *Reflexion* 1226.

322   Kant: *Religion Within the Limits of Reason Alone*, p. 32. Hereafter, this title will be shortened to *Religion*.

323   Cf. Anderson-Gold: "Kant's Rejection of Devilishness: The Limits of Human Volition."

324   Kant: *Religion*, pp. 24f.

325   Allison: *Kant's Theory of Freedom*, p. 40.

326   Kant: *Religion*, p. 19.

327   Kant: *Metaphysics of Morals* in *Practical Philosophy*, p. 536.

328   Cf. Kant: *Critique of Practical Reason* in *Practical Philosophy* pp. 187ff.

329   Kant: *Metaphysics of Morals* in *Practical Philosophy*, p. 380.

330   Kant: "Conjectural Beginning of Human History," p. 227.

331   Kant: *Religion*, p. 40; cf. Kant: *Anthropology From a Pragmatic Point of View*, p. 420, Kant: *Lectures on Pedagogy* in *Anthropology, History and Education*, p. 478.

332   Kant: *Religion,* p. 31.

333   Ibid., p. 26.

334   Kant: *Vorarbeiten zur Religion innerhalb der Grenzen der bloßen Vernunft*, p. 102

335   Kant: *Religion*, p. 25, 30.

336   Ibid., p. 27.

337   Ibid., pp. 16f.

338   Ibid., p. 66.

339   Ibid., p. 28.

340   Ibid., pp. 56f.

341   Kant: *Critique of Pure Reason*, p. B274, A551n./B579n.; Kant: *Reflections on Metaphysics, Reflection* 5612 and 5616.

342   Kant: *Religion*, p. 16.

343   Kant: *Religion*, pp. 34f.

344   Ibid., p. 27.

345   Kant: *Critique of Practical Reason* in *Practical Philosophy*, pp. 219f. Cf. *Religion*, p. 33.

346   *Romans*, 4:15, 5:13.

347   Kant: *Religion*, pp. 18ff.

348   Ibid., p. 38.

349   Ibid., p. 20.

350   Ibid., p. 18–19n.

351   Ibid., p. 25, 32.

352   Ibid., p. 43.

353   Ibid., p. 62.

354   Ibid., p. 3.

355   Ibid., pp. 17ff.

356   Becker: *Escape from Evil*, p. xvii.

357   Ibid., p. 148.

358   Novalis: *Teplitzer Fragments* in *Schriften*, p. 398.

359   Cohn: *Europe's Inner Demons*.

360   Nietzsche: *Beyond Good and Evil*, § 153.

361   For a historic thematisation of such idea pairs, see Koselleck: "Zur historisch-politischen Semantik asymmetrischer Gegenbegriffe."

362 Schmitt: *The Concept of the Political*, p. 37.

363 Novalis: *Notes for a Romantic Encyclopaedia*, p. 121.

364 Cf. Matthew 25:31–46.

365 Gourevitch: *We Wish to Inform You That Tomorrow We Will Be Killed With Our Families*, p. 95.

366 Cf. Naimark: *Fires of Hatred*, pp. 14f. and chap. 5.

367 Whether you consider the war to have been a war between two countries or an internal conflict, these deportations were a war crime. Forced deportation in war is prohibited by Article 29 of the Fourth Geneva Convention of 1949, a prohibition that was expanded in Protocol II from 1977 to include internal conflicts.

368 In part, Göring's defense strategy in the Nuremberg Trials was to proclaim that the war's victors, who were now putting him on trial, were guilty of similar crimes, both in the war against Germany and in earlier periods of nation building. And Göring was largely right: the United State's very existence is based upon the extermination of a whole people; England's riches were the result of an inhuman colonialism; the Soviet Union was at least as totalitarian as the Germans; the bombing of German civilians during World War II reached the proportions of an extreme war crime; and the dropping of the atomic bomb on Japanese civilians should similarly be regarded as criminal. In Casablanca in January 1943, Great Britain and the United States drew up a plan for a massive bombing campaign of German civilians meant to "destroy morale"—which was then carried out. If we put any stock in the concept of human rights, which holds that civilians should be protected as much as possible in war, than this—as much as the bombing of Hiroshima and Nagasaki—should be regarded as a serious breach. And what about the Allied blockade of Germany

after World War I, *after* the war had already been decided, which led to the death of hundreds of thousands of people? Göring was partially right in his assertions. His mistake was that be persisted in believing that these facts lessened his own guilt. Göring's guilt was just as great, but a number of the war's "victors" should also have been put on trial.

369   Alouni: "Transcript."

370   Numbers 31:1–19.

371   1 Samuel 15:3.

372   See for example Joshua 8:22ff., 10:28–40, 11:10–14.

373   Vetlesen: "Ondskap Bosnia," p. 96.

374   For a well-informed discussion of the social psychology of prejudice, see Duckitt: *The Social Psychology of Prejudice.*

375   Cf. Hochschild: *King Leopold's Ghost*, p. 16.

376   Anderson: *Imagined Communities*, p. 6.

377   Cf. Naimark: *Fires of Hatred*, chap. 5.

378   Kapuściński: *Soccer War*, pp. 157–85.

379   Cf. Gibbon: *The History of the Decline and Fall of the Roman Empire, Volume V*, pp. 66–72.

380   Freud: *Civilization and Its Discontents*, p. 72.

381   Ignatieff: *The Warrior's Honor*, p. 50.

382   Erwin Staub (*The Roots of Evil*, p. 58) tells the story of an English experiment where thirty-two young boys from Bristol were shown a number of dots on a screen, and afterwards asked to guess how many dots they'd seen. Half the boys were told that they belonged to the group that had overestimated the number, and the other half were told they belonged to the opposite group. After that, every boy was asked to divide up a sum of money between two other boys, and the only information they were given about these boys were that one belonged to the first group and one

belonged to the second. On this basis alone, the boys systematically discriminated between the recipients, and gave more money to those in the same category as themselves. Group solidarity provided no rational basis for handling the money, but it was nonetheless sufficient to lead to discriminatory behavior.

383   Aristotle: *Politics*, 1253a7ff.

384   Cf. Sofsky: *Traktat über die Gewalt*, p. 162.

385   Emerson: "Compensation," in *The Essential Writings of Ralph Waldo Emerson*, p. 167.

386   Blake: "Annotations in Lavater's *Aphorisms on Man*," in *The Complete Poetry of William Blake*, p. 589.

387   Todorov: *Facing the Extreme*, p. 200.

388   See for example May: *Power and Innocence*.

389   For a readable thematization of this problem, see Cruikshank: "Revolutions Within: Self-government and Self-esteem."

390   Cf. Berkowitz: *Aggression: Its Causes, Consequences, and Control*, pp. 143f. See also Baumeister: *Evil: Inside Human Violence and Cruelty*, chap. 5.

391   Generally speaking, we can distinguish between three different definitions of violence: (1) broad, (2) narrow, and (3) legitimacy-based. (1): Broad definitions of violence encompass a multitude of different phenomena, for example social injustice. One of the most common broad definitions of violence is Johan Galtung's idea of "structural violence," which suggests that violence occurs when people are influenced to such an extent that they cannot realize their full somatic and mental potential (Galtung: "Violence, Peace and Peace Research," p. 168.). The problem with this definition is that it makes it difficult to imagine a sphere of human life *not* permeated by violence. The concept of violence, therefore, becomes watered down. (2): Narrow definitions of violence are more

in keeping with the general use of the word and refer to human actions that deliberately cause psychical, or even emotional, damage. Galtung's idea of "personal violence" belongs to this category. (3): The third type of violence, legitimacy-based violence, is principally a narrower version of (2), where the concept of violence is reserved for deliberate actions that cause harm such that these actions are not legitimated by a country's laws. In my opinion, this definition is counter-intuitive, and a given action—for example, a police beating of protesters—is not made less violent just because it might be validated by law. I believe (2) is the most reasonable definition, and if not otherwise indicated, I use the term "violence" in the narrower sense.

392   Honderich: *Violence for Equality*, p. 153.

393   Cf. Baumeister: *Evil: Inside Human Violence and Cruelty*, pp. 274f.

394   Athens: *Violent Criminal Acts and Actors Revisited*, pp. 32–41.

395   Katz: *Seductions of Crime*, p. 19.

396   For an insightful discussion of this idea, see Emerson: "Experience," in *The Essential Writings of Ralph Waldo Emerson*, p. 323.

397   Cf. Katz: *Seductions of Crime*, p. 12.

398   Athens: *Violent Criminal Acts and Actors Revisited*, chap. 6 and 7.

399   See Katz: *Seductions of Crime*, chap. 3, about "the badass."

400   Arendt: *The Life of the Mind: Thinking*, p. 4

401   Arendt: *Eichmann in Jerusalem*, p. 276.

402   Ibid., p. 252, 287, 288.

403   Arendt: *The Life of the Mind: Thinking*, pp. 3ff.

404   Arendt: *Eichmann in Jerusalem*, p. 285, 288; Arendt: *The Life of the Mind: Thinking*, p. 3.

405   Arendt: *Eichmann in Jerusalem*, p. 276.

406   La Rochefoucauld: *Maxims*, § 269 (p. 55) and § 387 (p. 79).

407   Pascal: *Pensées*, p. 179.

408   Baudelaire: "The Counterfeit Coin," in *Prose Poems*, p. 74.

409   Camus: *The Plague*, p. 131.

410   Leopardi: "Memorable Sayings of Filippo Ottonieri" in *Operette Morali*, p. 307, 309.

411   Bonhoeffer: *Letters and Papers from Prison*, pp. 8f.

412   Arendt: *Eichmann in Jerusalem*, pp. 287f.

413   Arendt: *The Origins of Totalitarianism*, p. 459.

414   Ibid., p. 458.

415   Ibid., pp. 447f.

416   Ibid., pp. 451f.

417   Ibid., pp. 453f.

418   Ibid., p. 459.

419   Ibid., p. ix, 459.

420   Ibid., pp. 432f.

421   For a discussion of the purges under Stalin, see Getty and Naumov: *The Road to Terror*. This work is mainly composed of recently released internal documents from the Central Committee under Stalin together with commentary.

422   Ibid., pp. 470–81, 518–21, 583.

423   Ibid., pp. xiii, 272ff., 578.

424   Arendt: *Crises of the Republic*, p. 108.

425   Arendt: *The Origins of Totalitarianism*, p. 460.

426   Ibid., p. 468.

427   Arendt: *Vita Activa*, chap. 5.; *The Origins of Totalitarianism*, pp. 456f.

428   A selection of interrogation records by the Israeli police are published in Lang and Sibyll: *Eichmann Interrogated.*

429   For a discussion of this aspect, see Rosenthal: *A Good Look at Evil*, pp. 163–80.

430   Furthermore, I essentially limit myself to the picture Arendt paints of Eichmann. As David Cesarani points out in his book *Becoming Eichmann: Rethinking the Life, Crimes, and Trial of a "Desk Murderer*,*"* Arendt was only present for an extremely limited time during the trial. Cesarani finds many faults with Arendt's view of Eichmann, and I find Cesarini to be the more reliable biographer. However, since this chapter is more devoted to Arendt's thought than to an accurate portrayal of Eichmann, I have generally adhered to Arendt's interpretation of him.

431   Arendt: *Eichmann in Jerusalem*, pp. 25f., 48f.

432   Ibid., p. 92.

433   Lang and Sibyll: *Eichmann Interrogated*, p. 80.

434   Ibid., 104.

435   Ibid., pp. 96, 111, 118, 131. 197f.

436   Ibid., p. 104.

437   Ibid., p. 173.

438   Ibid., p. 199.

439   Weber: "Politics as a Vocation" in *Max Weber's Complete Writings*, p. 173.

440   Lang and Sibyll: *Eichmann Interrogated*, p. 144f, cf. pp. 157f., 197f., 208, 271f. Considered in this way, Eichmann is also reminiscent of Max Weber's protestant capitalist, who puts work above personal pleasure, because work is the way to salvation. The Weber capitalist completely dedicates himself to doing the best job possible in a system whose rules he never pauses to reflect on. Instead, he merely accepts the rules as a given.

441   Weber: "Bureaucracy" in *From Max Weber*, p. 228.

442   Cf. Nagel: *Mortal Questions*, p. 77.

443   Lang and Sibyll: *Eichmann Interrogated*, p. 288.

444   Cf. Arendt: *Eichmann in Jerusalem*, p. 136.

445   Kant: *Metaphysics of Morals* in *Practical Philosophy*, p. 505; Kant: *Religion*, p. 90n.

446   Lang and Sibyll: *Eichmann Interrogated*, p. 40f.

447   Arendt: *Eichmann in Jerusalem*, pp. 247f.

448   Ibid., p. 109.

449   Land and Sibyll: *Eichmann Interrogated*, p. 289.

450   Ibid., p. 150, 157.

451   Arendt: *Eichmann in Jerusalem*, p. 114.

452   Ibid., p. 287.

453   Cf. Luke 23:34; Acts 7:60.

454   Bauman: *Modernity and the Holocaust*.

455   Arendt: *Eichmann in Jerusalem*, pp. 48f., 53; Arendt: *The Life of the Mind: Thinking*, p. 4.

456   Arendt: *Eichmann in Jerusalem*, p. 287.

457   Ibid., p. 252.

458   Höss: *Commandant of Auschwitz*, p. 131.

459   Ibid., p. 178.

460   Levi: "Introduction."

461   Höss: *Commandant of Auschwitz*, p. 67.

462   Ibid., p. 71f.

463   Ibid., p. 67.

464   Ibid., pp. 80ff.

465   Ibid., pp. 178f.

466   Ibid., p. 116.

467   For a good examination of this idea, see Todorov: *Facing the Extreme*.

468   Höss: *Commandant of Auschwitz*, p. 111.

469   Ibid., p. 54.

470   Ibid., p. 76.

471   Ibid., p. 184.

472   Ibid., pp. 152f.

473   Ibid., p. 144.

474   Sereny: *Into that Darkness*, p. 39, 364.

475   Ibid., p. 364.

476   Ibid., p. 157.

477   Ibid., p. 229.

478   Ibid., p. 100.

479   Ibid., p. 101, 232.

480   Ibid., p. 201.

481   Ibid., p. 203.

482   Ibid., p. 35, 55, 110, 113, 134, 164, 233.

483   Ibid., p. 29, 364f.

484   Ibid., p. 113.

485   Ibid., p. 164.

486   Ibid., p. 164.

487   Ibid., p. 164.

488   Ibid., pp. 232f.

489   Ofstad: *Vår forakt for svakhet.*

490   *Hitler's Table Talk 1941–1944*, p. 396.

491   Sereny: *Into that Darkness*, p. 200. Seneca has already written about how evil tends to escalate, and that a person can develop his own blasé, routine form of evil (Seneca: "On Anger" in *Dialogues and Essays*, pp. 29f.). This habituation can happen terrifyingly fast. An SS doctor at Auschwitz, Johann Paul Kremer, who kept a diary during the time he was stationed at the camp, expressed his horror at what he saw there in the first two diary entries he wrote on arrival—after that, he never mentioned it again. (Cf. Katz: *Ordinary People and Extraordinary Evil*, p. 50–60. See also Lifton: *The Nazi Doctors*.)

492   Hegel discusses habit as being a "second nature" (Hegel: *The Encyclopaedia Logic*, § 410). In my opinion, this idea captures something essential about habits. If we distinguish between *instincts* and *habits*, we can describe instincts as belonging to our first nature (those things we were born with) and habits as belonging to our second nature (those things we learn along the way, but that are so strongly internalized that they approach pure instinct in terms of immediacy and necessity). The difference between our first and second natures is that the first is inborn and the second can be changed.

493   Adolf Hitler: *Mein Kampf*, p. 402.

494   Ibid., p. 297.

495   We can draw a parallel here with communism, especially as it played out under Stalin. Although there was no clearly articulated Führer principle, the party principle was just as strong. An individual was expected to subjugate himself to the party without reservation and there was no place for individual reflection and conscience. (Cf. Getty and Naumov: *The Road to Terror*.)

496   Cf. Emerson: "Politics," in *The Essential Writings of Ralph Waldo Emerson*, p. 65.

497   Himmler's famous speech in Posen in 1943 shows that the Nazis considered the mass exterminations to be a dirty secret. The speech reveals a contrast between the emphasis placed on honor and duty on the one hand, and the necessity to remain silent for all time on the other. The necessity for secrecy—not simply with regard to the strategic considerations of a certain situation, but for *all time*—reveals an awareness that these actions were immoral. Kant formulates a public principle for evaluating an action's legitimacy: "All actions that affect the rights of other human beings, the maxims of which are incompatible with publicity, are unjust." (Kant: *Toward Perpetual Peace* in *Toward Perpetual Peace*

and Other Writings, p. 104.) Kant emphasizes that this idea applies both to the moral and the juridical evaluations of an action.

498   Lifton: *The Nazi Doctors*, p. 418–65.

499   For example, we can think of the engineers who constructed the Nazis' cremation ovens. In 1950, one of these engineers, Martin Klettner, was still trying now and then to get a patent for one of the ovens he'd helped develop in Auschwitz. (Cf. Pressac: *Auschwitz: Technique and Operation of the Gas Chambers*, pp. 103, 105, 244.)

500   Cf. Glass: *Life Unworthy of Life*, pp. 88f.

501   For an excellent study of the doctors, see Lifton: *The Nazi Doctors*. The doctors in the concentration camps had taken the Hippocratic oath, but they committed actions that were diametrically opposed to that oath, seemingly without a single pang of conscience. They injected different organic material, including viruses and bacteria, into the prisoners, removed brain tissue and transplanted organs into living people without bothering to use anesthesia, stuck people in pressure chambers, in boiling and ice-cold water, etc. They were enacting an inverted Hippocratic oath. Of course, there were a few doctors who refused to take part, and none of these were punished in any way—they were simply given different jobs. However, the majority seemed to have very little objection to these experiments.

502   In Auschwitz, a large portion of the prisoners also had a number tattooed on their arm, and this number replaced their names, dehumanizing the prisoners even more. We can also remark in this context that these tattoos were yet another blow to orthodox Jews, because the Law of Moses forbids tattooing and the like (*Leviticus* 19:28, cf. *Deuteronomy* 14:1). However, I doubt that this was done intentionally, and I believe that the tattooing was mainly motivated by dehumanization and other "logistical" considerations.

503   Cited in Glass: *Life Unworthy of Life*, p. 27.

504   Lang: *Act and Idea in the Nazi Genocide*, p. 210.

505   Ibid., p. 29, 56.

506   Goldhagen: *Hitler's Willing Executioners*, p. 493n43, 593n23.

507   Finkelstein and Birn: *A Nation on Trial*.

508   Cited in Bauman: *Modernity and the Holocaust*, p. 75.

509   Bauman: pp. 109f., 165ff.

510   Goldhagen: *Hitler's Willing Executioners*, p. 194.

511   Ibid., p. 255.

512   Ibid., p. 580n108.

513   Ibid., p. 315.

514   Ibid., pp. 416, 479.

515   Glass: *Life Unworthy of Life*.

516   Goldhagen: *Hitler's Willing Executioners*, pp. 170f.

517   Johnson and Reuband: *What We Knew. Terror, Mass Murder and Everyday Life in Nazi Germany*.

518   Staub: *The Roots of Evil*, p. 38.

519   Aly: *Beneficiaries: Plunder, Racial War, and the Nazi Welfare State*.

520   Browning: *Ordinary Men*. Browning's study has been forcefully criticized by Goldhagen in *Hitler's Willing Executioners*, but in a new afterword to the 1998 edition of *Ordinary Men*, Browning gives a convincing response to this criticism. I am not a specialist in this area, but I find Browning's study more attractive than Goldhagen's, simply because Browning's assertions seem to be better supported than Goldhagen's. See also Bettina Birn's defense of Browning and critique of Goldhagen in Finkelstein and Birn: *A Nation on Trial*.

521   Browning: *Ordinary Men*, pp. 225f.

522   Ibid., p. 161.

523   Ibid., p. 57.

524   Ibid., pp. 61f.

525   Ibid., p. 74.

526   Goldhagen: *Hitler's Willing Executioners*, p. 553n68.

527   Browning: *Ordinary Men*, p. 214.

528   An especially shocking example is a group from Berlin, exclusively on hand to support the troops, who should have had no part in the killings. They asked for permission to participate in the shooting of the Jews, and received consent. (Ibid., p. 112.)

529   Ibid., pp. 73, 150ff., 184.

530   Ibid., p. 48.

531   Ibid., pp. 85ff.

532   Goldhagen: *Hitler's Willing Executioners*, p. 237.

533   Cited in Browning: *Ordinary Men*, p. 216.

534   Ibid., p. 72.

535   Ibid., p. 184.

536   During World War II, under thirty percent of the soldiers in the American Air Force expressed a hatred for the enemy, while between twenty-seven and thirty-eight percent of the soldiers in the infantry mentioned hatred as a motivation for killing. On the other hand, sixty percent cited loyalty to their comrades as the most important factor. In later wars, which take place at greater distances, this claim is more and more prevalent. (Cf. Bourke: *An Intimate History of Killing*, pp. 157f.)

537   Cited in ibid., pp. 171f.

538   Cited in ibid., p. 191.

539   Ibid., p. 226.

540   The following remarks concerning the protests against the trial against Calley are taken from Bourke: *An Intimate History of Killing*, pp. 193f.

541   Ibid., pp. 195f.

542   This example is taken from Conroy: *Unspeakable Acts, Ordinary People*, pp. 138f.

543   See Katz: *Ordinary People and Extraordinary Evil*, p. 84–90.

544   See Todorov: *Facing the Extreme*, p. 122.

545   A military tribunal in Tokyo (1946–48) uncovered examples of extreme cruelty in the treatment of prisoners of war, an investigation which, among other things, showed that twenty-seven percent of captured Allied soldiers died in Japanese custody, while corresponding tallies for soldiers in German and Italian custody were four percent. (Cf. Robertson: *Crimes Against Humanity*, p. 223.)

546   Cf. Glover: *Humanity*, p. 294.

547   Milgram: *Obedience to Authority*.

548   Baron: *Human Aggression*, pp. 260ff.

549   Milgram: *Obedience to Authority*, p. 205.

550   Levi: *The Drowned and the Saved*, p. 56.

551   Arendt: *Life of the Mind: Thinking*, p. 78.

552   Ibid., p. 193.

553   Ibid., p. 13.

554   Kant: *Critique of Judgment*, § 40, pp. 102f.

555   Kant: "An Answer to the Question: What is Enlightenment?" in *Toward Perpetual Peace and Other Writings*, p. 17.

556   Adorno: "Education After Auschwitz" in *Can One Live After Auschwitz?*, p. 23.

557   Cf. Arendt: *Life of the Mind: Thinking*, p. 5, 191.

558   Euripedes: *Orestes and Other Plays*, p. 59, line 396.

559   Ted Bundy, who certainly wasn't much troubled by his conscience, criticized the concept of guilt, which he believed to be a social control mechanism and "*very* unhealthy" (Hare: *Without*

Conscience, p. 41). It's uncertain how many women Bundy murdered, but it was at least seventeen, probably many more, and it's indisputable that Bundy would have been a far less "unhealthy" element in society if he'd been capable of feeling guilt.

560 Gelven: *The Risk of Being*, p. 22–37.

561 Conrad: *Heart of Darkness*, p. 87.

562 Ibid., p. 111.

563 Solzhenitsyn: *The Gulag Archipelago*, pp. 615f.

564 Sæterbakken: *Det onde øye,* p. 20.

565 Ricoeur: *Fallible Man*, p. 133.

566 Ibid., p. 142.

567 Ibid., p. 144.

568 Pascal writes: "There are only two kinds of men: the righteous who believe themselves sinners; the rest, sinners, who believe themselves righteous." (Pascal: *Penseés*, p. 194.)

569 Aristotle: *Nicomachean Ethics*, book 10.7–8.

570 Aurelius: *Meditations*, book IV. 39, p. 30.

571 Ibid., book VII. 71, p. 194.

572 Descartes: *The Philosophical Writings of Descartes*, 1: p. 122ff.

573 Ibid., 3: pp. 257f.

574 Engelmann: *Letters from Ludwig Wittgenstein with a Memoir*, p. 74.

575 Ibid., p. 79.

576 Wittgenstein: *Notebooks* 1914–1916, dated 11.6.16.

577 Ibid., dated 8.7.16.

578 Ibid., dated 13.8.16.

579 Ibid., dated 13.8.16.

580 Wittgenstein: *Culture and Value*, p. 45e.

581 Wittgenstein: *Philosophical Investigations*, § 124.

582 Wittgenstein: *Culture and Value*, p. 43e.

583   Aurelius: *Meditations*, book VII. 26, p. 60.

584   Romans 1:32.

585   Pascal: *Provincial Letters*, p. 249.

586   Kant: *Critique of Practical Reason*, p. 238.

587   Kant: *The Conflict of the Faculties*, p. 288.

588   Kant: *Critique of Judgment*, § 3, p. 39.

589   Kant distinguishes between philosophy as a school and philosophy's relevance to the world. Furthermore, Kant's philosophical endeavors were not undertaken as academic philosophy operating for its own sake (Kant: *Logic*, pp. 27f., cf. *Critique of Pure Reason*, p. A838f./B866f.).

590   Heller: "The Legacy of Marxian Ethics," p. 140.

591   A person is free if he exists for his own sake and not for the sake of another, Aristotle argues. (*Metaphysics*, 982b25, p. 9.) Unfortunately, Aristotle did not recognize that this principle applied to all human beings, and considered some people to be born slaves. Slaves are not accorded the same freedom as others: they do not have an individual *praxis*, but are tools for their owners' *praxis*.

592   Hume: *Enquiries Concerning Human Understanding and Concerning the Principles of Morals*, p. 229.

593   Hume: *A Treatise of Human Nature*, p. 408.

594   Ibid., pp. 401ff.

595   Freud: *Civilization and its Discontents*, p. 74.

596   Torture has been widespread for thousands of years. It isn't mentioned in antique Babylonian or Jewish texts, but both the Assyrians and the Egyptians made use of torture, and it was an everyday part of life for the Greeks and the Romans. In Aristophanes' comedy *The Frogs*, for instance, there are descriptions of numerous forms of torture. Then, for the Inquisition, torture wasn't just a legitimate practice—it was a holy exercise meant to snatch a person

out of Satan's claws. Up until the late eighteenth century, in fact, torture was common practice in most European countries. Prussia was the first nation to outlaw all torture, in 1754, and most European countries quickly followed suite. (Switzerland was the last country to hop on the bandwagon a hundred or so years later.) However, as Amnesty International has shown since they began their campaign against torture in 1973, torture has hardly disappeared from Europe.

Descriptions of torture tend to focus on the more obscure methods, but even the simplest can cause the same amount of pain. You can systematically beat someone. You can deny prisoners sleep and food or make them stand upright for long periods, which results in intense muscle pain. You can also shame your victims, for example by forcing them to eat an interrogator's snot or making them wear women's underwear on their heads. After that, different methods can be employed to break the prisoners mentally—for example by making them think they're going to be executed. These methods aren't as spectacular as the more medieval methods of torture, but can be just as effective. On top of this, they leave few physical traces behind. Torture is in violation of Article 5 in the UN Universal Declaration of Human Rights and Article 7 of the International Covenant on Civil and Political Rights. The UN Convention Against Torture in 1984 also prohibits all use of torture, defined as any action that consciously inflicts serious physical or mental harm on a person for the sake of punishing (excepting lawful cases of punishment), humiliating, or extracting information from the victim. One hundred and nineteen countries ratified the convention, and all pledged to punish any person who had carried out torture within their county's borders. The problem, however, is that the countries that did and do extensively use torture either did not ratify the convention or simply refuse to cooperate with the ongoing efforts of the Committee Against Torture.

597   Cf. Conroy: *Unspeakable Acts, Ordinary People*, pp. 27f.

598   Ibid., pp. 20f.

599   Goldhagen: *Hitler's Willing Executioners*, p. 119.

600   Staub: *The Roots of Evil*, p. 158.

601   In contrast to the usual assumption that the Allies neglected the Jews and could have saved a multitude of Jews from the extermination camps, William D. Rubenstein (*The Myth of Rescue: Why the Democracies Could Not Have Save More Jews from the Nazis*) has shown in detail that this was not a practical possibility.

602   Katz: *Seductions of Crime*, p. 20.

603   Darley and Latané: "Bystander Intervention in Emergencies: Diffusion of Responsibility."

604   Cf. Hochschild: *King Leopold's Ghost*.

605   Cf. Arendt: *Crises of the Republic*, p. 88.

606   Contrary to what you'd expect, an extensive investigation showed that people generally have a more pronounced feeling of guilt with regard to unpremeditated actions than to premeditated actions. (McGraw: "Guilt Following Transgression: An Attribution of Responsibility Approach.") The explanation for this is that premeditated actions already seem justified *before* they are carried out, and the agent, therefore, does not need to feel guilt, while unpremeditated actions do not necessarily appear justified afterward. Of course, agents will often try to rationalize their actions after the fact, and thereby spare themselves some humiliation.

607   Why do we punish offenders? Typically, we come up with two explanations: (1) prevention and (2) retribution. Most contemporary theories of punishment tend in the direction of the first,

but in my opinion, punishment should be something more serious, something more substantial than an all-around preventative. On the other hand, while it's understandable that a victim wants revenge, I don't think that thoughts of revenge should *legitimate* punishment . . . we should remember that there is an essential difference between pure revenge and punishment motivated by a concern for justice: (1) Punishment is "repayment" for an evil, while revenge is based on causing suffering; (2) punishment sets limits on the amount of "payback" that can be taken, while revenge is never proportional and has a tendency to escalate; (3) revenge is personal, but what is "repaid" by punishment doesn't have to have such personal overtones; and (4) revenge implies personal satisfaction at the sight of another's suffering—that is, revenge has an emotional aspect that punishment (ideally) lacks. Of course, it should be stated that it's not always easy to distinguish between revenge and punishment, but that doesn't mean that we shouldn't take pains to distinguish between the two. Hegel has given perhaps the most purely retributive justification of punishment: his theory states that a crime must always be punished, because the crime is a breach of justice—and, furthermore, that any possible beneficial consequences of punishment (for example, preventative effects) are chance occurrences and are utterly irrelevant to its legitimization (*Philosophy of Right*, § 99f.). Hegel expresses this idea quite strongly, insisting that a criminal *must* be punished, since by infringing on someone else's rights, the criminal has agreed to let his own rights be infringed upon. Punishment is the negation of a negation. The criminal's negative action should be annulled by subjecting him to a correspondingly negative action. Ideally, this process should annul the crime and provide the criminal with a new ethical grounding.

608   There are a number of juridical, political, and moral problems regarding the function and the legitimization of such war crimes tribunals. For a clear discussion of these problems, see Nino: *Radical Evil on Trial*.

609   Micah 4:3.

610   Joel 3:10.

611   Weber: "Politics as Vocation" in *Max Weber's Complete Writings on Academic and Political Vocations*, p. 197.

612   Ibid., p. 198.

613   See especially Matthew 5:39: "Do not resist an evil person." See also Romans 12:21.

614   See especially Psalms 37.

615   Immanuel Kant: "On a Supposed Right to Lie because of Philanthropic Concerns."

616   Weber: "Politics as Vocation" in *Max Weber's Complete Writings on Academic and Political Vocations*, p. 199.

617   Concerning the idea of a "moral algorithm" and fact that it doesn't exist, see O'Neill: *Constructions of Reason*.

618   Cf. Robertson: *Crimes Against Humanity*, p. 440.

619   For a discussion of "weak consequentialism," see Barry: *Liberty and Justice*, p. 40–77.

620   Ibid., p. 76.

621   Hegel: *Natural Law* p. 79. Cf. Hegel: *Philosophy of Right*, § 135.

622   Hegel: *Natural Law*, p. 80.

623   Cf. Castoriadis: *Philosophy, Politics, Autonomy*, p. 120. The reference to *Antigone* is in verse 707ff.

624   Sorel: *Reflections on Violence*.

625   Fanon: *The Wretched of the Earth*, p. 50.

626   Cf. Keane: *Reflections on Violence*, p. 88.

627   Ibid., p. 90.

628   On the development of the monopoly on violence, see Elias: *The Civilizing Process: Sociogenetic and Psychogenetic Investigations.*

629   Weber: "Politics as Vocation" in *Max Weber's Complete Writings on Academic and Political Vocations*, p. 156.

630   Arendt: *Crisis of the Republic*, p. 177. Arendt distinguishes sharply between power and violence. Power implies popular support, whereas violence largely occurs without such support. According to Arendt, power by definition belongs to a group, but violence can originate in a single individual. She admits that the two are often linked, but insists on the distinction, because the essential question is what *type* of power lies behind each individual instance of violence (ibid., p. 146). The essential question with regard to political violence is whether the violence has a *legitimate* power base behind it. We can even say that there is an inversely proportional relationship between the power base and the extent of the violence. This is illustrated by the Soviet terror of the 1930s: It was clear to the Central Committee that they didn't have the popular support they wanted, and they therefore drew the conclusion that they were threatened from all sides. A government that finds it necessary to arrest people who pose absolutely no threat—for example, students in small, insignificant towns—lacks security. These actions can be blamed on the implicit recognition that the power base is poor, that the government doesn't have enough support from the people as a whole. Violence is therefore a compensation for power. Of course, the power base may have been weak, but there's no reason to believe that there was any organized, domestic opposition after 1932 (cf. Getty and Naumov: *The Road to Terror*, p. 574). Despite the fact that the Bolsheviks weren't threatened by internal enemies, the Party felt itself to be steadily more threatened and regarded

all of their measures as "defensive." If only the Bolsheviks would have followed the rather more humble use of violence advocated by Machiavelli: strong, but short-lived. Totalitarian violence is almost without exception a "poor use of violence." And yet, from Arendt's perspective, Machiavelli's model doesn't work either. It's desirable that violence have as broad a power base as possible, because this minimizes the extent of the violence. The weaker the power base, however, the stronger the tendency that violence will increase, and this increase in violence only undermines the power base even more—with the result that we've taken a step in the direction of pure terror. A government structured around terror has little power, but always tends toward violence—though this type of violence doesn't gain the government any power, and can even undermine it (Arendt: *Crises of the Republic*, p. 155; cf. *Vita Activa*, p. 187). To governments built on terror, violence will have an inherent worth. That is, violence loses the instrumental character it has in governments who enjoy a larger power base. Arendt thus concludes that instead of stabilizing power, violence typically leads to more violence.

631 For a good discussion of the relationship between "genocide" and "ethnic cleansing," see Naimark: *Fires of Hatred*, pp. 2ff.

632 "Convention on the Prevention and Punishment . . ."

633 Cited in Keane: *Reflections on Violence*, p. 157.

634 For a discussion of this problem, see Ignatieff: *The Warrior's Honor*, p. 18, 109–63. See also William Shawcross: *Deliver Us From Evil*.

635 Ogata: "Peace, Security and Humanitarian Action," p. 275.

636 Cf. Seifert: "The Second Front."

637 The following remarks about rape in war are mainly based on Seifert, ibid.

638   Clausewitz: *On War*, pp. 127f.

639   Cf. Scarry: *The Body in Pain*, p. 61.

640   Seifert: "The Second Front," p. 150.

641   Mann: *Diaries 1919–1939*, dated August 13, 1936.

642   Adorno: *Negative Dialectics*, p. 380.

643   Cf. Morgenthau: *Politics among Nations*.

644   Kant: *Toward Perpetual Peace* in *Toward Perpetual Peace and Other Writings*, pp. 91f. See also Rawls: *The Law of Peoples*, p. 36.

645   Cf. Rawls: *The Law of Peoples*, § 10.

646   Walzer: *Just and Unjust Wars*.

647   For a good overview of this tradition, see Johnson: *The Just war Tradition and the Restraint of War*.

648   Augustine: *City of God*, book XIX. 11–13.

649   Military advocates evaluated every single bombing target (cf. Ignatieff: *Virtual War*, p. 197–201.) A few things went wrong—for example, the bombing of the Chinese embassy, a train filled with civilians, a refugee convoy, a Serbian nursing home, etc.—but for the most part, NATO seems to have done its utmost to distinguish between legitimate and illegitimate targets. A single instance, a television station in Beograd where ten to fifteen civilians were killed, appears to have been a gray zone, but the station also had a military use and can therefore be regarded as a legitimate bombing target. In contrast, it's doubtful that bombing from such great distance—a strategy the United States has used in multiple wars in the last century—is legitimate when it necessarily results in extensive loss to the civilian population.

650   Cf. Ignatieff: *Virtual War*, p. 72.

651   Habermas: "Bestiality and Humanity."

652   Cf. Kahn: "War and Sacrifice in Kosovo."

653   Baudrillard: *The Perfect Crime*, p. 141.

654   Rawls: "Kantian Constructivism in Moral Theory," p. 518.

655   Popper: *The Open Society and Its Enemies. Volume One: The Spell of Plato*, chap. 9.

656   Popper: *Conjectures and Refutations*, p. 361.

657   Hampshire: *Innocence and Experience*, p. 90.

658   Rawls: *A Theory of Justice*, p. 98.

659   Rawls: *The Law of Peoples*, § 16.

BIBLIOGRAPHY

Adams, Marilyn McCord. *Horrendous Evils and the Goodness of God*. Cornell University Press, Ithaca 1999.

Adams, Marilyn McCord and Robert Merrihew Adams, eds. *The Problem of Evil*. Oxford University Press, Oxford 1990.

Adorno, Theodor W. "Education After Auschwitz," in Rolf Tiedemann, ed.: *Can One Live After Auschwitz?* Trans. Rodney Livingstone, et. al. Stanford University Press, Stanford 2003.

—. *Minima Moralia: Reflections on a Damaged Life*. Trans. E. F. N. Jephcott. Verso, New York 2005.

—. *Negative Dialectics*. Trans. E. B. Ashton. Seabury Press, New York 1979.

Airaksinen, Timo. *The Philosophy of the Marquis de Sade*. Routledge, New York 1995.

Alford, C. Fred. *What Evil Means to Us*. Cornell University Press, Ithaca 1997.

Allison, Henry E. *Kant's Theory of Freedom*. Cambridge University Press, Cambridge 1990.

Alouni, Tayseer. "Transcript of Bin Laden's October Interview." CNN. 16 Nov. 2009 <http://archives.cnn.com/2002/WORLD/asiapcf/south/02/05/binladen.transcript/index.html>.

Aly, Götz. *Hitler's Beneficiaries: Plunder, Racial War, and the Nazi Welfare State*. Trans. Jefferson Chase. Metropolitan Books, New York 2006.

Amis, Martin. *London Fields*. Penguin, Harmondsworth 1990.

Andersen, Hans Christian. "The Snow Queen," in Jackie Wullschläger, ed.: *Hans Christian Andersen: Fairy Tales*. Trans. Tiina Nunnally. Penguin, New York 2004.

Anderson, Benedict. *Imagined Communities: Reflections on the Origin and Spread of Nationalism*. Verso, New York 1991.

Anderson-Gold, Sharon. "Kant's Rejection of Devilishness: The Limits of Human Volition." *Idealistic Studies* 14, 1984.

Anissimov, Myrian. *Primo Levi: Tragedy of an Optimist*. Trans. Steve Cox. Aurum Press, London 1998.

Aquinas, Thomas. *Summa Theologica*. Trans. Fathers of the English Dominican Province. Benziger Bros., New York 1948.

Arendt, Hannah. *Crises of the Republic*. Harcourt Brace, New York 1972.

—. *Eichmann in Jerusalem: A Report on the Banality of Evil*. Penguin, Harmondsworth 1994.

—. *The Life of the Mind*. Harcourt Brace, New York 1977.

—. *The Origins of Totalitarianism*. Harcourt Brace, New York 1979.

—. *Vita Activa*, in Peter Baehr, ed.: *The Portable Hannah Arendt*, Penguin, New York 2000.

Aristotle. *Metaphysics*. Trans. Hugh Lawson-Tancred. Penguin, New York 1998.

—. *The Nicomachean Ethics*. Trans. David Ross. Oxford University Press, New York 1998.

—. *The Politics*. Trans. T. A. Sinclair. Penguin, New York 1992.

Athens, Lonnie. *Violent Criminal Acts and Actors Revisited*. University of Illinois Press, Urbana 1997.

Augustine. *The City of God against the Pagans*. Trans. R. W. Dyson. Cambridge University Press, Cambridge 1998.

—. *Confessions*. Trans. Henry Chadwick. Oxford University Press, New York 1991.

—. *The Essential Augustine*, Vernon J. Burke, ed. Hacket Publishing Company, Indianapolis 1981.

Aurelius, Marcus. *Meditations*. Trans. R. B. Rutherford. Oxford University Press, New York 1998.

Barker, Kenneth L, ed. NIV Bible. Zondervan, Grand Rapids 2002.

Baron, Robert A. *Human Aggression*. Plenum Press, New York 1977.

Barry, Brian. *Liberty and Justice*. Clarendon Press, Oxford 1991.

Bataille, Georges. *Literature and Evil*. Trans. Alastair Hamilton. Marion Boyars, London 1997.

Baudelaire, Charles. *Baudelaire: Poems*. Trans. Richard Howard. Alfred A. Knopf, New York 1993.

—. *The Prose Poems and La Fanfarlo*. Trans. Rosemary Lloyd. The Oxford University Press, New York 2001.

Baudrillard, Jean. *Fatal Strategies*. Trans. Jim Fleming. Semiotext(e), New York 1990.

—. *The Perfect Crime*. Trans. Chris Turner. Verso, London 1996.

—. *The Transparency of Evil: Essays on Extreme Phenomena*. Trans. James Benedict. Verso, New York 1993.

Bauman, Zygmunt. *Modernity and the Holocaust*. Cornell University Press, Ithaca 2000.

Baumeister, Roy F. *Evil: Inside Human Cruelty and Violence*. W. H. Freeman and Company, New York 1999.

Becker, Ernest. *Escape from Evil*. The Free Press, New York 1975.

Benjamin, Walter. "The Work of Art in the Age of Mechanical Reproduction," in Hannah Arendt, ed.: *Illuminations: Essays and Reflections*. Trans. Harry Zohn. Harcourt Brace, New York 1968.

Berkowitz, Leonard. *Aggression: Its Causes, Consequences, and Control*. McGraw-Hill, New York 1993.

Bjørnvig, Thorkild. *Den æstetiske idiosynkrasi*. Cappelen, Oslo 1960. (Quotation trans. Kerri A. Pierce.)

Blake, William. *The Complete Poetry and Prose of William Blake.* Doubleday, New York 1988.

Blumenthal, David R. "Theodicy: Dissonance in Theory and Practice," in Hermann Häring and David Tracy, eds.: *The Fascination of Evil.* SCM Press, London 1998.

Boethius. *Consolation of Philosophy.* Trans. Joel C. Relihan. Hackett, Indianapolis 2001.

Bohrer, Karl Heinz. *Nach der Natur: Über Politik und Ästhetik.* Hanser, München 1988.

Bonhoeffer, Dietrich. *Letters and Papers from Prison: The Enlarged Edition.* Trans. Reginald Fuller, Frank Clark, et. al. Simon & Schuster, New York 1997.

Boom, Allan. "Introduction," in Jean-Jacques Rousseau: *Emile, or On Education.* Trans. Allan Bloom. Basic Books, New York 1979.

Bourke, Joanna. *An Intimate History of Killing: Face-to-Face Killing in Twentieth-Century Warfare.* Granta Books, London 1999.

Brecher, Bob. "Understanding the Holocaust. The Uniqueness Debate." *Radical Philosophy* 96, 1999.

Breidert, Wolfgang, ed. *Die Erschütterung der vollkommenen Welt: Die Wirkung des Erdbebens von Lissabon im Spiegel der europäischer Zeitgenossen.* Wissenschaftliche Buchgesellschaft, Darmstadt 1994.

Browning, Christopher R. *Ordinary Men: Reserve Police Battalion 101 and the Final Solution in Poland.* HarperCollins, New York 1998.

Calvin, Jean. *The Institutes of the Christian Religion*, in Mark Larrimore, ed.: *The Problem of Evil: A Reader.* Blackwell, Oxford 2001.

Camus, Albert. *The Plague.* Trans. Stuart Gilbert. Vintage Books, New York 1991.

Castoriadis, Corneslis. *Philosophy, Politics, Autonomy.* Oxford University Press, Oxford 1991.

Cenkner, William, ed. *Evil and the Response of World Religion.* Paragon House, St. Paul 1997.

Cesarini, David. *Becoming Eichmann: Rethinking the Life, Crimes, and Trial of a "Desk Murderer."* Da Capo Press, Cambridge MA 2006.

Cioran, E. M. *Drawn and Quartered.* Trans. Richard Howard. Arcade Publishing, New York 1998.

—. *On the Heights of Despair.* Trans. I. Zarifopol-Johnston. University of Chicago Press, Chicago 1992.

Clausewitz, Carl von. *On War.* Penguin, Harmondsworth 1982.

Cohn, Norman. *Europe's Inner Demons: The Demonization of Christians in Medieval Christendom.* University of Chicago Press, Chicago 2000.

Conrad, Joseph. *Heart of Darkness.* Penguin, Harmondsworth 1985.

Conroy, John. *Unspeakable Acts, Ordinary People: The Dynamics of Torture.* Knopf, New York 2000.

"Convention on the Prevention and Punishment of the Crime of Genocide." Human Rights Web. 16 Nov. 2009 <http://www.hrweb.org/legal/genocide.html>.

Courtois, Stéphane, Nicholas Werth, Jean-Louis Panné, Andrzej Paczkowski, Karel Bartošek, and Jean Louis Margolin. *The Black Book of Communism.* Trans. Jonathan Murphy and Mark Kramer. Harvard University Press, Cambridge MA 1999.

Cruikshank, Barbara. "Revolutions Within: Self-Government and Self-Esteem," in Andrew Barry et al., eds.: *Foucault and Political Reason: Liberalism, Neo-Liberalism and Rationalities of Government.* University of Chicago Press, Chicago 1996.

Darley, John M. and Bibb Latané. "Bystander Intervention in Emergencies: Diffusion of Responsibility." *Journal of Personality and Social Psychology* 8, 1968.

Davenport-Hines, Richard. *Gothic: 400 years of Excess, Horror, Evil and Ruin.* Fourth Estate, London 1998.

Davidson, Donald: "How is Weakness of the Will Possible?", in *Essays on Actions and Events.* Clarendon Press, Oxford 1982.

Delbanco, Andrew. *The Death of Satan: How Americans Have Lost the Sense of Evil.* Farrar, Straus and Giroux, New York 1995.

Descartes, René. *Meditations on First Philosophy*, in *Meditations and Other Metaphysical Writings.* Trans. Desmond M. Clark. Penguin, New York 1998.

—. *The Philosophical Writings of Descartes*, vol. 1. Trans. by John Cottingham, Robert Stoothoff, and Dugald Murdoch. Cambridge University Press, Cambridge 1999.

—. *The Philosophical Writings of Descartes*, vol. 3. Trans. by John Cottingham, Robert Stoothoff, and Dugald Murdoch. Cambridge University Press, Cambridge 1999.

Dostoevsky, Fyodor. *The Brothers Karamasov.* Trans. Andrew R. MacAndrew. Bantam Books, New York 2003.

—. "Environment," in *A Writer's Diary: Volume 1, 1873–1876.* Trans. Kenneth Lantz. Northwestern University Press, Evanston, 1994.

—. "Pushkin (A Sketch)," in *A Writer's Diary: Volume 2, 1877–1881.* Trans. Kenneth Lantz. Northwestern University Press, Evanston 2000.

—. *Selected Letters of Fyodor Dostoevsky.* Trans. Andrew R. MacAndres. Joseph Frank and David I. Goldstein, eds. Rutgers University Press, New Brunswick 1987.

Duckitt, John. *The Social Psychology of Prejudice.* Praeger Publishers, Westport CT 1992.

Elias, Norbert. *The Civilizing Process: Sociogenetic and Psychogenetic Investigations*. Trans. Edmund Jephcott. Blackwell Publishers Ltd., Oxford 2000.

Emerson, Ralph Waldo. *The Essential Writings of Ralph Waldo Emerson*. The Modern Library, New York 2000.

Engelmann, Paul. *Letters from Ludwig Wittgenstein with a Memoir*, B. F. McGuinness, ed. Blackwell, Oxford 1967.

Euripides. *Orestes and Other Plays*. Trans. Robin Waterfield. Oxford University Press, New York 2001.

Fanon, Frantz. *The Wretched of the Earth*. Trans. Richard Philcox. Grove, New York 2004.

Ferry, Luc. *Man Made God: The Meaning of Life*. Trans. David Pellauer. University of Chicago Press, Chicago 2002.

Finkelstein, Norman G. and Bettina Birn. *A Nation on Trial: The Goldhagen Thesis and Historical Truth*. Henry Holt and Company, New York 1998.

Forges, Alison des. *Leave None to Tell the Story: Genocide in Rwanda*. Human Rights Watch, New York 1999.

Freud, Sigmund. *Civilization and Its Discontents*. Trans. and ed. James Strachey. W. W. Norton & Company, New York 1989.

Gaita, Raimond. *A Common Humanity: Thinking About Love and Truth and Justice*. Routledge, New York 2000.

Galtung, Johan. "Violence, Peace and Peace Research." *Journal of Peace Research* 6:3, 1969.

Gauchet, Marcel. *The Disenchantment of the World: A Political History of Religion*. Trans. Oscar Burge. Princeton University Press, Princeton NJ 1997.

Gelven, Michael. *The Risk of Being: What It Means to Be Good and Bad*. Pennsylvania State University Press, University Park PA 1997.

Genet, Jean. *The Thief's Journal*. Trans. B. Frechtman. Olympia Press, Paris 2008.

Getty, J. Arch and Oleg V. Naumov. *The Road to Terror: Stalin and the Self-Destruction of the Bolsheviks, 1932–39.* Yale University Press, New Haven 1999.

Gibbon, Edward. *The History of the Decline and Fall of the Roman Empire, Volume V: Justinian and the Roman Law.* The Folio Society, London 1998.

Gillespie, Michael Allan. *Nihilism Before Nietzsche.* University of Chicago Press, Chicago 1998.

Glass, James M. *"Life Unworthy of Life": Racial Phobia and Mass Murder in Hitler's Germany.* Basic Books, New York 1997.

Glover, Jonathan. *Humanity: A Moral History of the Twentieth Century.* Yale University Press, New Haven 2000.

Goethe, Johann Wolfgang von. *Goethe's Faust.* Trans. Walter Kaufmann. Anchor Books, New York 1990.

Goldhagen, Daniel Jonah. *Hitler's Willing Executioners: Ordinary Germans and the Holocaust.* Abacus, London 1999.

Gourevitch, Philip. *We Wish to Inform You That Tomorrow We Will Be Killed With Our Families: Stories from Rwanda.* Farrar, Strauss and Giroux, New York 1998.

Grant, Ruth W. *Hypocrisy and Integrity: Machiavelli, Rousseau, and the Ethics of Politics.* University of Chicago Press, Chicago 1997.

Griffin, David. *God, Power and Evil.* Westminster Press, Philadelphia 1976.

Gutman, Roy and David Rieff, eds. *Crimes of War: What the Public Should Know.* W. W. Norton & Company, New York 1999.

Habermas, Jürgen. "Bestiality and Humanity: A War on the Border Between Legaity and Morality." *Constellations* 6:3, 1999.

Hampshire, Stuart. *Innocence and Experience.* Harvard University Press, Cambridge MA 1989.

Hamsun, Knut: *Fra det ubevidste Sjæleliv.* Gyldendal, Oslo 1994. (Quotation trans. Kerri A. Pierce.)

Hare, Robert D. *Without Conscience: The Disturbing World of the Psychopaths among Us*, Guilford Press, London 1999.

Häring, Hermann and David Tracy, eds. *The Fascination of Evil*. SCM Press, London 1998.

Harris, Thomas. *The Silence of the Lambs*. St. Martin's Press, New York 1988.

Hegel, G. W. F. *The Encyclopaedia Logic: Part 1 of the Encyclopaedia of Philosophical Sciences*. Trans. T. F. Geraets, et. al. Hackett, Indianapolis, 1991.

—. *Hegel's Aesthetics: Lectures on Fine Art, Volume I*. Trans. T. M. Knox. Oxford University Press, Oxford 1998.

—. *Natural Law*. Trans. T.M. Knox. University of Pennsylvania Press, Philadelphia 1975.

—. *The Philosophy of History*. Trans. J. Sibree. Dover Publications, New York 2004.

—. *Philosophy of Right*. Trans. S. W. Dyde. Dover Publications, Mineola, 2005.

Heidegger, Martin. *Being and Time*. Trans. John Macquarrie and Edward Robinson. Harper & Row, New York 1962.

—. *Contributions to Philosophy (From Enowning)*. Trans. Parvis Ernad and Kenneth Maly. Indiana University Press, Bloomington 1989.

—. *Feldweg-Gespräche, Gesamtausgabe Band 77*. Klostermann, Frankfurt a. M. 1989.

—. *Hölderlins Hymne "Andenken," Gesamtausgabe Band 52*. Klostermann, Frankfurt a. M. 1982.

—. *Hölderlin's Hymn "The Ister."* Trans. William McNeill and Julia Davis. Indiana University Press, Bloomington 1996.

Heller, Agnes. "The Legacy of Marxian Ethics," in A. Heller & F. Feher, eds.: *The Grandeur and Twilight of Radical Universalism*. New Brunswick 1987.

Heraclitus. *Fragments*. Trans. Brooks Haxton. Penguin, New York 2003.

Herder, Johann Gottfried. *Another Philosophy of History for the Education of Mankind*. Trans. Ioannis D. Evrigenis and Daniel Pellerin. Hackett, Indianapolis 2004.

Hick, John. *Evil and the God of Love*. Harper and Row, New York 1978.

Hitler, Adolf. *Hitler's Table Talk 1941–1944. His Private Conversations*. Trans. Norman Cameron and R. H. Stevens. Enigma Books, New York 2000.

—. *Mein Kampf*. Trans. Ralph Manheim. Houghton Mifflin, New York 1999.

Hobbes, Thomas. *De Cive*. Clarendon Press, Oxford 1983.

—. *Leviathan*. Cambridge University Press, Cambridge 1991.

Hochschild, Adam. *King Leopold's Ghost: A Story of Greed, Terror, and Heroism in Colonial Africa*. Papermac, London 2000.

Hollander, Paul. "Revisiting the 'Banality of Evil': Political Violence in Communist Systems," in *Partisan Review* 1, 1997.

Honderich, Ted. *Violence for Equality: Inquiries in Political Philosophy*. Penguin, Harmondsworth 1980.

Höss, Rudolf. *Commandant of Auschwitz: The Autobiography of Rudolf Höss*. Trans. Constantine Fitzgibbon. Phoenix Press, London 2000.

Howard-Snyder, Daniel, ed. *The Evidential Argument from Evil*. Indiana University Press, Bloomington 1996.

Hume, David. *Enquiries Concerning Human Understanding and Concerning the Principles of Morals*. Clarendon Press, Oxford 1989.

—. *A Treatise of Human Nature*. Penguin, Harmondsworth 1984.

Ignatieff, Michael. *Virtual War: Kosovo and Beyond*. Vintage, London 2001.

—. *The Warrior's Honor: Ethnic War and the Modern Conscience*. Henry Holt and Company, New York 1997.

Irlenborn, Bernd. *Der Ingrimm des Aufruhrs: Heidegger und das Problem des Bösen*. Passagen Verlag, Vienna 2000.

Jaspers, Karl. *Von der Wahrheit*. Piper, Munich 1947.

Johnson, Eric and Karl-Heinz Reuband. *What We Knew. Terror, Mass Murder and Everyday Life in Nazi Germany*. John Murray, London 2005.

Johnson, James T. *The Just War Tradition and the Restraint of War*. Princeton University Press, Princeton NJ 1981.

Kahn, Paul W. "War and Sacrifice in Kosovo," *Philosophy and Public Policy* 19:2/3, 1999.

Kant, Immanuel. "An Answer to the Question: What is Enlightenment?" Trans. David L. Colclasure, in Pauline Kleingeld, ed.: *Toward Perpetual Peace and Other Writings on Politics, Peace, and History*. Yale University Press, New Haven, 2006.

—. *Anthropology from a Pragmatic Point of View*. Trans. Robert B. Louden, in Gunter Zöller and Robert B. Louden, eds.: *Anthropology, History, and Education*. Cambridge University Press, Cambridge 2007.

—. *The Conflict of the Faculties*. Trans. Mary J. Gregor and Robert Anchor, in Paul Guyer and Allen W. Wood, eds.: *Religion and Rational Theology*. Cambridge University Press, Cambridge 2005.

—. "Conjectural Beginning of Human History." Trans. David L. Colclasure. In Pauline Kleingeld, ed.: *Toward Perpetual Peace and Other Writings on Politics, Peace, and History*. Yale University Press, New Haven 2006.

—. *Critique of Judgment.* Trans. J. H. Bernard. Dover Publications, Mineola 2005.

—. *Critique of Practical Reason.* Trans. Mary J. Gregor. In Allen W. Wood, ed.: *Practical Philosophy.* Cambridge University Press, Cambridge 1996.

—. *Critique of Pure Reason.* Ed. and trans. Marcus Weigelt. Penguin, New York 2007.

—. *Fundamental Principles of the Metaphysics of Morals.* Trans. Thomas K. Abbott. In Allen W. Wood, ed.: *Basic Writings of Kant.* The Modern Library, New York 2001.

—. "Idea for a Universal History from a Cosmopolitan Perspective." Trans. David L. Colclasure. In Pauline Kleingeld, ed.: *Toward Perpetual Peace and Other Writings on Politics, Peace, and History.* Yale University Press, New Haven 2006.

—. *Lectures on Ethics.* Trans. Peter Heath. J. B. Schneewind, ed. Cambridge University Press, Cambridge 2001.

—. *Lectures on Pedagogy.* Trans. Robert B. Louden. In Gunter Zöller and Robert B. Louden, eds.: *Anthropology, History, and Education.* Cambridge University Press, Cambridge 2007.

—. *Logic.* Trans. Robert S. Hartman and Wolfgang Schwarz. Dover Publications, New York 1988.

—. *Metaphysics of Morals.* Trans. Mary J. Gregor. In Allen W. Wood, ed.: *Practical Philosophy.* Cambridge University Press, Cambridge 1996.

—. "On the Common Saying: This May be True in Theory, But It Does Not Apply in Praxis." Trans. N. S. Nisbet, in H. S. Reiss, ed.: *Political Writings.* Cambridge University Press, Cambridge 1991.

—. "On the Miscarriage of All Philosophical Trials in Theodicy." Trans. George di Giovanni. In Paul Guyer and Allen W. Wood, eds.: *Religion and Rational Theology*. Cambridge University Press, Cambridge 2005.

—. "On a Supposed Right to Lie because of Philanthropic Concerns." Trans. James W. Ellington. In *Ethical Philosophy*. Hackett, Indianapolis 1994.

—. *Reflexionen zur Anthropologie*. In *Kants gesammelte Schriften*, bind XIV, Preußischen Akademie der Wissenschaften ed. de Gruyter, Berlin 1902.

—. *Reflexionen zur Metaphysik*. In *Kants gesammelte Schriften*, bind XIV, Preußischen Akademie der Wissenschaften ed. de Gruyter, Berlin 1902.

—. *Religion Within the Limits of Reason Alone*. Trans. Theodore M. Greene and Hoyt H. Hudson. HarperCollins, New York 2008.

—. "Reviews of Herder's Ideas on the Philosophy of the History of Mankind." Trans. N. S. Nisbet. In H. S. Reiss, ed.: *Political Writings*. Cambridge University Press, Cambridge 1991.

—. *Toward Perpetual Peace*. Trans. David L. Colclasure. In Pauline Kleingeld, ed.: *Toward Perpetual Peace and Other Writings on Politics, Peace, and History*. Yale University Press, New Haven 2006.

—. *Vorarbeiten zur Religion innerhalb der Grenzen der bloßen Vernunft*, i *Kants gesammelte Schriften*, bind XXIII, Preußischen Akademie der Wissenschaften ed. de Gruyter, Berlin 1902.

Kapuściński, Ryszard. *The Soccer War*. Trans. William Brand. Vintage Books. New York 1992.

Katz, Fred E. *Ordinary People and Extraordinary Evil: A Report on the Beguilings of Evil*. State University of New York Press, Albany 1993.

Katz, Jack. *Seductions of Crime: Moral and Sensual Attractions in Doing Evil*. Basic Books, New York 1988.

Keane, John. *Reflections on Violence*. Verso, New York 1996.

Keats, John. "To George and Georgina Keats, February 14 to May 8, 1819," in Mark Larrimore, ed.: *The Problem of Evil: A Reader*. Blackwell, Oxford 2001.

Kekes, John. *Facing Evil*. Princeton University Press, Princeton NJ 1990.

Kittsteiner, Heinz Dieter. "Die Abschaffung des Teufels im 18. Jahrundert. Ein kulturhistorisches Ereignis und seine Folgen," in Alexander Schuller und Wolfgang von Rahden, eds. *Die andere Kraft: Zur Renaissance des Bösen*. Akademie Verlag, Berlin 1993.

Koselleck, Reinhard. "Zur historisch-politischen Semantik asymmetrischer Gegenbegriffe," in *Vergangene Zukunft. Zur Se mantik geschichtlicher Zeiten*. Suhrkamp, Frankfurt a. M. 1979.

Lacroix, Michel. *Das Böse*. Trans. Thomas Laugstien. BLT, Bergisch Gladbach 1999.

Lactantius. *The Wrath of God*. Trans. Sister Mary Frances McDonald, in Mark Larrimore, ed.: *The Problem of Evil: A Reader*. Blackwell, Oxford 2001.

Lang, Berel. *Act and Idea in the Nazi Genocide*. University of Chicago Press, Chicago 1990.

Lang, Jochen von and Claus Sibyll, eds. *Eichmann Interrogated: Transcripts from the Archives of the Israeli Police*. Da Capo Press, New York 1999.

Lautréamont, Comte de. *Maldoror and Poems*. Trans. Paul Knight. Penguin, New York, 1978.

Leibniz, Gottfried Wilhelm von. *Theodicy: Essays on the Goodness of God, the Freedom of Man, and the Origin of Evil*. Trans. E. M. Huggard. Open Court, Chicago 1985.

Leopardi, Giacomo. *The Canti with a Selection of His Prose*. Trans. J. G. Nichols. Routledge, New York 2003.

—. "Memorable Sayings of Filippo Ottonieri." Trans. Giovanni Ceccetti, in *Operette Morali: Essays and Dialogues*. University of California Press, Berkeley 1982.

Lerner, M. *The Belief in a Just World: A Fundamental Delusion*. Plenum Press, New York 1980.

Levi, Primo. *The Drowned and the Saved*. Trans. Raymond Rosenthal. Vintage, New York 1989.

—. "Introduction." Trans. Joachim Neugroschel, in Rudolf Höss: *Commandant of Auschwitz: The Autobiography of Rudolf Höss*. Phoenix Press, London 2000.

Levinas, Emmanuel. *Humanism of the Other*. Trans. Nidra Poller. University of Illinois Press, Urbana 2006.

—. *Of God Who Comes to Mind*. Trans. Bettina Bergo. Stanford University Press, Stanford 1998.

—. "Useless Suffering." Trans. Richard Cohen, in Mark Larrimore, ed.: *The Problem of Evil: A Reader*. Blackwell, Oxford 2001.

Leyhausen, Paul et. al. *Krieg oder Frieden*. Piper, Munich 1970.

Lifton, Robert J. *The Nazi Doctors: Medical Killing and the Psychology of Genocide*. Basic Books, New York 1986.

Lissman, Konrad Paul, ed. *Fascination des Bösen: Über die Abgründe des Menschlichen*. Paul Zsolnay Verlag, Vienna 1997.

Lyotard, Jean-François. *The Postmodern Condition: A Report on Knowledge*. Trans. Geoff Bennington and Brian Massumi. Manchester University Press, Manchester 1984.

Machiavelli, Niccolò. *Discourses*. Trans. Peter Bondenella and Mark Muse. Penguin, Harmondsworth 1979.

Mackie, John. "Evil and Omnipotence," in Marilyn McCord Adams and Robert Merrihew Adams, eds.: *The Problem of Evil*. Oxford University Press, New York 1990.

Mann, Thomas. *Diaries 1918–1939*. Trans. C. Winston and R. Winston. Hermann Kesten, ed. André Deutsch, London 1983.

—. "The Problem of Freedom: An Address to the Undergraduates and Faculty of Rutgers University at Convocation on April the 28th, 1939." Rutgers University Press, New Brunswick, 1939.

Marquard, Odo. *In Defense of the Accidental: Philosophical Studies*. Trans. Robert M. Wallace. Oxford University Press, New York 1991.

Masters, Brian. *The Evil That Men Do*. Doubleday, London 1996.

May, Rollo. *Power and Innocence: A Search for the Sources of Violence*. Norton, New York 1972.

McGinn, Bernard. *Antichrist: Two Thousand Years of the Human Fascination with Evil*. Columbia University Press, New York 2000.

McGinn, Colin. *Ethics, Evil, and Fiction*. Clarendon Press, Oxford 1997.

McGraw, Kathleen M. "Guilt Following Transgression: An Attribution of Responsibility Approach." *Journal of Personality and Social Psychology* 53, 1987.

Melville, Herman. *Billy Budd and Other Stories*. Penguin, New York 1986.

Midgley, Mary. *Wickedness: A Philosophical Essay*. Routledge, New York 2001.

Milgram, Stanley. *Obedience to Authority: An Experimental View*. Harper & Row, New York 1974.

Mill, John Stuart. *An Examination of Sir William Hamilton's Philosophy*, in Mark Larrimore, ed.: *The Problem of Evil: A Reader*, Blackwell, Oxford 2001.

Milton, John. *Paradise Lost*, Penguin, London 2000.

Montaigne, Michel de. "On Cruelty," in *The Essays: A Selection*. Trans. M.A. Screech. Penguin, New York 2003.

Morgenthau, Hans. "Love and Power," in *Commentary* 33, 1962.

—. *Politics among Nations.* Knopf, New York 1948.

Morris, David B. "The Plot of Suffering: AIDS and Evil," in Jennifer L. Geddes, ed.: *Evil After Postmodernism.* Routledge, Lon- New York 2001.

Nagel, Thomas. *Mortal Questions.* Cambridge University Press, Cambridge 1979.

Naimark, Norman M. *Fires of Hatred: Ethnic Cleansing in Twentieth-Century Europe.* Harvard University Press, Cambridge MA 2001.

Nancy, Jean-Luc. *The Experience of Freedom.* Trans. Bridget McDonald. Stanford University Press, Stanford 1993.

Nietzsche, Friedrich. *Beyond Good and Evil.* Trans. Walter Kaufmann. Vintage Books, New York 1989.

—. *Nachgelassene Fragmente 1884–1885,* in *Kritische Studienausgabe,* Bd. 11, dtv/de Gruyter, Berlin 1988.

—. *Nachgelassene Fragmente 1885–1887,* in *Kritische Studienausgabe,* Bd. 12, dtv/de Gruyter, Berlin 1988.

—. *On the Genealogy of Morals.* Trans. Douglas Smith. Oxford University Press, New York 1996.

—. *Thus Spoke Zarathustra.* Trans. R. J. Hollingdale. Penguin, New York, 2003.

—. *Writings from the Late Notebooks.* Trans. Kate Sturge. Rüdiger Bittner, ed. Cambridge University Press, New York 2003.

Nino, Carlos Santiago. *Radical Evil on Trial.* Yale University Press, New Haven 1996.

Norris, Joel. *Serial Killers. The Growing Menace.* Doubleday, New York 1988.

Novalis. *Notes for a Romantic Encyclopaedia.* Trans. David W. Wood. State University of New York Press, Albany 2007.

—. *Schriften, Band 2, Das Philosophisch-theoretische Werk.* Wissenschaftliche Buchgesellschaft, Darmstadt 1999.

Ofstad, Harald. *Our Contempt for Weakness: Nazi Norms and Values—and Our Own.* Trans. C. von Sydow. Almquist & Wiksell International, Stockholm 1989.

Ogata, Sadako. "Peace, Security and Humanitarian Action," in Frank J. Lechner and John Boli, eds.: *The Globalization Reader*, Blackwell, Oxford 2000.

O'Neill, Onora. *Constructions of Reason: Explorations of Kant's Practical Philosophy.* Cambridge University Press, Cambridge 1989.

Oppenheimer, Paul. *Evil and the Demonic: A New Theory of Monstrous Behaviour.* New York University Press, New York 1996.

Pakenham, Thomas. *The Scramble for Africa: The White Man's Conquest of the Dark Continent from 1876–1912.* Random House, New York 1991.

Parkin, David, ed. *The Anthropology of Evil.* Blackwell, Oxford 1985.

Pascal, Blaise. *Penseés and Other Writings.* Trans. Honor Levi. Oxford University Press, New York, 1999.

—. *The Provincial Letters.* Trans. Thomas M'Crie. BiblioBazaar, Charleston 2009.

Pauen, Michael. *Pessimismus: Geschichtsphilosophie, Metaphysik und Moderne von Nietzsche bis Spengler.* Akademie Verlag, Berlin 1997.

Plack, Arno. *Die Gesellschaft und Das Böse: Eine Kritik der herrschenden Moral.* Fischer, Frankfurt a. M. 1991.

Plantinga, Alvin. *The Nature of Necessity.* Oxford University Press, Oxford 1974.

Plato. *Gorgias.* Trans. Robin Waterfield. Oxford University Press, New York 1994.

—. *Meno and Other Dialogues.* Trans. Robin Waterfield. Oxford University Press, Oxford 2005.

—. *Philebus.* Trans. Dorothea Frede. Hackett, Indianapolis 1993.

—. *Protagoras.* Trans. C. C. W. Taylor. Oxford University Press, Oxford 2002.

—. *The Republic.* Trans. G. M. A. Grube. Hackett, Indianapolis 1992.

—. *Timaeus.* Trans. Peter Kalkavage. Focus Publishing, Newburyport 2001.

Plotinus. *The Enneads.* Trans. Stephen MacKenna. Paul Brunton, New York 1992.

Poe, Edgar Allen. *The Complete Illustrated Stories and Poems.* Chancellor Press, London 1994.

Pope, Alexander. *The Poems of Alexander Pope.* John Butt, ed. Yale University Press, New Haven 1963.

Popper, Karl R. *Conjectures and Refutations.* Routledge, London 1989.

—. *The Open Society and Its Enemies. Volume One: The Spell of Plato.* Routledge, London 2005.

Portmann, John. *When Bad Things Happen to Other People.* Routledge, New York 2000.

Pressac, Jean-Claude. *Auschwitz: Technique and Operation of the Gas Chambers.* The Holocaust History Project. 16 Nov. 2009 <http://www.holocaust-history.org/auschwitz/pressac/technique-and-operation/pressac0005.shtml>.

Pseudo-Dionysius. *On the Divine Names.* Trans. John D. Jones, in Mark Larrimore, ed.: *The Problem of Evil: A Reader.* Blackwell, Oxford 2001.

Rapp, Friedrich. *Fortschritt: Entwicklung und Sinngehalt einer philosophischen Idee.* Wissenschaftliche Buchgesellschaft, Darmstadt 1992.

Rawls, John. "Kantian Constructivism in Moral Theory," in *Journal of Philosophy* 77:9, 1980.

—. *The Law of Peoples*. Harvard University Press, Cambridge MA 1999.

—. *A Theory of Justice*. Oxford University Press, Oxford 1971.

Ricoeur, Paul. *The Conflict of Interpretations*. Don Ihde, ed. Northwestern University Press, Evanston 1974.

—. *Fallible Man*. Trans. Charles A. Kelbley. Fordham University Press, New York 2000.

—. *The Symbolism of Evil*. Trans. Emerson Buchanan. Beacon Press, Boston 1969.

Robertson, Geoffrey. *Crimes Against Humanity: The Struggle for Global Justice*. Penguin, Harmondsworth 2000.

Rochefoucauld, François de La. *Maxims*. Trans. Leonard Tancock. Penguin, New York 1959.

Rosenbaum, Ron. *Explaining Hitler: The Search for the Origins of His Evil*. HarperCollins, New York 1999.

Rosenkranz, Karl. *Ästhetik des Häßlichen*. Reclam, Leipzig 1990.

Rosenthal, Abigail L. *A Good Look at Evil*. Temple University Press, Philadelphia 1987.

Rousseau, Jean-Jacques. *A Discourse on Inequality*. Trans. Maurice Cranston. Penguin, New York 1984.

—. *Emile, or On Education*. Trans. Allan Bloom. Basic Books, New York 1979.

—. "Letter from J.-J. Rousseau to Mr. de Voltaire, August 18, 1756." Trans. Judith R. Bush, Roger D. Masters, Christopher Kelly, and Terence Marshall. In Mark Larrimore, ed.: *The Problem of Evil: A Reader*. Blackwell, Oxford 2001.

—. *Reveries of a Solitary Walker*. Trans. Peter France. Penguin, New York, 1979.

Rowe, William L. "The Problem of Evil and Some Varieties of Atheism," in Marilyn McCord Adams and Robert Merrihew Adams, eds.: *The Problem of Evil*. Oxford University Press, New York 1990.

Rubenstein, William D. *The Myth of Rescue: Why the Democracies Could Not Have Saved More Jews from the Nazis*. Routledge, New York 1997.

Russell, Jeffrey Burton. *The Devil: Perceptions of Evil from Antiquity to Primitive Christianity*. Cornell University Press, Ithaca 1977.

—. *Lucifer: The Devil in the Middle Ages*. Cornell University Press, Ithaca 1984.

—. *Mephistopheles: The Devil in the Modern World*. Cornell University Press, Ithaca 1986.

—. *The Prince of Darkness: Radical Evil and Power of Good in History*. Cornell University Press, Ithaka/London 1988.

—. *Satan: The Early Christian Tradition*. Cornell University Press, Ithaca 1981.

Sade, Donatien-Alphonse-François de. *Justine, Philosophy in the Bedroom and other writings*. Trans. Richard Seaver and Austryn Wainhouse. Grove Press, New York 1965.

Sæterbakken, Stig. *Det onde øye*. Cappelen, Oslo 2001. (Quotation trans. Kerri A. Pierce.)

Sartre, Jean-Paul. *Baudelaire*. Trans. Martin Turnell. New Directions, New York 1967.

Scarry, Elaine. *The Body in Pain: The Making and the Unmaking of the World*. Oxford University Press, New York 1985.

Schelling, F. W. J. *Philosophical Investigations into the Essence of Human Freedom*. Trans. Jeff Love and Johannes Schmidt. State University of New York, Albany 2006.

Schmitt, Carl. *The Concept of the Political*. Trans. George Schwab. University of Chicago Press, Chicago 1996.

Schopenhauer, Arthur. *On the Basis of Morality*. Trans. Arthur Brodrick Bullock. McMillan, New York 1915.

—. *Parerga and Paralipomena: Volume II*. Trans. E. F. J. Payne. Oxford University Press, Oxford 1974.

—. *The World as Will and Representation: Volume I*. Trans. E. F. J. Payne. Dover Publications, Mineola 1966.

—. *The World as Will and Representation: Volume. II*. Trans. E. F. J. Payne. Dover Publications, Mineola 1966.

Schrader, Wolfgang H. *Ethik nd Anthropologie in der englischen Aufklärung: Der Wandel der moral-sense-Theorie von Schaftesbury bis Hume*. Felix Meiner, Hamburg 1984.

Schuller, Alexander and Wolfgang von Rahden, eds. *Die andere Kraft: Zur Renaissance des Bösen*. Akademie Verlag, Berlin 1993.

Seifert, Ruth. "The Second Front: The Logic of Sexual Violence in Wars," in Manfred B. Steger and Nancy S. Lind, eds.: *Violence and Its Alternatives: An Interdisciplinary Reader*. Macmillan, London 1999.

Seneca, Lucius Annaeus. *Dialogues and Essays*. Trans. John Davie. Oxford University Press, New York 2007.

Sereny, Gitta. *Into that Darkness: An Examination of Conscience*. Vintage Books, New York 1983.

Shakespeare, William. *Hamlet*, Sylvan Barnet, ed. New American Library, New York 1998.

Shawcross, William. *Deliver Us From Evil: Peacekeepers, Warlords and a World of Endless Conflict*. Simon & Schuster, New York 2000.

Smith, Adam. *The Wealth of Nations*. The Modern Library, New York 2000.

Sofsky, Wolfgang. *Traktat über die Gewalt*, Fischer. Frankfurt a. M. 1996.

Solzhenitsyn, Alexander. *The Gulag Archipelago*. Trans. Thomas P. Whitney. Harper and Row, New York 1975.

Sorel, Georges. *Reflections on Violence*. Jeremy Jennings, ed. Cambridge University Press, Cambridge 2001.

Spinoza, Baruch. *The Ethics and Selected Letters*. Trans. Samuel Shirley. Hackett, Indianapolis 1982.

Staub, Ervin. *The Roots of Evil: The Origins of Genocide and Other Group Violence*. Cambridge University Press, Cambridge 1989.

Stump, Eleonore. "Knowledge, Freedom, and the Problem of Evil," in Michael L. Peterson, ed.: *The Problem of Evil: Selected Readings*. University of Notre Dame Press, Notre Dame 1992.

Svendsen, Lars. *The Philosophy of Boredom*. Trans. John Irons. Reaktion Books, London 2005.

Swinburne, Richard. *The Existence of God*. Clarendon Press, Oxford 1991.

—. "Natural Evil," in Michael L. Peterson, ed.: *The Problem of Evil: Selected Readings*. University of Notre Dame Press, Notre Dame 1992.

Todorov, Tzvetan. *Facing the Extreme: Moral Life in the Concentration Camps*. Trans. Arthur Denner and Abigail Pollack. Phoenix Press, London 2000.

Trevor-Roper, Hugh. *The European Witch-Craze of the Sixteenth and Seventeenth Centuries*. Penguin, New York, 1969.

Vetlesen, Arne Johan. "Ondskap i Bosnia," in *Norsk filosofisk tidsskrift* 1/2, 1997.

Voltaire, François-Marie Arouet de. *Candide, or Optimism*. Trans. Theo Cuffe. London, Penguin 2005.

Walzer, Michael. *Just and Unjust Wars*. Basic Books, New York 1977.

Watson, Lyall. *Dark Nature: A Natural History of Evil*. HarperCollins, New York 1995.

—. *From Max Weber: Essays in Sociology.* Trans. and ed. H. H. Gerth and C. Wright Mills. Routledge, London 2001.

Weber, Max. *Max Weber's Complete Writings on Academic and Political Vocations.* Trans. Gordon C. Wells. John Dreijmanis, ed. Algora Publishing, New York 2008.

Weil, Simone. *Gravity and Grace.* Trans. Emma Crawford and Mario von der Ruhr. Routledge, New York 2008.

—. "The Power of Words." Trans. Richard Rees, in Siân Miles, ed.: *Simone Weil: An Anthology.* Grove Press, New York 1986.

Wittgenstein, Ludwig. *Culture and Value.* Trans. Peter Winch. The University of Chicago Press, Chicago 1984.

—. *Notebooks 1914–1916: 2nd Edition.* Trans. G. E. M. Anscombe. G. H. von Wright and G. E. M. Anscombe, eds. University of Chicago Press, Chicago 1979.

—. *Philosophical Investigations: 2nd Edition.* Trans. G. E. M. Anscombe. R. Rhees and G. E. M. Anscombe, eds. Blackwell Publishers, Malden 1999.

Xenophon. *The Memorabilia.* Trans. H. G. Dakyns. BiblioBazaar, Charleston 2007.

LARS SVENDSEN is Professor in the Department of Philosophy at the University of Bergen, Norway. He is the author of several books, including *A Philosophy of Boredom* (2005), *Fashion: A Philosophy* (2006), *Work* (2008), and *A Philosophy of Fear* (2008). His books have been translated into twenty-two languages.

KERRI A. PIERCE is the translator of Mela Hartwig's *Am I a Redundant Human Being?* for Dalkey Archive Press. She translates from German, Danish, Dutch, Portuguese, Spanish, Norwegian, and Swedish.

PETROS ABATZOGLOU, *What Does Mrs. Freeman Want?*
MICHAL AJVAZ, *The Golden Age.*
The Other City.
PIERRE ALBERT-BIROT, *Grabinoulor.*
YUZ ALESHKOVSKY, *Kangaroo.*
FELIPE ALFAU, *Chromos.*
Locos.
IVAN ÂNGELO, *The Celebration.*
The Tower of Glass.
DAVID ANTIN, *Talking.*
ANTÓNIO LOBO ANTUNES, *Knowledge of Hell.*
ALAIN ARIAS-MISSON, *Theatre of Incest.*
JOHN ASHBERY AND JAMES SCHUYLER, *A Nest of Ninnies.*
HEIMRAD BÄCKER, *transcript.*
DJUNA BARNES, *Ladies Almanack.*
Ryder.
JOHN BARTH, *LETTERS.*
Sabbatical.
DONALD BARTHELME, *The King.*
Paradise.
SVETISLAV BASARA, *Chinese Letter.*
MARK BINELLI, *Sacco and Vanzetti Must Die!*
ANDREI BITOV, *Pushkin House.*
LOUIS PAUL BOON, *Chapel Road.*
My Little War.
Summer in Termuren.
ROGER BOYLAN, *Killoyle.*
IGNÁCIO DE LOYOLA BRANDÃO, *Anonymous Celebrity.*
Teeth under the Sun.
Zero.
BONNIE BREMSER, *Troia: Mexican Memoirs.*
CHRISTINE BROOKE-ROSE, *Amalgamemnon.*
BRIGID BROPHY, *In Transit.*
MEREDITH BROSNAN, *Mr. Dynamite.*
GERALD L. BRUNS, *Modern Poetry and the Idea of Language.*
EVGENY BUNIMOVICH AND J. KATES, EDS., *Contemporary Russian Poetry: An Anthology.*
GABRIELLE BURTON, *Heartbreak Hotel.*
MICHEL BUTOR, *Degrees.*
Mobile.
Portrait of the Artist as a Young Ape.
G. CABRERA INFANTE, *Infante's Inferno.*
Three Trapped Tigers.
JULIETA CAMPOS, *The Fear of Losing Eurydice.*
ANNE CARSON, *Eros the Bittersweet.*
CAMILO JOSÉ CELA, *Christ versus Arizona.*
The Family of Pascual Duarte.
The Hive.
LOUIS-FERDINAND CÉLINE, *Castle to Castle.*
Conversations with Professor Y.
London Bridge.
Normance.
North.
Rigadoon.
HUGO CHARTERIS, *The Tide Is Right.*
JEROME CHARYN, *The Tar Baby.*
MARC CHOLODENKO, *Mordechai Schamz.*

JOSHUA COHEN, *Witz.*
EMILY HOLMES COLEMAN, *The Shutter of Snow.*
ROBERT COOVER, *A Night at the Movies.*
STANLEY CRAWFORD, *Log of the S.S. The Mrs Unguentine.*
Some Instructions to My Wife.
ROBERT CREELEY, *Collected Prose.*
RENÉ CREVEL, *Putting My Foot in It.*
RALPH CUSACK, *Cadenza.*
SUSAN DAITCH, *L.C.*
Storytown.
NICHOLAS DELBANCO, *The Count of Concord.*
NIGEL DENNIS, *Cards of Identity.*
PETER DIMOCK, *A Short Rhetoric for Leaving the Family.*
ARIEL DORFMAN, *Konfidenz.*
COLEMAN DOWELL, *The Houses of Children.*
Island People.
Too Much Flesh and Jabez.
ARKADII DRAGOMOSHCHENKO, *Dust.*
RIKKI DUCORNET, *The Complete Butcher's Tales.*
The Fountains of Neptune.
The Jade Cabinet.
The One Marvelous Thing.
Phosphor in Dreamland.
The Stain.
The Word "Desire."
WILLIAM EASTLAKE, *The Bamboo Bed.*
Castle Keep.
Lyric of the Circle Heart.
JEAN ECHENOZ, *Chopin's Move.*
STANLEY ELKIN, *A Bad Man.*
Boswell: A Modern Comedy.
Criers and Kibitzers, Kibitzers and Criers.
The Dick Gibson Show.
The Franchiser.
George Mills.
The Living End.
The MacGuffin.
The Magic Kingdom.
Mrs. Ted Bliss.
The Rabbi of Lud.
Van Gogh's Room at Arles.
ANNIE ERNAUX, *Cleaned Out.*
LAUREN FAIRBANKS, *Muzzle Thyself.*
Sister Carrie.
LESLIE A. FIEDLER, *Love and Death in the American Novel.*
JUAN FILLOY, *Op Oloop.*
GUSTAVE FLAUBERT, *Bouvard and Pécuchet.*
KASS FLEISHER, *Talking out of School.*
FORD MADOX FORD, *The March of Literature.*
JON FOSSE, *Melancholy.*
MAX FRISCH, *I'm Not Stiller.*
Man in the Holocene.
CARLOS FUENTES, *Christopher Unborn.*
Distant Relations.
Terra Nostra.
Where the Air Is Clear.

JANICE GALLOWAY, *Foreign Parts*.
   The Trick Is to Keep Breathing.
WILLIAM H. GASS, *Cartesian Sonata*
      and Other Novellas.
   Finding a Form.
   A Temple of Texts.
   The Tunnel.
   Willie Masters' Lonesome Wife.
GÉRARD GAVARRY, *Hoppla! 1 2 3*.
ETIENNE GILSON,
   The Arts of the Beautiful.
   Forms and Substances in the Arts.
C. S. GISCOMBE, *Giscome Road*.
   Here.
   Prairie Style.
DOUGLAS GLOVER, *Bad News of the Heart*.
   The Enamoured Knight.
WITOLD GOMBROWICZ,
   A Kind of Testament.
KAREN ELIZABETH GORDON, *The Red Shoes*.
GEORGI GOSPODINOV, *Natural Novel*.
JUAN GOYTISOLO, *Count Julian*.
   Juan the Landless.
   Makbara.
   Marks of Identity.
PATRICK GRAINVILLE, *The Cave of Heaven*.
HENRY GREEN, *Back*.
   Blindness.
   Concluding.
   Doting.
   Nothing.
JIŘÍ GRUŠA, *The Questionnaire*.
GABRIEL GUDDING,
   Rhode Island Notebook.
MELA HARTWIG, *Am I a Redundant*
      Human Being?
JOHN HAWKES, *The Passion Artist*.
   Whistlejacket.
ALEKSANDAR HEMON, ED.,
   Best European Fiction 2010.
AIDAN HIGGINS, *A Bestiary*.
   Balcony of Europe.
   Bornholm Night-Ferry.
   Darkling Plain: Texts for the Air.
   Flotsam and Jetsam.
   Langrishe, Go Down.
   Scenes from a Receding Past.
   Windy Arbours.
ALDOUS HUXLEY, *Antic Hay*.
   Crome Yellow.
   Point Counter Point.
   Those Barren Leaves.
   Time Must Have a Stop.
MIKHAIL IOSSEL AND JEFF PARKER, EDS.,
   Amerika: Russian Writers View the
      United States.
GERT JONKE, *The Distant Sound*.
   Geometric Regional Novel.
   Homage to Czerny.
   The System of Vienna.
JACQUES JOUET, *Mountain R*.
   Savage.
CHARLES JULIET, *Conversations with*
      Samuel Beckett and Bram van
      Velde.
MIEKO KANAI, *The Word Book*.

HUGH KENNER, *The Counterfeiters*.
   Flaubert, Joyce and Beckett:
      The Stoic Comedians.
   Joyce's Voices.
DANILO KIŠ, *Garden, Ashes*.
   A Tomb for Boris Davidovich.
ANITA KONKKA, *A Fool's Paradise*.
GEORGE KONRÁD, *The City Builder*.
TADEUSZ KONWICKI, *A Minor Apocalypse*.
   The Polish Complex.
MENIS KOUMANDAREAS, *Koula*.
ELAINE KRAF, *The Princess of 72nd Street*.
JIM KRUSOE, *Iceland*.
EWA KURYLUK, *Century 21*.
ERIC LAURRENT, *Do Not Touch*.
VIOLETTE LEDUC, *La Bâtarde*.
SUZANNE JILL LEVINE, *The Subversive*
      Scribe: Translating Latin
      American Fiction.
DEBORAH LEVY, *Billy and Girl*.
   Pillow Talk in Europe and Other
      Places.
JOSÉ LEZAMA LIMA, *Paradiso*.
ROSA LIKSOM, *Dark Paradise*.
OSMAN LINS, *Avalovara*.
   The Queen of the Prisons of Greece.
ALF MAC LOCHLAINN,
   The Corpus in the Library.
   Out of Focus.
RON LOEWINSOHN, *Magnetic Field(s)*.
BRIAN LYNCH, *The Winner of Sorrow*.
D. KEITH MANO, *Take Five*.
MICHELINE AHARONIAN MARCOM,
   The Mirror in the Well.
BEN MARCUS,
   The Age of Wire and String.
WALLACE MARKFIELD,
   Teitlebaum's Window.
   To an Early Grave.
DAVID MARKSON, *Reader's Block*.
   Springer's Progress.
   Wittgenstein's Mistress.
CAROLE MASO, *AVA*.
LADISLAV MATEJKA AND KRYSTYNA
   POMORSKA, EDS.,
   Readings in Russian Poetics:
      Formalist and Structuralist Views.
HARRY MATHEWS,
   The Case of the Persevering Maltese:
      Collected Essays.
   Cigarettes.
   The Conversions.
   The Human Country: New and
      Collected Stories.
   The Journalist.
   My Life in CIA.
   Singular Pleasures.
   The Sinking of the Odradek
      Stadium.
   Tlooth.
   20 Lines a Day.
ROBERT L. MCLAUGHLIN, ED.,
   Innovations: An Anthology of
      Modern & Contemporary Fiction.
HERMAN MELVILLE, *The Confidence-Man*.
AMANDA MICHALOPOULOU, *I'd Like*.

STEVEN MILLHAUSER,
The Barnum Museum.
In the Penny Arcade.
RALPH J. MILLS, JR.,
Essays on Poetry.
MOMUS, *The Book of Jokes.*
CHRISTINE MONTALBETTI, *Western.*
OLIVE MOORE, *Spleen.*
NICHOLAS MOSLEY, *Accident.*
Assassins.
Catastrophe Practice.
Children of Darkness and Light.
Experience and Religion.
God's Hazard.
The Hesperides Tree.
Hopeful Monsters.
Imago Bird.
Impossible Object.
Inventing God.
Judith.
Look at the Dark.
Natalie Natalia.
Paradoxes of Peace.
Serpent.
Time at War.
The Uses of Slime Mould:
Essays of Four Decades.
WARREN MOTTE,
Fables of the Novel: French Fiction
since 1990.
Fiction Now: The French Novel in
the 21st Century.
Oulipo: A Primer of Potential
Literature.
YVES NAVARRE, *Our Share of Time.*
Sweet Tooth.
DOROTHY NELSON, *In Night's City.*
Tar and Feathers.
ESHKOL NEVO, *Homesick.*
WILFRIDO D. NOLLEDO,
But for the Lovers.
FLANN O'BRIEN,
At Swim-Two-Birds.
At War.
The Best of Myles.
The Dalkey Archive.
Further Cuttings.
The Hard Life.
The Poor Mouth.
The Third Policeman.
CLAUDE OLLIER, *The Mise-en-Scène.*
PATRIK OUŘEDNÍK, *Europeana.*
FERNANDO DEL PASO,
News from the Empire.
Palinuro of Mexico.
ROBERT PINGET, *The Inquisitory.*
Mahu or The Material.
Trio.
MANUEL PUIG,
Betrayed by Rita Hayworth.
The Buenos Aires Affair.
Heartbreak Tango.
RAYMOND QUENEAU, *The Last Days.*
Odile.
Pierrot Mon Ami.
Saint Glinglin.

ANN QUIN, *Berg.*
Passages.
Three.
Tripticks.
ISHMAEL REED,
The Free-Lance Pallbearers.
The Last Days of Louisiana Red.
Ishmael Reed: The Plays.
Reckless Eyeballing.
The Terrible Threes.
The Terrible Twos.
Yellow Back Radio Broke-Down.
JEAN RICARDOU, *Place Names.*
RAINER MARIA RILKE,
The Notebooks of Malte Laurids
Brigge.
JULIÁN RÍOS, *Larva: A Midsummer*
Night's Babel.
Poundemonium.
AUGUSTO ROA BASTOS, *I the Supreme.*
OLIVIER ROLIN, *Hotel Crystal.*
ALIX CLEO ROUBAUD, *Alix's Journal.*
JACQUES ROUBAUD, *The Form of a*
City Changes Faster, Alas, Than
the Human Heart.
The Great Fire of London.
Hortense in Exile.
Hortense Is Abducted.
The Loop.
The Plurality of Worlds of Lewis.
The Princess Hoppy.
Some Thing Black.
LEON S. ROUDIEZ,
French Fiction Revisited.
VEDRANA RUDAN, *Night.*
STIG SÆTERBAKKEN, *Siamese.*
LYDIE SALVAYRE, *The Company of Ghosts.*
Everyday Life.
The Lecture.
Portrait of the Writer as a
Domesticated Animal.
The Power of Flies.
LUIS RAFAEL SÁNCHEZ,
Macho Camacho's Beat.
SEVERO SARDUY, *Cobra* & *Maitreya.*
NATHALIE SARRAUTE,
Do You Hear Them?
Martereau.
The Planetarium.
ARNO SCHMIDT, *Collected Stories.*
Nobodaddy's Children.
CHRISTINE SCHUTT, *Nightwork.*
GAIL SCOTT, *My Paris.*
DAMION SEARLS, *What We Were Doing*
and Where We Were Going.
JUNE AKERS SEESE,
Is This What Other Women Feel Too?
What Waiting Really Means.
BERNARD SHARE, *Inish.*
Transit.
AURELIE SHEEHAN,
Jack Kerouac Is Pregnant.
VIKTOR SHKLOVSKY, *Knight's Move.*
A Sentimental Journey:
Memoirs 1917–1922.
Energy of Delusion: A Book on Plot.

FOR A FULL LIST OF PUBLICATIONS, VISIT:
www.dalkeyarchive.com